Praise for *Culture Making*

"American evangelicals in the last hundred years have found it easy to condemn culture, critique culture, copy culture and consume culture. It has been much harder for them to actively and imaginatively create culture. Andy Crouch is out to change that. I confess I doubt whether they can rise to the challenge. But I am persuaded by Crouch's case that the Christian calling requires it. Here is a voice worth taking very seriously."

CHRISTIAN SMITH, professor of sociology, University of Notre Dame

"In this graceful, articulate volume Crouch challenges Christian common wisdom about creation and challenges as well our traditional understandings about the Revelation to John and how it articulates with the rest of Holy Writ. As refreshing as it is smart, *Culture Making* is a significant addition to contemporary Christian thought."

PHYLLIS TICKLE, compiler, *The Divine Hours*, and former religion editor, *Publishers Weekly*

"Andy Crouch's *Culture Making* models what it argues: that a kingdom imagination that takes our richly enculturated lives seriously shows grace to be real, immanent and compelling. Surely this vocation must be central to God's call!"

MARK LABBERTON, pastor, First Presbyterian Church of Berkeley, and author of *The Dangerous Act of Worship*

"In *Culture Making*, Andy Crouch has given us a vision for creativity that is not reserved for the practitioners of high art, but that reveals the dignity of the most ordinary sorts of cultural creation. It is a transformative vision that inspires to action and—in the face of the almost inevitable failures—perseverance. In the end, cultural creativity is not a gift we own, exercise and grow anxious over, but one that we receive and nurture—and through which we come to know grace."

DAVID NEFF, editor-in-chief and vice president, Christianity Today Media Group

"*Culture Making* is one of the few books taking the discussion about Christianity and culture to a new level. It is a rare mix of the theoretical and the practical, its definitions are nuanced but not abstract, and it strikes all kinds of fine balances. I highly recommend it."

TIM KELLER, pastor, Redeemer Presbyterian Church, New York City, and author of *The Reason for God*

"Good books are either brilliant or helpful, but the best books are both—and Andy Crouch has attained that rare combination of virtues in *Culture Making.* As a Christian, as a parent and as an organizational leader, I would like to make a difference in the world. Crouch not only helps me understand where that yearning comes from, but how to pursue it with passion, commitment, power and spiritual health. *Culture Making* is a joyful gift of intelligence and practical provocation for thoughtful Christians."

GARY HAUGEN, president, International Justice Mission, and author of *Good News About Injustice* and *Just Courage*

"In this marvelous book Andy Crouch makes the case for cultural discipleship by giving us an exciting overview of the drama of creation, fallenness and renewal. And along the way he offers much wisdom about the very real cultural realities that we face as twenty-first-century Christians."

RICHARD J. MOUW, president and professor of Christian philosophy, Fuller Theological Seminary

"This is not a good book, because it provokes and prods, incites and inspires. It takes you on an uncomfortable journey, defying the status quo and questioning accepted perspectives. It offers a fresh voice with trenchant thinking, forcing you to blow the dust off the mantle of your own settled proclivities. It resonates deeply within you, even on those points you may question. It addresses the heart of the challenge of our day. No, this is not a good book. It is a great one."

JAMES EMERY WHITE, pastor, professor and author of *Serious Times*

"A deep and thoughtful reminder that the resurrection of Jesus empowers us to cultivate the garden, to build in the ruins of our world, and to create within and around us cultures of life."

KELLY MONROE KULLBERG, author of *Finding God Beyond Harvard: The Quest for Veritas,* and founder and director of Project Development, The Veritas Forum

"Andy Crouch's book is thoughtful, stimulating and challenging."

STEVE TURNER, writer, poet and author of *Conversations with Eric Clapton, U2: Rattle and Hum* and *Imagine: A Vision for Christians in the Arts*

"Grappling with 'the culture' has become an obsession for contemporary Christians, but a misunderstanding of what cultures are and how they behave results in a great deal of frustration. Andy Crouch's *Culture Making* draws on both his broad experience and originality of insight to offer a bracing and clear-eyed view of the way forward."

FREDERICA MATHEWES-GREEN, author and columnist, www.frederica.com

ANDY CROUCH

CULTURE MAKING

RECOVERING OUR CREATIVE CALLING

IVP Books

An imprint of InterVarsity Press
Downers Grove, Illinois

InterVarsity Press
P.O. Box 1400, Downers Grove, IL 60515-1426
World Wide Web: www.ivpress.com
E-mail: email@ivpress.com

InterVarsity Press® is the book-publishing division of InterVarsity Christian Fellowship/USA®, a student movement active on campus at hundreds of universities, colleges and schools of nursing in the United States of America, and a member movement of the International Fellowship of Evangelical Students. For information about local and regional activities, write Public Relations Dept., InterVarsity Christian Fellowship/USA, 6400 Schroeder Rd., P.O. Box 7895, Madison, WI 53707-7895, or visit the IVCF website at <www.intervarsity.org>.

Scripture quotations, unless otherwise noted, are from the New Revised Standard Version of the Bible, *copyright 1989 by the Division of Christian Education of the National Council of the Churches of Christ in the USA. Used by permission. All rights reserved.*

Design: Cindy Kiple
Images: ballyscanlon / Getty Images

ISBN 978-0-8308-3394-8 (hardcover)
ISBN 978-0-8308-3755-7 (paperback)
ISBN 978-0-8308-7484-2 (digital)

Printed in the United States of America ∞

Library of Congress Cataloging-in-Publication Data

Crouch, Andy.
  Culture making: recovering our creative calling/Andy Crouch.
    p. cm.
  Includes bibliographical references.
  ISBN 978-0-8308-3394-8 (cloth: alk. paper)
  1. Christianity and culture. I. Title.
  BR115.C8C77 2008
  261.0973—dc22
                2008008913

P	21	20	19	18	17	16	15	14	13	12	11	10	9	8	7	6	5	4
Y	32	31	30	29	28	26	25	24	23	22	21	20	19	18	17	16	15	

In memory of my grandparents,

Homer and Alice Crouch

and Asa and Ann Bennett,

and in hope for my children's children.

Posterity will serve him;
future generations will be told about the Lord.
They will proclaim his righteousness
to a people yet unborn—
for he has done it.

CONTENTS

PREFACE TO THE PAPERBACK EDITION

Culture making is a risky business. You never know what will happen once you launch a cultural good into the world. It's a cliché (one that seems mostly to occur to male authors) to say that publishing a book is like giving birth to a child. Actually, it's more like sending a child off to college. You've invested years of your life in this creation of yours, and it bears your own unmistakable imprint and image, but now it makes its own way into the world. You watch nervously to see whether it will delight or disappoint you (and others), but the results from now on are mostly out of your control.

I wrote *Culture Making* on a hunch that the language of "engaging the culture," let alone the "culture wars," fell far short of what we were really meant to do and be as Christians in the world. I also sensed that most churches were neglecting the centrality of culture to the biblical story and the gospel itself.

I couldn't have dared to hope for the generous and enthusiastic response that this book has received so far. Most of all, I am thrilled by the acts of culture making it has helped to encourage, and grateful for the new friends I've made since its publication. The best part of writing the book has been discovering that we are in the midst of a great recovery of the themes of vocation and human flourishing, not as thin substitutes for the gospel but as rich dimensions of the gospel. To have been a witness to this recovery, and to assist it in a small way with this book, is one of the great joys of my life.

Among the gratifying responses have been some important and humbling critical ones. Some friends have pointed out that in my eagerness to convey just how embodied (dare I say, incarnate) culture is, I sometimes let particular artifacts stand in too readily for the more complex reality of institutions—the deep structures of human behavior and belief. Indeed, cultural artifacts that lose their link to these systems are reduced to artifacts in the thinnest, archaeological sense, totems dug up from ancient graves whose meanings to their makers we can only dimly guess. I devote a whole section of my next book, *Playing God*, to institutions, for institutions are indeed more important than you might imagine if you only read *Culture Making*.

The second area where some have expressed dissatisfaction with this book is its perceived populism—its lack of attention to the importance of cultural elites. If I'm not mistaken, behind these critiques seems to be a fear that this book might encourage too *much* culture making, by the wrong sort of people, those with neither the preparation, talent, nor ambition to make culture from the "center" where truly influential and valuable cultural goods are shaped. Such populist excesses of cultural creativity might actually make the work of the elites more difficult, or distract Christians from their calling to invest more seriously in the most influential cultural institutions.

I hope no one comes away from this book thinking that shoddy or facile culture making is adequate to our Christian—or human—calling. We are called to help shape "the glory and the honor of the nations," and that should fuel a godly ambition to do our very best, wherever grace may take us.

But my Christian hope for culture does not rest on access to the "centers" of cultural influence—and that is partly because I have seen those centers up close. I am grateful for friends (not to mention my wife!) who live and work at the very heart of elite institutions, and I celebrate their commitment to the flourishing of those important sources of cultural capital. And indeed, when I look at the great sweep of redemptive history, I note the inescapable involvement of "elites"—Pharaoh's daughter and Pharaoh himself, Pontius Pilate and Caiaphas, Felix and Festus, Jairus and his twelve-year-old daughter. But I also remark the consistent involvement of those no one counted as "central"—the subjugated Hebrew people, the Nazarene whose followers could be identified by their strong regional accents, the trader in purple named Lydia and the runaway slave named Onesimus, and the "daughter," unnamed to us, who had suffered a chronic illness for twelve years.

If you want to change the world, generally speaking, you do well to scale the ladders that lead to elite influence. But we are not here to change the world, generally speaking. Indeed, the good news is *the world is already changed, in a specific and astonishing way.* God's ways are not our ways. The culture he would have us make will undoubtedly be far more influential, and far more marginal, than our ambitions could ever fathom.

It bears repeating: The good news about culture is that culture is finally not about us, but about God. May you sense that good news in this book, and may your life and work surprise you as wonderfully as this book's own life has surprised me.

Pentecost 2013

INTRODUCTION

The essence of childhood is innocence. The essence of youth is awareness. The essence of adulthood is responsibility. This book is for people and a Christian community on the threshold of cultural responsibility.

For several decades now, many of American Christianity's most dynamic expressions have been youth ministries—even when they seem to serve grownups. Our goal, like that of many a plugged-in teenager, has been cultural awareness. We've paid the culture around us the ultimate compliment: careful study and, often, imitation. We have put in countless hours (often enjoyable ones!) "engaging culture"—looking, with surprising success, for hopeful signs of God in the world outside the church and also finding, with depressing frequency, signs of the enduring emptiness of that same world. Indeed, the desire to engage culture—to listen to it, learn from it and affirm it while also critiquing it—is one of the most hopeful developments of recent decades.

Our youth ministries have been astonishingly successful. Many of the most influential leaders of the evangelical movement began their careers with parachurch organizations like Youth for Christ, Campus Crusade for Christ, Youth Specialties, InterVarsity Christian Fellowship and a host of others. Some of our most prominent churches began literally as youth groups. In more recent years there has been a surge of events for college students and young adults that combine passionate faith with fluency in our media-saturated youth culture (along with media's large production budgets), as well as churches that seem to rip each month's sermon series directly from YouTube and BoxOfficeMojo.com. I am who I am because of culturally relevant ministries like these—and I spent fifteen years doing ministry in those contexts.

But what happens after youth ministry? What does it mean to be not just culturally aware but culturally responsible? Not just culture consumers or even just culture critics, but culture makers? Our newly regained cultural awareness means that we are not satisfied, as earlier generations might have been, with separating our faith from our "worldly" activities. We want our lives—our whole lives—to matter for the gospel. But what exactly does that mean?

This book is an attempt to point my fellow Christians toward new, and also very old, directions for understanding our calling in culture. I hope to offer us a new vocabulary, a new story and a new set of questions.

First, a new vocabulary, because our ways of talking about culture—how it works, how it changes, how it influences us and what we hope for from it—often do not serve us well. We talk about "the culture" even though culture is always cultures, plural: full of diversity, variety and history. We talk about culture as if it were primarily a set of ideas when it is primarily a set of tangible goods. We talk about "engaging," "impacting" and "transforming the culture" when in fact the people who most carefully study culture tend to stress instead how much we are transformed by it. If we are to be at all responsible agents in the midst of culture, we need to learn new ways of speaking about what we are doing.

Of course little of what I offer in this book is truly new. The first section borrows heavily from the field of sociology, which has developed an imposing apparatus for understanding this most characteristic and complex of human phenomena. (The literary critic Terry Eagleton observes, not reassuringly, that *culture* has been called the second most complicated word in the English language, after *nature*.) Most of the seminal writing in sociology, alas for us plainspoken Americans, bears the unmistakable imprint of the German language in which its central insights were first formulated. In trying to translate from the language of specialists, I have trampled merrily through the carefully tended gardens of any number of scholars, and they will no doubt look on with horror at my attempts at simplification. In particular, the sociologists who are cited in the notes and thanked in the acknowledgments should be absolved of all responsibility for my ham-handedness—still, I hope that I have captured some of the essential ideas that Christians need to be more careful and creative in the world.

In the second section I'll be offering a new story or, more precisely, a new way of reading a very old story: the story of culture as told through the pages of Scripture, from its opening chapters to its surprise ending.

Until recently, Christians seem to have forgotten how to tell the story of Scripture as a story that is both a genuine disclosure of God's presence in the world and a deeply cultural artifact that intersects over and over with concrete historical realities. Liberal Christians, enamored with the historical-critical method, have done a fine job of dismantling the claims of Scripture in light of its cultural context, but evangelical Christians have often done a fine job of ignoring the cultural import of Scripture while defending its divine inspiration.

I am by no means the first writer in recent years to recapture a cultural way of reading the good news. We believe that rediscovering the cultural context of the gospel does nothing to prevent it from being good news from above, before and beyond us, and is actually the key to it being fully good news for us. I have benefited most of all from the many thinkers in the Reformed community who have followed the Dutch statesman Abraham Kuyper's call to Christian cultural responsibility. I have tried to credit a representative sampling of them in the notes, but my simplifications will be all too apparent to those who have made more pilgrimages to Geneva and Grand Rapids than I.

Finally, I want to offer a new set of questions about our calling. What is it, exactly, that we are called to do in the world? Are we called to "transform culture" or to "change the world"? If we are to be culture makers, where in the world do we begin? How do we deal with power, that most difficult of all cultural realities, and its inescapably uneven distribution?

Readers who are looking for seven easy steps to cultural influence will have to look elsewhere—because I do not happen to believe that anything lasting is easy. What we most have to learn about being creators of culture is the very thing we human beings find hardest to learn: everything about our calling, from start to finish, is a gift. What is most needed in our time are Christians who are deeply serious about cultivating and creating but who wear that seriousness lightly—who are not desperately trying to change the world but who also wake up every morning eager to create.

The worst thing we could do is follow that familiar advice to "pray as if it all depended on God, and work as if it all depended on you." Rather, we need to become people who work as if it all depends on God—because it does, and because that is the best possible news. We work for, indeed work in the life and power of, a gracious and infinitely resourceful Creator, Redeemer and Sustainer. And we need to know ourselves well enough that the thought that it might in fact all depend on us would drive us straight to fasting and trembling prayer. I'm grateful that in the creation of the small cultural good that is this book, I've tasted both that kind of work and that kind of prayer.

•   •   •

I hope that most people who read this book will read it together with someone else. One of the most mysterious and beautiful things about culture is that it has to be shared. I can walk out alone into the wilderness, and from time to time I should. But I am never alone in culture. I am always accompanied by those who created it before me and share it with me; I can never really escape my responsibility to those who come after me, whose horizons of possibility I will move in some way, for better or worse.

I hope friends will read this book and begin to envision their friendships not just as the companionship of compatible individuals but as potentially transformative partnerships in the places where they live, study, work and play.

I hope families will read this book and discover that the family, so seemingly insignificant in an age of technology and celebrity, is still the heart of culture, the primary place where most of us are called to cultivate and create.

I hope churches will read this book and take the risky path of celebrating their members who do not go into "full-time Christian service" but who serve Christ full time in their own arena of culture.

I hope that those with evident cultural power will read this book and discover God's purpose for their power; I hope that those who feel small and neglected in the world will discover that God has something great for them to do, that they are not forgotten but are at the very center of his plan, the heroes of his surprise ending.

It could seem like a book about culture is likely somehow to be a book about us—about what we do, what we accomplish, our ambitions and dreams and schemes.

I hope that when you finish this book, you will have discovered that culture is not finally about us, but about God.

PART ONE

CULTURE

1

THE HORIZONS
OF THE POSSIBLE

This book addresses a huge topic, so let's begin by making it clear just how huge the topic is.

We are not just talking about culture in the sense of what "cultured" people do—hushed art museums and symphony orchestras—although art and music, as well as museums and orchestras, as well as the very idea that some people are "cultured" and others are not, are all part of a particular culture.

We are not just talking about culture in the sense of the trends, fads and fashions of the self-proclaimed culture mavens who focus our collective attention on the latest single-named celebrity or the latest piece of technology—though celebrity, technology and mavens are all part of a particular culture, the mass-mediated culture in which we participate every day.

We are not just talking about culture in the sense of ethnic identity, the collection of practices, beliefs and stories that carve out a sense of distinctiveness and pride or failure and shame, or perhaps some of both, in a world where cultural pluralism is widely affirmed and yet the hard realities of history render some cultures more equal than others. Before we finish we will indeed have to consider our particular cultures, not just culture in general. But not yet.

We are not even just talking about culture in the sense of the governing ideas, values and presuppositions of our society—as it is used in phrases like "culture wars," "the culture of disbelief" or "the decline of our culture"—although ideas, values and presuppositions are indeed at the heart of every human cultural effort, and the fact that we find them there gives us some clues about culture's ultimate significance. Nor are we just talking about the ongoing contest in democratic societies to advance one set of ideas, values and presuppositions in the realm of politics and legislation—though laws are among the most dramatic ways that culture is expressed and enforced.

Many attempts, especially Christian attempts, to come to terms with culture have fallen short because they paid too much attention to one of these categories of culture. High culture, pop culture, ethnic culture, political culture—all are part of culture and worthy of attention, reflection and action.

But culture is more than any of these things. And to grasp how much more it is, we need to go deeper down and further back, to the beginning. Actually, we need to go back to three beginnings.

BIRTH

Begin with your own beginning.

You emerged wrinkled and wet, squinting against the light. You wailed in a thin and raspy voice, taking in gulps of unfamiliar air, until someone placed you near a heartbeat you knew even better than your own. Close to your mother's warmth, you became calm and alert. You opened your eyes, feeling the air on your skin, hearing sounds and voices that once had echoed through your watery cradle, now vivid and distinct. Perhaps your eyes even found a face, somehow recognizing the significance of eyes, nose and mouth, and fixed on it with rapt attention.

A human baby is the strangest and most wonderful creature this world can offer. No other mammal emerges so helpless from the womb, utterly unable to cope with the opportunity and adversity of nature. Yet no other creature holds such limitless possibility. While arguments about nature and nurture have raged for centuries and will do so for centuries more, everyone agrees that human beings come into the world primed for culture.

Without culture—which begins, for the baby, with recognition of relationship, finding her mother and her father, and goes on in the first few years to what is in some ways the most stupendous of human achievements, the acquisition of language—we simply do not become anything at all. We are hard-wired for nothing but learning. All we begin with are possibilities.

HISTORY

Begin at history's beginning.

We hold lanterns up to cave walls and see that our earliest ancestors were artists. They traced patterns in the clay with their fingers. They sculpted figures, from bison to the female human form, into the rocks, seemingly prompted by the natural shape of the surface. They mixed pigments with mortar and pestle and created dramatically large paintings—a painting of a bison in the cave at Altamira, Spain, is over six feet wide. This highly developed artistic activity was well underway 14,000 years ago. So complex is the work that we find in the caves of Europe, says the writer Paul Johnson, that "it is likely that art was the first of the human professions."

But we find more than art in humankind's early history. We find tools, like the arrowheads that I collected as a boy on my grandparents' Georgia farm. We find charred circles where our forebears harnessed fire. We find domesticated animals—the skulls of two dogs found in central Russia in 2003 are roughly contemporary with the cave art of Europe. We find toys. And we find tombs.

Those earliest traces of culture do not preserve language. But soon we have records not just of language but of stories. The most durable stories—the ones we call "myths"—wrestle directly with the questions provoked by the existence of the world. Like astronomers who can peer into the history of the universe with powerful telescopes, when we listen to the ancient myths we are encountering the human consciousness just beginning to awaken, and as it awakens it asks: Why are we here? Where did this world come from? Who or what is responsible for the bison so carefully and lovingly portrayed on the cave wall?

Take the *Enuma Elish*, one of those texts from the dawn of human story-telling preserved for us in tantalizingly fragile form on clay tablets from Ashurbanipal's great library at Nineveh. To the people who told and heard this epic, it must have seemed obvious that the world needed a story. The story they told, which archaeologists believe goes back at least to the third millennium before Christ, was the victory of the god Marduk over the serpent Tiamat and her company of monsters. Having vanquished Tiamat, Marduk fillets her, turning one fillet into the heavens and the other into the earth. In one version of the myth, he turns her brood of monsters into the Zodiac, the twelve constellations through which the sun passes in the course of a year.

This is what human beings do: we extract stories even from the stars.

SCRIPTURE

All human beings share the first two beginnings—the universal experience of infancy, and the history of the species. But biblical people emphasize a different beginning, the story recounted in the first pages of the Hebrew Bible.

Genesis begins with a Creator, purposeful and pleased with his work. Already in the first sentence, the writer of Genesis stakes out a story very different from the creation myths that were circulating at the time. "In the beginning when God created the heavens and the earth, the earth was a formless void and darkness covered the face of the deep, while a wind from God swept over the face of the waters." There is no violent conflict among gods and monsters here, no irrepressible and threatening chaos, just the hushed sound of divine breath in the dark. Then comes the stately and measured progression toward the sixth day, the pinnacle of creation:

> So God created humankind in his image,
>> in the image of God he created them;
>> male and female he created them. (Gen 1:27)

You can fill many bookshelves with the three thousand years of conversation sparked by Genesis 1:27. The claim—repeated, poetically and emphatically, twice in one verse—that human beings are made in God's image takes on all the more resonance when we realize that the same people

who wrote and preserved Genesis 1:27 also knew the second commandment, which insisted, "you shall not make a graven image." The writers
of the Bible would have been the first to insist that human attempts at
fashioning images of God are doomed to failure or worse. But God, it
seems, has no such limitation. God himself makes an "image" of himself.
Humankind's "images of God" are always deficient and destructive, the
Hebrew Bible insists, but God's own "image of God" is the summary of
everything he has made, crowned with the words, "It was very good."

What does it mean that we are made in the image of God? Perhaps the
best way to answer this question is to ask another: What "image of God"
is conveyed by Genesis 1:1-26? The God we meet in these verses, so unlike
the alternative gods on offer in the ancient Near East, is first of all a source
of limitless, extraordinary *creativity*. For the writers of the *Enuma Elish*, the
world was a byproduct of divine conflict. The cosmos of the *Enuma Elish*
is grim, with chaos always near. Even human beings, who are Marduk's
crowning achievement, are a response to a divine political problem (as near
as we can tell from the fragmentary text): the other gods complain that there
is no one to worship them, and Marduk's "cunning plan" is to create human
beings to serve that purpose. In contrast, the writer of Genesis looks at the
world, from stars to starfish, and sees a purposeful, engaged, creative intelligence at work. Every "kind" of animal is further testimony to the extraordinary fruitfulness of this Creator's imagination. The world is not the product
of accident or heavenly politics, but of a free, even relaxed, blessed Creator.

However, this Creator also addresses the fundamental concern that lies
underneath the *Enuma Elish* and other creation myths—the human sense
that chaos is never far away. Genesis 1 is a sequence of acts of *ordering*, as
the Creator gradually carves out a habitable environment. The first chapter of Genesis records a series of divisions—order from chaos, light from
darkness, heaven from earth, sea from land—each of which makes the
world more amenable for the flourishing of creativity.

Another way of putting these two features of creation is to say that
Genesis presents God as both Creator and Ruler of the universe. Creators
are those who make something new; rulers are those who maintain order
and separation.

As an American I'm aware that I tend to celebrate creators and am suspicious of rulers—our nation's history began, after all, with the over-throw of a ruler and the creation of a novel form of government. In America, though not at many other times and places in history, innovation is prized more than conservation. The idea that the world's Creator is also its Ruler—that order accompanies creativity—may strike us as suspicious and unfamiliar.

Yet creativity cannot exist without order—a structure within which creation can happen. On a cosmic level the extraordinary profusion of species could never survive if the world were an undifferentiated soup of elements. This is true of human creativity too. Without the darkened box of a theater, films would lose their compelling power. Without the lines and spaces that make up written English, this book would be a soup of letters. Creativity requires cosmos—it requires an ordered environment.

So in a way the Creator's greatest gift to his creation is the gift of structure—not a structure which locks the world, let alone the Creator himself, into eternal mechanical repetition, but a structure which provides freedom. And those who are made in his image will also be both creators and rulers. They will have a unique capacity to create—perhaps not to call something out of nothing in quite the way that God does in Genesis 1:1, but to reshape what exists into something genuinely new. And they will have a responsibility to care for what God has made—"The LORD God took the man and put him in the garden of Eden to till it and keep it" (Gen 2:15). They will sort out the cultivated from the wild. Human beings will be gardeners.

MAKING SOMETHING OF THE WORLD

This, then, is the picture of humanity we find in Genesis: creative cultivators. We'll return to the Genesis story in chapter six. But for the moment notice how much it has in common with our other beginnings—the beginnings we have in common with every human being. The man and the woman in the Garden, just like every newborn baby and just like human beings at the dawn of their history—indeed, just like the human beings in the myths that the Genesis story was clearly written to rebut—find themselves already in the midst of a world. We can't escape the fact that the world came before us.

They also find themselves, as we find ourselves, as human beings always and everywhere have found themselves, sensing that they are in the midst of a story. For the baby, it is the story of her family, a story that will be put together using words like *mama* and *daddy*. For our earliest ancestors, according to the archaeological record, it is the mysterious story of a world with stars and rocks and bison, a world that cries out for explanation.

And God gives the primordial man and woman the same task that the baby almost immediately undertakes with the raw materials of her vocal cords, lungs and mouth—the same thing that our human ancestors did with stone and fire and pigment on cave walls. They go to work with these recalcitrant raw materials (even the Garden before the Fall, it seems, required tilling and keeping), forming and reshaping the world they find themselves in. They begin "making something of the world."

This phrase, which I have adapted from the Christian cultural critic Ken Myers, distills what culture is and why it matters: *Culture is what we make of the world.* Culture is, first of all, the name for our relentless, restless human effort to take the world as it's given to us and make something else. This is the original insight of the writer of Genesis when he says that human beings were made in God's image: just like the original Creator, we are creators. God, of course, began with nothing, whereas we begin with something. But the difference is not as great as you might think. For every act of creation involves bringing something into being that was not there before—every creation is *ex nihilo*, from nothing, even when it takes the world as its starting point. Something is added in every act of making. This is clearest in the realm of art, where the raw materials of pigment and canvas become more than you ever could have predicted. Even a five-year-old's finger painting is more than the sum of paper and paint. But creation, the marvelous making of more than was there before, also happens when a chef makes an omelet, when a carpenter makes a chair, when a toddler makes a snow angel.

Culture is all of these things: paintings (whether finger paintings or the Sistine Chapel), omelets, chairs, snow angels. It is what human beings make of the world. It always bears the stamp of our creativity, our God-given desire to make something more than we were given.

But culture is not just what we make of the world in the first, most obvious sense. Culture also is what we make of the world in a deeper sense of that phrase. When we find ourselves perplexed by a scene in a movie or the lyrics of a song, we say to our friends, "What do you make of that?" We aren't usually asking our friends to write a new scene or sing new lyrics—we aren't asking for more creation. We mean, what sense do you make of it? We are asking for interpretation.

Indeed, the world that every baby, every human society and our primordial parents found themselves in clearly needs some interpreting. One of the most striking things about the world is just how little it discloses to us about its true meaning. It is full of mystery—at its best, full of wonder; at its worst, full of terror. Making sense of the wonder and terror of the world is the original human preoccupation. And it is this deeper sense of culture that most clearly distinguishes us from all the rest of creation. Ants and birds and chimpanzees make something of the world, in the sense of reshaping their environment with anthills and nests and even rudimentary tools and techniques—but we simply have no indication that any other creature wonders about the mystery of the world. Making sense of the world, interpreting its wonder and its terror, is left up to human beings alone.

So how do we make sense of the world? The two senses turn out to be more intertwined than we might have thought. We *make sense* of the world by *making something* of the world. The human quest for meaning is played out in human making: the finger-painting, omelet-stirring, chair-crafting, snow-swishing activities of culture. Meaning and making go together—culture, you could say, is the activity of making meaning.

Think about the baby again. As she tries out the infinite combinations of sounds that her tongue and throat and lungs can produce, she happens upon a few that elicit an excited response from her parents. Quite by accident, her tongue bumps against her upper teeth while she vocalizes, making the sound "da." She does it again, over and over. Her father wanders into the room. "Da." "Da." "Da-da." Suddenly her daddy is leaning close, smiling, exclaiming, picking her up, hugging her. "She said *daddy!*" The baby might not have meant any such thing, but this smiling, hugging, loving man is clearly pleased. The next day, when she's trying out vocalizations again, it happens once more. Over the coming weeks the baby begins to connect that sound—"da-da"—with the hugs and the smiles. Perhaps she hears other people making the same sounds and is inspired to make them some more. Over time "da-da" becomes more than just a random and intriguing combination of sounds. The baby has made sense of daddy—given a name to an exceedingly important feature of her world—by making something of the world. Meaning and making have come together.

THE WORLD OF CULTURE

But notice something else about the baby: the world that she must make something of is not just the natural, created world of sound, teeth, lungs and air. Nor is it even just the other creatures, mommy and daddy, that inhabit that world with her. The father's excitement at hearing "da-da" comes because in our language (and in most other languages, as it happens) that sequence of sounds resembles a word. The existence of that word is itself a part of the world that the baby is trying to make something of. But the word is not "natural"—it is cultural. Culture, not just creation, is part of the baby's world.

One of the key insights that emerged over several centuries' worth of study in the fields we now call sociology and anthropology was summed up by Peter Berger and Thomas Luckmann in their book *The Social Construction of Reality*. Berger later expanded on its religious implications in his book *The Sacred Canopy*, which begins, "Every human society is an enterprise of world-building." Culture is not just what human beings make of the world; it is not just the way human beings make sense of the world; it is in fact *part of the world* that every new human being has to make something of.

So the baby must make something not just of sounds but of words. Words and language are as inescapable a part of "the world" with which she must work as are lungs and tongues. Omelets and chairs and paintings are just as much a part of the world as eggs and wood and pigments, preexisting and waiting for both interpretation and further creation. The world the baby arrives in encompasses not just the original stuff of prehuman creation but all the myriad things that humans themselves have already made from that stuff. The world with which the baby will have to come to terms as she grows is just as much cultural as it is natural.

So culture is cumulative: our cultural products become part of the world that a future generation must make something of—in both senses. It's important to appreciate how deep this goes, which is why Berger and Luckmann gave their book the startling title *The Social Construction of Reality*. It is not that nature is somehow deeply real and culture is shadowy, vague or transient. Culture really is part of our world, just as central to our lives and our being human as nature. In some ways it is more central. A baby who is born without hearing may never experience sound or understand the significance of the sounds that he produces by chance with his own vocal tract. But he can survive and even thrive in the world if he is taught language—whether a sign language or a written language—and thus inducted into a culture. The cultural world of language is more essential to human flourishing than the natural world of sound.

THE RIVER AND THE HIGHWAY

Culture has quite literally reshaped the world. In the nineteenth century, if you had asked well-traveled Americans to sketch a map of their country, including its most significant features, they would almost certainly have drawn you a continent full of rivers. The Mississippi, of course, but also the Connecticut, the Ohio, the Missouri, the St. Lawrence and a dozen more. Rivers—part of the created, "uncultured" world—were a crucial part of the world that early Americans had to make something of. And make something of them they did indeed—the rivers, in their dual role as transportation routes for cargo and people on the one hand, and barriers to travel on the other, prompted myriad cultural innovations. Just to name the rivers is to realize that they gave their names to many of the states created as America expanded westward. Cities arose at the juncture of rivers. Technologies were developed to harness the river for transportation. Songs and stories arose that depended on rivers for their setting and meaning—try to imagine *Huckleberry Finn* without Huck and Jim on the barge floating down the Mississippi.

But if you asked similarly well-traveled Americans in the twenty-first century to sketch a map of the continent, I suspect they would have a hard time identifying any river but the Mississippi. Here's a quick quiz: where on a map is the Missouri River? If you know the answer, you probably either live in St. Louis or have a lifelong obsession with geography. Rivers, so central to the world of the nineteenth century, are now peripheral at best. Interstate highways, on the other hand, are the principal means of travel by land, and most Americans can sketch out the rough lines of Interstate 90, cutting east to west across the continent from Boston to Seattle, and the highway Southern Californians call "the 5," stretching from San Diego to the Pacific Northwest.

Highways are our rivers. Cities arise and economies thrive where they intersect. New forms of commerce flourish alongside the interstate. The extraordinarily complex web of modern intermodal transport, depending on containers that can be transferred seamlessly from ship to rail to truck, depends on the highway system. Songs and stories arise from the highway system too—if nothing quite so romantic and durable as *Huckleberry Finn*, then at least the enduring tradition of the American "road movie" and Jack Kerouac's Beat classic *On the Road*.

The transition from river to highway is a transition from one world to another. We can argue about whether interstate highways make the world better or worse, but we cannot deny that they make a new kind of world. They do so partly by reshaping the physical world itself, blasting through hills and bridging rivers so smoothly that we don't even know the names of the rivers we cross. And they do so more profoundly by reshaping our imagination, our mental picture of what is in the world and what matters in it. The difference they make, however, is not "imaginary"—it is real. It really is possible to drive from Boston to Seattle in fifty hours or less (if you have a partner to drive when you get sleepy). And you can do so without knowing the name of a single river or port. It's possible because of Interstate 90, a purely cultural product, along with the myriad other cultural products that interact with and support it. Culture, not just nature, has become the world that we must make something of.

THE HORIZONS OF THE POSSIBLE

Up to now I've indulged in a risky shortcut: talking about culture in the abstract, almost as if it were an ethereal Big Idea, written with Capital

Letters, floating through History. Yet no one—not even those who read books with titles like *Culture Making*—makes Culture. Rather, Culture, in the abstract, always and only comes from particular human acts of cultivation and creativity. We don't make Culture, we make omelets. We tell stories. We build hospitals. We pass laws. These specific products of cultivating and creating—borrowing a word from archaeology and anthropology, we can call them "artifacts," or borrowing from philosophy, we can call them "goods"—are what eventually, over time, become part of the framework of the world for future generations.

Likewise, the word *culture*, when it is reserved for art, music, literature and the like, tends to make us think of vague interior states. We think of a beautiful symphony or a provocative work of art in a museum—powerful ideas and images, perhaps, but not artifacts that seem to do anything real, anything tangible, to the world outside the walls where we enjoy or endure them. Yet culture, in its more fundamental sense, really does remake the world, because culture shapes the horizons of the possible.

Think again of that fifty-hour journey from Boston to Seattle. Before the vast, culture-making act that was the construction of Interstate 90, such a journey, in terms of speed and comfort, was impossible. Now it is possible. What made the difference was a concrete cultural good—in this case, quite literally made of concrete. Of course, most of us are too impatient to drive across the country, so if we can afford it, we avail ourselves of an even more audacious kind of culture—air travel—and cover the distance in a few hours. What was previously impossible, culture has made possible.

And even more remarkably, culture can make some things impossible that were previously possible. Reading David McCullough's biography of John Adams a few years ago, I was reminded that not that long ago, a vast cultural infrastructure made it possible to travel the three hundred miles from Boston to Philadelphia by horse. There were roads, wayside inns, stables and turnpikes along which travelers could make a slow but steady journey from one city to the other. For more than a century these cultural goods made interstate horse travel possible. But I dare say it would be impossible now. The inns and stables of the nineteenth century are long gone. Horses are forbidden from the shoulders of the highways that connect Boston and Philadelphia, even if horses could stand the roar of the traffic that would be rushing by them just a few feet away. To ride a horse any distance in what is now called "the Northeast Corridor" would be a feat of bravery, to say the least, and quite possibly also an act of cruelty to animals. Culture has made travel by horse, once eminently possible, impossible.

And these two functions—making things possible that were impossible, and perhaps even more importantly making things impossible that were once possible—when put together add up to "world-building." *World*, after all, is a shorthand way of describing all those forces outside ourselves, beyond our control and will, that both constrain us and give us options and opportunities. After many thousands of years of accumulating human culture, the world which we must make something of—the environment in which we carry on the never-ending human cultural project—is largely the world others before us have made. Culture, even more than nature, defines for us the horizons of possibility and impossibility. We live in the world that culture has made.

DIAGNOSING CULTURE

If we want to understand culture, then, it's always best to begin and end with specific cultural goods. I've found five questions to be particularly helpful in understanding how a particular artifact fits into its broader cultural story.

The first two questions arise from culture's meaning-making function—culture's role in making sense of the world. (1) *What does this cultural artifact assume about the way the world is?* What are the key features of the world that this cultural artifact tries to deal with, respond to, make sense of? (2) *What does this cultural artifact assume about the way the world should be?* What vision of the future animated its creators? What new sense does it seek to add to a world that often seems chaotic and senseless?

Then come two questions that acknowledge culture's extraordinary power to shape the horizons of possibility. (3) *What does this cultural artifact make possible?* What can people do or imagine, thanks to this artifact, that they could not before? Conversely, (4) *what does this cultural artifact make impossible (or at least very difficult)?* What activities and experiences that were previously part of the human experience become all but impossible in the wake of this new thing? Often this is the most interesting question of all, especially because so much technological culture is presented exclusively in terms of what it will make *possible*. Yet few cultural artifacts serve only to move the horizons of possibility outward and leave the horizons of impossibility unchanged. Almost every cultural artifact, in small or large ways, makes something impossible—or at least more difficult—that was possible before.

Finally, because culture inevitably begets more culture, we have to look at the effect of this artifact on future culture. (5) *What new forms of culture are created in response to this artifact?* What is cultivated and created that could not have been before?

To be sure, these five questions may yield more interesting answers with some cultural artifacts than others. *What do omelets assume about the world?* may not seem to be the kind of question you'd want to spend much time on. Then again, even to answer that question is to remind ourselves just how much culture is part of the "world" we must make something of—since omelets assume that the world includes not just the natural phenomena called eggs (obtained from chickens that have been domesticated through millennia in order to produce reliably large, tasty eggs for human consumption) but cultural phenomena, including a ready source of high heat, nonstick or well-seasoned frying pans, natural ingredients like peppers or mushrooms and processed ingredients like cheese or ham, a meal called breakfast where eggs figure prominently, utensils that are well suited to eating a large mass of eggs, and hearty appetites that are inclined to consume several eggs in a sitting. Just for starters.

What do omelets assume about the way the world should be? Well, I suppose they assume that the tasty, protein-laden nutrients of an egg are better eaten cooked than raw—and perhaps also that the world should have an alternative to the blandness of plain cooked eggs. The world should be multicolored, with green peppers and pink ham and white cheese contrasting pleasingly with the pale yellow eggs; the world should have many textures, both crunchy and smooth. The world should hold together—a haphazard pile of scrambled eggs is antithetical to the vision of the well-turned-out omelet, semicircular and perfectly bronzed. The world should be filling, satisfying, rich in the mouth, large on the plate—an overflow of plenitude from the small, unremarkable beginning of an egg (or three). Life, or at least breakfast, should leave us stuffed.

Perhaps there is more here than we realized. Even a simple breakfast dish encodes a whole set of assumptions and hopes about the world, which we could summarize this way: the world has eggs, but it should have omelets too. The world, the cultural artifact of the omelet says, always has room for more. The givens of our natural environment, as satisfying and nutritious as they are, are nothing compared to what can happen with a little culture—or, in the case of the omelet, centuries and centuries of gradual perfecting of all the cultural ingredients, from cheese to frying pans, that make the omelet possible. Culture fulfills the latent promise of nature. To echo biblical language, the egg is good, but the omelet is very good—but now we're really getting ahead of ourselves.

What does the omelet make possible? To balance out our meditations on the glories of omelets, perhaps we should engage in a bit of culinary realpolitik. The omelet, fully cooked as it is, helps make it possible for salmonella to contaminate our egg supply without causing a public health disaster. For that matter, the omelet, generally a good source of cholesterol, saturated fat and sodium, might make heart disease possible, or a lot more likely, for many of its satisfied customers. It also may contribute to the fortunes of the egg industry and the wallets of egg industrialists. *What does the omelet make impossible, or at least a lot more difficult?* Perhaps the omelet doesn't make anything truly impossible, though you may be able to think of something I haven't. It certainly makes eating raw eggs—not unknown in human history—a lot less appealing. It may even make plain old scrambled eggs seem rather second rate. It makes it harder to sit down to a "continental" breakfast of bread, butter and jam, and feel fully satisfied. It makes it harder to pay for breakfast at a restaurant, in many American cities at any rate, without getting into double digits. It may make it harder for many of us to stay thin.

What new culture is created in response to the omelet? New kinds of omelets—omelets with egg whites only (a response to the original omelet's deficiencies for cholesterol watchers) and omelets with new combinations of ingredients. New kinds of kitchen implements—better surfaces for executing the all-important omelet flip, pan sizes suited to creating the perfect omelet half-moon shape. The "omelet station" in fancy hotel restaurants, staffed by a chef whose only job is to make omelets to order. Books about omelet preparation. Websites (or at least sections of egg websites) about omelets. And these very paragraphs in this book, themselves a small cultural artifact seeking to "make something of" omelets and the world they make.

THE INTERSTATE HIGHWAY SYSTEM

As fascinating, and revealing, as these questions may be when applied to omelets, they are even more helpful when we try to understand large-scale cultural goods like the interstate highway system, established when President Dwight Eisenhower signed into law the "National System of Interstate and Defense Highways Act" on June 29, 1956. Encoded into its very beginnings was America's preoccupation with being prepared to meet the military threat from the Soviet Union. Eisenhower had been impressed by Germany's autobahn system while serving there in the United States Army—so that the interstate highway system's origins, like so many other cultural artifacts in post–World War II America, were shaped by the experiences and values of military men, many of which can be discerned in our answers to our diagnostic questions.

What does the interstate highway assume about the way the world is? Of course it assumes the existence of the automobile, which in turn assumes combustion engines and combustible fuel—so that the interstate highway system depends on other exceedingly complex cultural artifacts for its existence. It assumes the political unification of relatively distant places, the modern nation-state that stretches from "sea to shining sea," so different from the arrangements of an earlier time when each valley could be a kingdom. It assumes millennia of accumulated experience in road building, reaching back at least to the Romans' engineering achievements that made possible their own far-flung empire. The highway system also assumes a preexisting map of significant cities, most of which will be incorporated into its grid (thus reinforcing the viability of the cities it passes through, while sidelining those it passes by). It assumes significant national wealth that provides the capacity to invest in such a massive project, and it assumes the population pressures and economic growth that have produced that wealth.

What does it assume about the way the world should be? The world should be smoother and faster, and the world should be safer—its corners, hills and valleys literally rounded off in the interests of efficiency. Rivers and mountains should be scenery, not obstacles. The perceived distance from one place to the next should shrink—the mile should seem like a short distance rather than a long one. Consistency from place to place is more valuable than the particulars of each place—uniform signage and road markings, fixed radii for curves and angles for exit ramps, and identical rules of the road should make local knowledge unnecessary. We should be able to go anywhere and feel more or less at home. Goods from far away should become more economically competitive with goods from nearby; goods nearby should have new markets in places far away.

What does the interstate highway system make possible? If you are reading this in the United States, it is overwhelmingly likely that everything you can touch nearby—your clothes, the chair, the coffee you're sipping or the food you're eating—traveled at some point by interstate, more cheaply and more quickly than it would have otherwise. So the interstates have indeed made smooth and efficient commerce more possible. The interstates also spawned entirely new forms of commerce—from fast-food restaurants to Cracker Barrel, that paradoxical restaurant chain that reveres "old country cooking" and inhabits apparently time-weathered old buildings, but is in fact only available next to interstate highways. They helped make America's car culture not only possible but, in most parts of the country, necessary. We wouldn't have green-lawned suburbs without the interstates that made it possible to live far from workplaces in central cities. And without the interstates we wouldn't have the abandoned-lot "inner cities," created when middle-class families moved to the suburbs. In fact, when the Fannie Mae Foundation asked urban planners to name the top ten factors in the way American cities developed (and decayed) in the twentieth century, the interstate highway system was number one.

So the interstate highway system has also made some things impossible, or at least much more difficult. It has become more difficult for many Americans to work without commuting. It has become impossible to sustain economic growth without reasonably priced oil—an impossibility that becomes more ominous the more oil we use. In many small towns that were bypassed by the interstates, vibrant commercial life has become impossible; even as in cities that were at the intersection of major interstates (like Atlanta), vibrant commercial growth has become more possible, and new forms of culture have arisen at otherwise forsaken highway exits.

And yet the story of interstate highway culture, and the broader automotive culture it enables, is not over. *What new culture is being created in response?* A Toyota Prius hatchback owned by the nonprofit organization PhillyCarShare has a permanent parking space a few blocks from my home. PhillyCarShare's executive director, Tanya Seaman, was working as a city planner when she and a few friends conceived the vision of hundreds of cars parked in convenient locations around the city, freeing many residents of both central and suburban Philadelphia from the need to own their own cars. The organization, which was operating in the black with a $10 million budget in 2007, has grown to thirty thousand members and over four hundred cars. City planners estimate that each shared car makes it possible for up to twenty-five people to forego buying a private car of their own—so there are perhaps ten thousand fewer vehicles crammed onto Philadelphia's streets and highways in 2007 than when the organization was founded in 2002. PhillyCarShare would never have been necessary before the interstate highway system changed the horizons of metropolitan Philadelphia—but its creative and sustainable solution to urban driving would never have been possible either.

CULTURE IS NOT OPTIONAL

So this is what culture does: it defines the horizons of the possible and the impossible in very concrete, tangible ways. I don't just believe in fast and convenient travel by highway; I don't just value it; it isn't just something I can imagine that I couldn't imagine before. It is something I can actually do. And the only reason I can do it is because someone (President Eisenhower, the members of the United States Congress, and untold numbers of civil engineers, road builders, zoning commission members and accountants) created something that wasn't there before.

And, for that matter, I might believe that we'd be better off if we didn't spend eighty-one minutes a day in our cars (the American average, according to the *Wall Street Journal*), that the days of horse travel were actually better for people and animals, and that the rapid consumption of our planet's limited supply of fossil fuels is both greedy and foolish. But it's impossible for me to live as if the highways don't exist. And, again, those impossibilities are there, whether I like it or not, because someone created something that wasn't there before. Surely interstate highways have removed many appealing possibilities from American life, from viable Main Streets to travel by horse (though both may be more appealing from a safe historical distance than they were up close).

But however constricting culture's horizons of impossibility may seem, culture is indispensable for any human possibility. Culture is the realm of human freedom—its constraints and impossibilities are the boundaries within which we can create and innovate. This is clearly true of a cultural artifact like this book: when I write about omelets for a North American audience, I can expect that nearly every reader will know what an omelet is, and most will have eaten one. I can be all but certain that anyone who purchases this book will have driven on an interstate highway. (This book itself, the physical object, almost certainly traveled on an interstate highway on its way to you, and as an author I rely on that too.) But even if my book finds its way to an omelet-innocent, interstate-free corner of the world, I can be absolutely sure that we share the cultural heritage of spoken and written language. Because of language, interstates and even omelets, we are able to engage in a conversation that would be impossible otherwise. To whatever extent you have been engaged by, enlightened by or even confused by the content of this chapter, culture has made that possible. Indeed, without culture, literally nothing would be possible for human beings. To say that culture creates the horizons of possibility is to speak literal, not just figurative or metaphorical, truth.

This truth is embedded in the Genesis story of beginnings. Not only does God himself function as both Creator and Ruler, breather of possibilities and setter of limits, he intends the same for those who are made in his image. Without the task of gardening—cultivating, tending, ruling and creating using the bountiful raw material of nature—the woman and man would have had nothing to do, nothing to be. Whatever distortions may arise as the man and the woman carry out their cultural task (and as we know from experience and will see in part two, the distortions are grave indeed), culture begins, just as human beings begin, in the realm of created blessing. The beginning of culture and the beginning of humanity are one and the same because culture is what we were made to do.

There is no withdrawing from culture. Culture is inescapable. And that's a good thing.

2

CULTURAL WORLDS

Culture is what human beings make of the world, but not everything that human beings make shapes culture.

In 1979 the flamboyant artist couple Christo and Jeanne-Claude (in our culture, people signal artistic flamboyancy by using only their first names) conceived of a project called *The Gates*. They imagined lining the paths of New York City's Central Park with saffron-colored curtains mounted on steel arches. A proposal to the New York City Parks Department was rejected—the department said that Christo and Jeanne-Claude's proposal was "in the wrong place and the wrong time and in the wrong scale"—and the idea languished in their studio, dormant though never forgotten, for more than twenty years. Only a few people in the community of artists knew about the project.

The vision for *The Gates*, as with all art and all culture, was to make something of the world—in this case, the "world" of Central Park, which is itself a grand exercise in world making by the landscape designers Frederick Law Olmsted and Calvert Vaux. Even when *The Gates* was just a set of sketches and pastel drawings, it was already a cultural good in one sense—the work of human beings trying to make something of the world.

But if *The Gates* had never been actually produced, it would never have become a fully realized cultural good. Go back to the diagnostic questions we asked in chapter one and imagine asking them of *The Gates* in the year 1999 when it was just a collection of sketches, proposals and maps, along with further ideas found only in the artists' imaginations and conversations. *What does* The Gates, *circa 1999, assume about the way the world is? What does it assume about the way the world ought to be?* We could certainly answer these questions. *The Gates*, circa 1999, assumes the existence of Central Park, its significance in the life of New York City and its wider significance as an emblem of the possibilities of urban spaces. It assumes the chilly, leafless, barren terrain of a New York February (the project was always envisioned for midwinter). It assumes that the world should be adorned, at least from time to time and temporarily, with billowing fabrics that reveal and yet sometimes also conceal paths, hills and valleys. It assumes—in significant tension with many artists' convictions, especially in the modern and postmodern eras—that art should be colorful, accessible, fun and free to the public.

But then move on to the next three questions. *What does* The Gates, *circa 1999, make possible? What does it make impossible, or at least much more difficult? What new forms of culture are created in response?* We're stuck. There is little to say because *The Gates*, twenty years after it was first proposed, had had almost no effect to speak of. About the only cultural artifacts that had been created in response were a few bureaucratic documents categorically rejecting the artists' proposal. And perhaps those documents did make some things impossible, or at least much more difficult, if they discouraged other would-be flamboyant artists from proposing any such works for Central Park. *The Gates*, circa 1999, was an artifact—a human effort to make something of the world—but it was not yet fully culture. Which is another way of saying that it was not yet—and as far as its creators knew, might never be—shared by a public.

Culture requires a public: a group of people who have been sufficiently affected by a cultural good that their horizons of possibility and impossibility have in fact been altered, and their own cultural creativity has been spurred, by that good's existence. This group of people does not necessarily have to be large. But without such a group the artifact remains exclusively personal and private. It may be deeply meaningful to its owners—Christo and Jeanne-Claude may have treasured their sketches and maps in the privacy of their studio—but it has not reshaped the world for anyone. At least not yet.

As it happened, in 2003 a new mayor and new parks commissioner finally approved a somewhat revised proposal for *The Gates*. Michael Bloomberg, a successful businessman turned mayor, was clearly motivated more by millions of dollars in potential tourist revenue than any intrinsic artistic merits of the work itself. Christo and Jeanne-Claude had modified their plan so that no trace would be left when the installation was removed, and they themselves underwrote the $20 million in costs with proceeds from sales of their other works. And Central Park was a different place than it was in 1979, thanks to various cultural developments—cleaner, safer, more hospitable and far more widely visited by New Yorkers and out-of-town visitors alike. On February 12, 2005, "*The Gates*, Central Park: 1979-2005" unfurled for a sixteen-day run.

Hundreds of thousands of city residents and visitors walked through the park during those sixteen days. And suddenly it became possible to answer the three questions that were unanswerable before. *What did* The Gates *make possible?* Artists and city officials answered this question differently: the artists could point to the ways that the installation helped visitors see Central Park's winding paths afresh; the mayor pointed to the revenue the city earned from the influx of tourists. *What did* The Gates *make impossible, or at least much more difficult?* It made it impossible to reserve a hotel room in Manhattan during the two weekends of the installation—normally not a problem in the dead of winter. The artists' willingness to fully fund their own artwork, praised by Mayor Bloomberg, might well make it more difficult for public support of the arts, especially grand public installations, to gain widespread support. *What new culture was created in response?* Newspapers and magazines published articles celebrating, criticizing and interpreting the project; reproductions of the artists' sketches and drawings, formerly languishing in their studio, were sold at a premium to eager buyers, with the proceeds funding a New York arts foundation; and no doubt, the fertile imaginations of Christo and Jeanne-Claude were already at work on an even grander project somewhere in the world, its prospects enhanced by the popular success of their venture in Central Park.

REAL ARTISTS SHIP

Culture making requires shared goods. Culture making is *people* (plural) making something of the world—it is never a solitary affair. Only artifacts that leave the solitude of their inventors' studios and imaginations can move the horizons of possibility and become the raw material for more culture making. Until an artifact is shared, it is not culture. In the pithy words attributed to Apple Computer founder Steve Jobs when his engineers were tempted to put off the release date of the first Macintosh: "Real artists ship." Jobs was willing to flatter his engineers, with their attention to detail and passion for perfection, by calling them artists—but he also was calling them back to the fundamental requirement of every software developer, to "ship" a working product to a wider public.

In February 2005, *The Gates* shipped. It crossed the threshold from personal project to shared cultural good. And yet, at another scale, *The Gates* never set sail at all. For billions of people, *The Gates* came and went without notice, moving no horizons and generating no new cultural artifacts. Indeed, if you live far from New York City, *The Gates* may not have had the slightest cultural effect on you until you read these pages. For a few million people, at least for a few weeks in February 2005, *The Gates* was culture, but for most of the world it might as well have stayed in Christo and Jeanne-Claude's studio.

So just as we can't speak of culture without speaking of particular artifacts and specific things, we can't speak of culture without speaking of particular "publics": specific groups of people who are affected by particular acts of making something of the world. Once again, we're reminded of the danger of talking about "the Culture," as if it were an undifferentiated, single thing. Just as we must always ask which cultural goods are meant by a reference to "Culture," we must also ask which public receives and responds to those goods. If real artists—and real engineers, lawmakers, novelists and general contractors—ship, they have to have a real shipping address. Beyond the addresses where their cultural artifacts arrive, those artifacts are not culture at all.

The insight that culture has many different addresses, and that not every cultural good affects the same public, is the most basic form of "multiculturalism." Multiculturalism begins with the simple observation that the cumulative, creative process of human culture has happened in widely different places, with widely different results, throughout human history. Before the rise of modern technologies of communication and transportation, the work of culture making could be going on simultaneously in myriad locations, each cut off from the next. Over thousands of years, one generation made something of the world and handed on an enriched (but perhaps also, in other ways, impoverished) world to the next. As this process was repeated over and over, in realms from the preparation of food to the nature of political authority to the stories that were told to make sense of the stars, cultures developed—historically continuous traditions of a particular, multigenerational public who shared a set of common cultural goods, handed on and honed by countless culture makers who "shipped" to their neighbors and their descendants. The Greeks, and the writers of the New Testament, called these various cultural traditions *ta ethnē*—the "peoples" or "nations."

So when we speak of "ethnic" cultures we (making something of the cultural good that is the Greek word *ethnē*) are referring to these extraordinarily complex, rich collections of traditions of culture making, each rooted in a particular set of times and places. But we should not be misled by the common associations of the word *ethnic*. In many American supermarkets you can still find an "ethnic food" aisle—as if only some kinds of food participate in a particular cultural tradition. Nonsense—all food is "ethnic." Real cooks ship too, and they ship to particular addresses.

COURTHOUSE CULTURE

My first—and so far, only—visit to a court of law came when I was twenty-six years old, a newlywed in search of a new name.

Few aspects of any culture's world-making project are as deeply rooted as the traditions of marriage, the set of cultural practices that make sense of men and women, our passionate and sometimes unruly affections for one another, and our capacity to conceive and nurture children. In my case, my culture, as expressed in the laws of the Commonwealth of Massachusetts, didn't quite make sense of the world as I understood it. When Catherine Hirshfeld and I had filled out our marriage certificate, it was easy enough for her to change her name to reflect the biblical teaching that we were creating a new family by making our marriage vows to one another—she could simply change her last name to match mine, and change her former family name to her middle name. But on the "groom" side of the marriage certificate there was no way to change my name—even though my religious tradition, perhaps hinting at the matriarchal assumptions of one stage of Jewish history, said that "a man leaves his father and mother and clings to his wife, and they become one flesh." Why couldn't my name, too, reflect that new identity that had been sealed in our promises to one another?

So I was off to probate court to legally change my name to match Catherine's: we would each have her family name as our middle name, and my family name as our last name. I would leave behind my middle name Bennett, along with its ties to my mother's family, not to mention my childhood pride in the initials ABC, and become Andrew Hirshfeld Crouch.

But first I had to find the courtroom.

I walked into a vast hall echoing with footsteps and voices. Corridors led in several directions, marked with cryptic signs. A bored-looking woman wearing a badge sat behind a desk. When I explained my purpose, she pointed vaguely down one of the hallways.

After wandering in that general direction I finally found the courtroom where my petition could be heard. When I finally reached the judge's bench to make my simple request, I found my heart pounding and my throat dry. I stammered out my reason for changing my name, answered a few questions from the brusque though not unkind judge, and was done. I left the courthouse feeling the same mixture of triumph and exhaustion one sees on the faces of people who finish a triathlon.

I learned several things about culture during my visit to probate court.

The courthouse was, in one sense, part of my culture as an American citizen. But it was a sphere of culture I had no prior experience in. My feelings of dislocation and unease visiting the courthouse were not so different from the way I have felt when traveling in countries where I don't speak the language. In both cases, I found myself thrust into a world-making tradition, with its own history, its own initiates who were fluent in the culture. Though I hadn't left America—or even my own regional, ethnic and linguistic corner of America—in visiting the courthouse I had still entered a new sphere of culture, where I felt anxious and helpless. I suddenly understood why lawyers are such a good idea.

I also learned something about cultural power. Within the courthouse, of course, there were people with official power. The bailiff at the desk had a degree of power, the judge at the bench had even more. But quite aside from roles and titles, the daily inhabitants of the courthouse, whatever their position in its hierarchy, had a kind of power that came merely from being fluent in that sphere of culture. They knew their way around; they even knew who had official forms of power, and that knowledge was a kind of power in itself.

For a few moments, in an admittedly very limited way, I experienced what it is like to be poor. Poverty is not just a matter of lacking financial resources; it can also simply mean being cut off from cultural power. To be poor is to be unable to "make something of the world." On first entering the courthouse I had no idea how to make something of its world. Only because I actually was not at all poor—I speak English, I am a fairly confident person, and I have the good fortune to live in a country where however vague and bored they may be, bailiffs are still expected to help ordinary citizens—was I able to navigate through the courthouse's unfamiliar culture and remake one of the most fundamental aspects of my world: my name.

SPHERES OF CULTURE

The courthouse is just one of a host of spheres of culture. Thinking just in terms of buildings, consider the unique cultural features and the particular forms of world making embodied in a mall, a sewage treatment plant, a bank, a high-school cafeteria, an auto dealership, a prison, a television studio, a resort hotel, a hospital, a high-rise office building, a library, a dentist's office, a semiconductor fabrication plant, a bar or—last but not least—a church. In each of these places, people are making something of the world. But the culture of each building, and the culture of the more abstract sphere they represent—retail, water treatment, banking, education and so on—has its own history of making and remaking, of possibility and impossibility. Many things that are entirely possible in a cafeteria—say, a food fight—are all but impossible in a dentist's office, and vice versa.

These various spheres do overlap and influence each other—that is to say, they affect one another's horizons of possibility and impossibility. The culture of the sewage treatment plant has a great deal to do with the culture of the resort hotel, though the guests may never realize it: without sewage treatment for hundreds of rooms, the hotel could not exist. The bank's formal and informal lending policies affect how many cars the dealership can afford to have on its lot. Workers in the high-rise office building may prefer their church culture to be like their office's—pleasantly anonymous, professionally cleaned and well supplied with parking.

Certain spheres of culture also have special powers. Every building required the approval of local (and sometimes regional and national) government officials before it was built. Furthermore, the culture that each building represents is constrained by laws that the government enforces. Other spheres of culture do not have the same coercive power as the government, but they are no less influential. Educational institutions pass on some kinds of knowledge and not others; mass media select a certain set of images and ideas to set before the public; retailers choose to offer some products and not others to consumers. These spheres of culture can profoundly shape the horizons of possibility and impossibility far beyond their own borders, as when a cell phone sold in the mall is carried into the library, the dentist's office and the church, creating the possibility of instant communication, and instant interruption, in all of those places.

SCALES OF CULTURE

Just as there are many different *spheres* of culture—different encapsulated traditions of world making—so culture happens at many different scales. I wrote a good portion of this book in the Gryphon Café in Wayne, Pennsylvania, a friendly coffee shop presided over by a pony-tailed thirty-something owner named Rich, staffed by artfully scruffy twenty-somethings and patronized by the bourgeois bohemians of Philadelphia's Main Line, a crowd that includes birdlike suburban moms with chirping cell phones, groups of intermittently studious students from nearby colleges, and realtors looking over property listings with anxious-looking young strivers.

The fact that I can give you a fairly complete description of the Gryphon Café depends on its participation in a broader culture, one that includes coffee shops, ponytails, realtors and bourgeois bohemians. But the culture of the Gryphon Café—the things it makes of the world, the horizons of possibility it creates within its walls, the new culture that its denizens make in response—is not exactly like any other coffee shop. The Gryphon Café is not just making something of the vast world of coffee or the current boom in "third places" all over America fueled by the growth of Starbucks; it is also making something of the lovely building it inhabits at the corner of Wayne and Lancaster Avenues, of local artists who hang their work on its walls, of the availability of artfully scruffy twenty-somethings who somehow can afford to live in an affluent community on a barista's wages. The horizons of possibility are ever so subtly different here from the horizons at the Starbucks half a mile from my house, which is why I often find it worthwhile to drive the ten miles to the Gryphon to wrestle with ideas and words. Within those horizons, people create new culture—a band called The Bitter Sweet plays on a Tuesday night, a parents' association gathers here on Thursdays to talk about the public schools, teenagers practice their flirting over hot chocolate on a February afternoon after school.

The Gryphon Café, all seventeen tables and one thousand square feet of it, is a convergence of shared cultural goods. It is a culture. The scale of the Gryphon Café's culture is small, compared to Christo's *Gates*, and it certainly depends on many other forms of culture on a larger scale. But it is a real enterprise in making something of the world, with real cultural effects, and just because it is small does not mean it is insignificant or simple. A full description of the Gryphon's culture could occupy a particularly hedonistic anthropologist for years.

But there are even smaller scales at which culture happens. A basic unit of culture is the family, where we first begin making something of the world. Food and language, two of culture's most far-reaching forms, begin in the home, which may encompass a "public" as small as two people. It can take us decades to appreciate all the ways in which the culture of our families set our horizons of the possible and the impossible. Until we leave our families and venture into the homes of our neighbors and friends, or perhaps the family home of our future spouse, we are likely not even to realize all the ways that our family sets our horizons. In one family's culture it is "impossible" for people who love each other to argue with one another; in another family's culture it is "impossible" for people who love each other *not* to argue with one another. One family makes it possible for the whole extended family of aunts, uncles, nephews, nieces, cousins and grandparents to gather nearly every week for Sunday dinner; another family barely manages to reunite at Thanksgiving. In one family elaborately spiced meals appear every night from the kitchen; in another comfort food comes by way of the freezer and the microwave. Family is culture at its smallest—and its most powerful.

It is easy to talk as if the culture that matters is culture whose public encompasses millions of people. Certainly a cultural artifact like the English language, which in one way or another touches perhaps two-thirds of the world's population, is of tremendous importance. But to focus only on cultural artifacts of such grand scale is to miss a crucial point, which is that the larger the scale of culture, the less anyone can plausibly claim to be a "culture maker." Who makes the English language? Who decides which new words get admitted into the common vocabulary? Who even can grasp the profusion of forms of English around the world, from the Scottish brogue to an American Southern drawl to the lingua franca of the Indian subcontinent? Culture that is everyone's property is in no one's grasp.

But as we consider smaller scales of culture, we begin to have more meaningful influence over what culture makes of the world. As parents of two children, Timothy and Amy, my wife Catherine and I truly have the ability to make some things possible and others impossible for them and for ourselves—even though our culture making takes place within larger horizons over which we have less control. So the culture of our family makes possible, or at least much easier, music making, bread baking, reading, storytelling, baseball watching and Sunday afternoon tea (and also occasional spasms of collective busyness, prolonged sessions on the Internet and frantic Sunday mornings before church); it makes impossible, or at least much more difficult, video games, football prowess and fashion-forward dressing (also, all too often, quiet time for mom and dad, a clean kitchen and prayer). I can do very little about the horizons of the English language, but I can do a lot about the culture of my family. For better and for worse, it is what Catherine and I have made it.

Likewise, in her work as a professor of physics, Catherine can do much to shape the culture of her courses and her research lab. In the somewhat sterile and technological environment of a physics laboratory, she can play classical music to create an atmosphere of creativity and beauty. She can shape the way her students respond to exciting and disappointing results, and can model both hard work and good rest rather than frantic work and fitful procrastination. By bringing her children with her to work occasionally she can create a culture where family is not an interruption from work, and where research and teaching are natural parts of a mother's life; by inviting her students into our home she can show that she values them as persons, not just as units of research productivity. At the small scale of her laboratory and classroom, she has real ability to reshape the world.

As we move out from our own home or workplace, we move into larger scales of culture. When we moved to Swarthmore, the small town in Pennsylvania where we now live, we entered a cultural world very different from Cambridge, the city we had just left. And our town's local culture participates in larger layers of culture—the culture of southeast Pennsylvania, the culture of the United States, the culture of the North Atlantic nations. To understand the culture of my little four-person nuclear family, you also need to understand the myriad scales of culture that surround it, radiating out like concentric circles from our household to the four-thousand-year-old project of Western civilization. To understand the culture of Catherine's laboratory, you also need to understand the college where she teaches, the broader worlds of physics and academia, and the extraordinary human enterprise of scientific investigation and discovery. Each of those circles contributes to what Catherine, our children and I can imagine as possible and impossible—each circle constrains us and sets us free.

FINDING OUR PLACE IN CULTURAL DIVERSITY

If human beings stayed in one place for eons, then the different scales of culture might look like the ripples outward from a single pebble landing in a lake. But because people are constantly on the move, cultural circles overlap almost everywhere in the world, and nowhere in such an intricate pattern of mutual influence as the United States. My family preserves some of the cultural heritage of the American Midwest and South. Down the street is a Jewish family who participate in a set of concentric circles that trace their way back to the ancient nation of Israel. Across from them is a couple who have been shaped by the concentric circles that made twentieth-century China. Two blocks over is a family whose African American culture was decisively shaped by the Atlantic slave trade centuries ago.

When we talk about cultural diversity, we are often thinking of the ripples that have been imported through centuries of such voluntary and involuntary movement across cultures. The diversity of a country like America is sustained by countless choices about which cultural world we will inhabit, where we will settle down to our world-making project. My choice to drive to the Gryphon Café, to make something of (and make something within) the horizons it generates, reinforces certain cultures—the culture of the independently owned coffee shop, the culture of bourgeois bohemia, the culture of the automobile—and leaves other cultural spheres and scales untouched and untended. When my African American neighbor passes by the Italian American–owned barbershop in our town on his way to a black-owned barbershop six miles away, he is not just prudently calculating that the culture of Italian American barbering has no idea what to make of what the prophet Daniel called "hair like pure wool"—he is also reinforcing his link to a culture that could otherwise become distant and irrelevant.

So finding our place in the world as culture makers requires us to pay attention to culture's many dimensions. We will make something of the world in a particular ethnic tradition, in particular spheres, at particular scales. There is no such thing as "the Culture," and any attempt to talk about "the Culture," especially in terms of "transforming the Culture," is misled and misleading. Real culture making, not to mention cultural transformation, begins with a decision about which cultural world—or, better, worlds—we will attempt to make something of.

Some people choose a set of cultural ripples that was not originally their own. When they do so in pursuit of economic or political opportunities, we've traditionally called them "immigrants"; when they do so in pursuit of evangelistic or religious opportunities, we've called them "missionaries." But as the wheels within wheels overlap more and more in a mobile world, most of us have some choice about which cultures we will call our own. We are almost all immigrants now, and more of us than we may realize are missionaries too.

3

TEARDOWNS, TECHNOLOGY
AND CHANGE

Culture changes, and the evidence is in this sentence—in the spelling.

Until the Renaissance, there were no "silent *e*s" in the English language. In fact, there were hardly any silent letters at all—people wrote down what they spoke, sound by sound (and until the rise of the dictionary, their spellynges often did not agree). They wrote the *e* at the end of words like, well, *like*, because they heard an *e*, not because their second grade teacher told them to. Somewhere along the way pronunciation changed, but spelling did not. And because the English people traded with, conquered and were conquered by a host of other peoples, the English language acquired words, and unpredictable spellings, from all their languages as well, a process that has only accelerated in the era of cheap and frequent worldwide travel. It's not only *e*s that are silent—every letter in English can be silent except *j* and *v*. Even for those two letters, to the chagrin of second-graders everywhere, it's probably only a matter of time.

The difference between the way we spell and the way we talk gives us a glimpse into cultural change. Our language is the result of centuries of adaptation, accommodation and assimilation. Embedded in the words we speak and the way we write is a history that includes Viking raiders despoiling coastal villages, French armies advancing over England, British colonizers co-opting Indian maharajahs, Arab traders making their way along the spice routes, slave traders crossing the Atlantic with ships packed with human cargo, and Celtic missionaries walking and praying their way through pagan northern England. Even further back are Phoenicians setting out on the Mediterranean and nomadic peoples spreading out from the Indus River valley.

And within these grand and often terrible movements of history there is the complex history of language and writing itself—the tales told around fires in the old north of England that a bard wrote down in the epic poem we call *Beowulf,* the plays performed by the sometimes-starving artists of the Lord Chamberlain's Men, the edict of King James that set dozens of scholars to producing a translation of the Bible into English, the clipped cadences of a woman in Amherst, Massachusetts, dressed in white, the thundering voice of an African American preacher on the Washington Mall in 1963. Even if we do not know their names or what they said, they still shape the way we speak and what we listen for. We live in their world—the world made of what they made.

FROM LANGUAGE TO LASERS

Language changes slowly, and for much of human history that was true of nearly all forms of culture. But the last few centuries have brought change of a much speedier sort. In 1951 a scientist named Charles Townes was sitting on a park bench in Washington, D.C., when he suddenly had an idea for a device he would come to call "microwave amplification by stimulated emission of radiation," or, for short, a maser. Within two years he and his colleagues had built a working model.

There was no obvious use for a maser. But Townes and his group kept experimenting. By 1958 they had begun to lay the theoretical groundwork for an "optical maser" that would emit visible light rather than microwaves. In 1960, another research group in California built the first laser. In 1964, Townes and several other researchers shared the Nobel Prize for physics for their discovery. One of the most consequential inventions of the twentieth century had gone from obscurity to celebrity in the space of a decade.

Any piece of technology, like all culture, has countless unpredictable effects, but lasers rank with transistors and integrated circuits as one of the most startlingly versatile and mutable inventions of our time. Townes and his colleagues could never have foreseen all the uses to which lasers were put in the next few decades. They are in living rooms (powering DVD players), in surgical suites (performing delicate cosmetic procedures and correcting nearsightedness), under oceans (transmitting terabits of data per second from one continent to another), in offices (in printers and color copiers) and in supermarkets (scanning bar codes, another amazingly versatile invention, with its own countless knock-on effects, that would not be possible without lasers). In 1960 there were a handful of lasers in the entire world; now the chances are that as you read this book, you are no more than fifty feet from one.

THE TROUBLE WITH PROGRESS

The English language has changed little enough in four hundred years that we can read Shakespeare without too much effort; in forty years, devices like the laser have become ubiquitous and all but essential to our culture. But the difference between language and lasers is not just a matter of the speed with which they change. We find it natural to speak of lasers as an "advance" over masers—because they use a wider spectrum of light than masers were able to harness—just as the tiny low-powered lasers that make LASIK treatments and DVDs possible are an "advance" over the unwieldy lab-bench lasers of the 1960s. Not only does technological knowledge clearly build on previous scientific and engineering achievements, the results for human beings, whether measured in the acuity of our eyesight or the vividness of our home movies, seem clearly to have improved.

Americans love improvement. Whether in the can-do spirit of American engineers solving a technological problem, American leaders setting out to change history by building democracy in far-off lands, American dieters embracing the latest plan, or American Christians dreaming of cultural renewal, we tell ourselves stories of progress.

But the language of improvement can be dangerous and misleading when applied to many of the most important features of culture. Language, like lasers, changes. Yet is twenty-first-century American English an *improvement* over the Anglo-Saxon of *Beowulf?* This is not an easy question to answer. Human languages, as they develop, do not seem to become either more complex or more simple—or, strangely enough, they seem to become both. The language of *Beowulf* includes grammatical "cases," different endings signaling a word's function in the sentence, that have all but disappeared from modern English. So English has become simpler. On the other hand, the number of words in modern English vastly outnumbers the vocabulary of *Beowulf*'s first hearers. In this sense English has become more complex. As far back as historical linguists can peer into the processes of change that gave us our modern languages, there is no clear pattern of either progress or decay. Long-lost languages were no more or less complex than our own. As far as linguists can tell, language is always changing—but it never "improves."

What is true for language is true for many cultural goods that rely on it. Is *The Great Gatsby* an improvement over *Beowulf?* Is *The Waste Land* an improvement over Dante's *Divine Comedy?* These questions are not only difficult to answer, they strike us as very possibly absurd. Indeed, one of the simplest ways to distinguish between the subjects we call the "sciences" and the subjects we call the "humanities" is that the humanities deal with topics where there is no unambiguous measure of improvement. Charles Townes's Nobel Prize–winning paper of 1958 describing the laser is no longer read by working scientists—it has long since been superseded. But serious students of literature still read *The Waste Land*, *Beowulf* and Homer because, while the stories told by the great writers and poets may change, they never improve.

A few years ago we moved into a house that had just been thoroughly renovated by a contractor named Ken Crowther. It had been neglected, inside and out, for many years, to the point of being the subject of at least one admonishing letter in the local weekly paper. Its owners, grown old and infirm, had ceased to make something of their cultural world—and more to the point, were sufficiently cut off from kin and community that there was no one to come alongside them and take up the cultural work they were no longer able to carry out.

Ken tore out the weeds in the front yard and planted flowering shrubs.

Inside, he restored the worn, wooden floors, tore down a few walls and resurfaced the rest, installed new cabinets and tile in the kitchen. He applied fresh paint inside and out. We have been fending off compliments from grateful passersby, who think we did the work ourselves, ever since.

Is our home an improvement over the tired building on a weed-infested lot that stood here just a few years ago? Yes. But is it an improvement over the solid, modest house that was built on this site in the 1940s? I'm not so sure. In certain technological senses, it is. Its kitchen counters are granite instead of Formica, which is an unmixed blessing when I am making bread or chopping parsley. Its windows are more energy-efficient—though that efficiency is more than offset by the addition of central air conditioning. But in the broader sense, in its function of being a home, a building that makes something of the corner lot on which it sits, a structure that participates in the cultural world of our small town, I don't see that it represents progress. Our home has changed dramatically over its sixty years of existence, but the most important changes have not so much improved it as maintained it—which is to say, kept it faithful to its possibilities, made the most of its opportunities and minimized its limitations.

If progress is not the right word for buildings or poems, what is the right way to evaluate cultural change? I suggest *integrity*. We can speak of progress when a certain arena of culture is more whole, more faithful to the world of which it is making something. That world includes the previous instances of culture created by generations before us. Progress in a house, as Stewart Brand suggests in his rich study of cultural change, *How Buildings Learn*, really means effectively adapting a building to the requirements of its surroundings and the needs of its occupants. Our house is a lovely and valuable home because it has been lived in—it has settled into the landscape and surrounding neighborhood in subtle ways—and it has been restored with an eye to making the most of its history and its possibilities.

Sometimes the cycle of culture making breaks down. Buildings are allowed to fall into such disrepair that they must be razed to the ground rather than lovingly maintained and improved. Or owners demolish even well-maintained homes in search of the maximum square footage per acre—the phenomenon of "teardowns" that has arrived in many high-priced suburban communities. The teardown may represent a kind of progress: the new house is superior in nearly every technological way to the building it replaced. But it also represents a kind of cultural failure—the failure to make something of the world that was given to the owners of that piece of property. Such failure is sometimes inevitable—the world we must make something of includes, for better or worse, the economic realities of the real estate markets and the construction business, the unwise and slipshod architectural choices of previous generations, and laws governing land use that impose relatively stiff taxes on small buildings. But while responsibility for the cultural failure of a teardown may be shared by many parties, it is a failure still.

Even cultural change that seems unambiguously positive is often more complicated. In industrial England, children as young as six were sent to work in the mines. The passage of laws barring child labor strikes us as clear cultural progress. But in fact there was child labor in England long before industrialization. In an agricultural world children worked alongside their parents from an early age. Such an arrangement was not necessarily exploitative—a fact recognized even today by the exceptions child labor laws make for farm families.

It was only with the rise of industrialization—hailed as the clearest sort of "progress" at the time—that the conditions emerged within which children's labor, previously acceptable, became a distortion of human life and dignity. The "progress" of child labor laws simply restored a kind of equity and safety to childhood that the "progress" of industrialization had undone.

A world where children do not have to toil in dangerous conditions far from their parents is clearly an improvement over one where mine owners treat children as dispensable units of labor. But what about a world where children never get to participate in the economy of the family, never see their parents at work and are never given responsibility for cultivating the earth? Is that really an improvement over the world where families shared responsibility for their corner of the created world, where boys and girls learned skills alongside their fathers and mothers, and where culture was created largely by the communal effort of families rather than commercial enterprises? At one scale, we see clear progress; at another, larger scale we realize that while much has been gained, something real has been lost.

RATES OF CHANGE

Culture is constantly changing, and different kinds of culture change at different rates. In *How Buildings Learn*, Brand observes that every building consists of six layers. From the inside out, he labels them Stuff, Space Plan, Services, Skin, Structure and Site. Each layer changes at its own rate. The stuff in a home—the furniture and fixtures—may change in just a few years. The space plan—the arrangement of interior walls, the placement of doors—may change once a decade or so; the services—electricity, water, heat, waste disposal—may need replacing every twenty years. At the other end of the spectrum, the site, the physical land and legally defined property on which the building sits, bounded by streets and other properties, may not change for hundreds of years.

In *The Clock of the Long Now*, Brand applies the same model to culture as a whole, dividing it into Fashion, Commerce, Infrastructure and Governance. These layers "[work] down from fast and attention-getting to slow and powerful. Note that as people get older, their interests tend to migrate to the slower parts of the continuum. . . . Adolescents are obsessed by fashion, elders bored by it." We could argue with Brand's four layers. Where do omelets fit in his scheme? How about lasers? How about language? But the core insight is crucial. Some aspects of culture change rapidly—at the level of fashion, where hemlines or sideburns go up and down, they change chaotically and cyclically, with no real long-term trend at all. Woe to the cultural observer or would-be culture maker who ascribes great importance to this year's preference for tucked or untucked shirts. Fashion rarely changes in any particular direction from year to year; it simply comes and goes.

Brand's most important insight is that there is an inverse relationship between a cultural layer's *speed of change* and its *longevity of impact*. The faster a given layer of culture changes, the less long-term effect it has on the horizons of possibility and impossibility. My life as an American citizen is profoundly shaped by centuries of development in our political system, especially the ideals of governance ratified by the Constitutional Convention in 1787 and shaped by countless legislative and judicial decisions since. But my life is not at all affected by the fashions for men's wigs in 1787. By the same token, any change that will profoundly move the horizons of possibility and impossibility will almost always, by definition, take lots of time. The bigger the change we hope for, the longer we must be willing to invest, work and wait for it.

What about revolutions—sudden changes at the level of governance and other large-scale, long-term structures of culture? Or what about revivals—the sudden, precipitous, spiritually motivated turning points in culture that many Christians pray for, sometimes as their sole hope for change in the culture? There can be no doubt that we can point to moments in history when cultural change accelerated or changed course. What about the Constitutional Convention of 1787, the battle of Waterloo, or the New York City "businessmen's revivals" that dramatically increased support for the abolitionist cause?

These moments tend to be foreshortened by hindsight. They appear to us as moments, but to those who lived through them they often were lengthy, unpredictable series of smaller events. The Constitutional Convention debated for months, with many moments of tedium, many blind alleys and many revisions, before they produced the document that has so shaped American governance. Furthermore, that Convention could not have come to its conclusions without two hundred years of writing, mostly in England, about political philosophy.

Even aside from the development of technological devices like lasers, some culture-changing events do seem to happen in the blink of an eye. In the course of a few hours on the morning of September 11, 2001, nineteen men radically changed the culture of the United States. But even such nearly instantaneous events are not as instantaneous as they seem. They are like earthquakes, which seem to happen suddenly, without warning. But we know that earthquakes are only the climactic events of a process that has taken years, sometimes decades, centuries or millennia, of accumulated stresses deep under the earth. From the point of view of many Americans, September 11 was a revolution, but for the terrorists themselves that was just one day in a much longer process with a history stretching back at least to the Crusades and a future extending to a far-off but devoutly hoped for culmination of a worldwide caliphate, and indeed an envisioned afterlife of heavenly rewards for their martyrdom. Nothing that matters, no matter how sudden, does not have a long history and take part in a long future.

And like earthquakes, revolutions are much better at destroying than building. There is an important asymmetry here, whose roots go all the way down to the laws of physics: It is possible to change things quickly *for the worse*. It only took two hours after the collision between a 767 and the South Tower of the World Trade Center to destroy it. But no one can build the World Trade Center in two hours. The only thing you can do with Rome in a day is burn it.

The revolutionaries—and terrorists—of the world put their hope in cataclysmic events. But even they are likely to be disappointed by the long-term effects of their actions. After the 2005 bombings in the London Underground, the *Economist* observed, "No city . . . can stop terrorists altogether. What can be said, though, is that terrorists are unable to stop cities, either." The attacks of September 11, 2001, undoubtedly set in motion huge, and very likely tragic, changes. But they did not change as much as all of us who witnessed them thought they would. At the largest scale of culture, even horrific revolutionary events cannot easily destroy. All the more so, the most beneficial events possible have little positive effect in the short run.

THE INVISIBLE RESURRECTION

As Christians tell the story, the three days encompassing the condemnation, crucifixion, burial and resurrection of Jesus of Nazareth were the most extraordinary sequence of events in human history—events accompanied by physical earthquakes, splitting the temple veil and opening tombs, which mirrored the historical and spiritual drama of that divine intervention.

In chapter eight we will look in more depth at the cultural implications of Jesus' resurrection. As we will see, believers and nonbelievers alike can agree that whatever happened that early Sunday morning was the most culturally significant event in history. Surely here is evidence that the best hope for dramatic cultural change is in singular acts of divine intervention?

And yet the cultural implications of Jesus' resurrection, one day or one week after the event, were exactly nil. The following Sunday, according to the Gospels, the witnesses to that earth-shattering event were hidden in an obscure corner of Jerusalem in fear for their lives. The event that would do more than any other in history to alter the horizons of possibility and impossibility had not yet had the slightest effect on the life of a typical resident of Jerusalem. Arguably, it had not even had much effect on the few who had seen evidence of the event with their own eyes.

A few decades later there was a burgeoning movement of witnesses to the resurrection and those who believed their testimony. But their cultural impact was still minimal, meriting only the most cursory references in the correspondence of Roman officials and the annals of contemporary historians. It was not until several hundred years had passed that the Christian movement, with the assistance of a possibly converted and certainly savvy emperor named Constantine, began to shape the horizons of the Roman Empire. Even the resurrection of Jesus, the most extraordinary intervention of God in history, took hundreds of years to have widespread cultural effects.

So hope in a future revolution, or revival, to solve the problems of our contemporary culture is usually misplaced. And such a hope makes us especially vulnerable to fashion, mistaking shifts in the wind for changes in the climate. Fads sweep across the cultural landscape and believers invest outsized portions of energy and commitment in furthering the fad, mistaking it for real change. The mass media, which are largely driven by fashion, can amplify the effect of a fad—for a few weeks, everyone is humming the number one song, the band is on *Saturday Night Live* and talking with Leno, the video is in heavy rotation. If the song or the band has Christian affinities, websites will spring up overnight celebrating a new victory for the gospel in the culture. The short-term effects may be startling. But the long-term effects are negligible.

When we celebrate the arrival of the new Christian band, we are treating them as a technological device—the cultural equivalent of a laser that will in a few short years reshape the culture in significant ways. Strangely, we rarely fail to be surprised when the device fails to deliver at the scale that we had hoped. Culture watchers sometimes talk about the "silver bullet" theory of Christian influence—the dream that someday, someone will write "the perfect song" that will, in four minutes of pure inspiration, bring about a wave of repentance and conversion in our land. This is treating a song like a device. It is turning music into technology. Christians are not the only ones who cherish this fantasy—advertisers of all sorts have mastered the art of transmuting music and art into the technology of persuasion. In fact, it might not be too much to say that the four-minute pop song is itself a device, a technologically massaged tool for the delivery of pleasing or cathartic emotions.

The record of technology as science—relieving human beings of specific burdens and diseases—is splendid. The record of technology as a metaphor for being human is disastrous. When technology is used to win wars, it becomes the atomic bomb. When it is used to control human sexuality, it becomes the destruction of millions of unborn lives and, in contraception, all too often fosters the disengagement of fruitfulness from love. The biggest cultural mistake we can indulge in is to yearn for technological "solutions" to our deepest cultural "problems."

CULTURE IS MORE THAN WORLDVIEW

By now we should be completely cured of talking about "the culture." Not only does this shorthand way of speaking gloss over culture's many *spheres;* not only does it ignore the difference between culture's different *scales;* not only does it pass too quickly over *ethnic diversity;* we can now add to the lengthy list of charges against this beguiling abstraction that it is far too static a way of talking about a phenomenon that is always changing. The only meaningful use of the phrase "the culture" is embedded in a longer phrase: the culture of a particular sphere, at a particular scale, for a particular people or public (ethnicity), at a particular time. And even this much more careful way of speaking needs to always be accompanied by the awareness that the culture we are describing is changing, perhaps slowly, perhaps quickly.

But there is one more easy abstraction we need to clear up in order to appreciate how culture changes. To define culture as *what human beings make of the world* is to make clear that culture is much more than a "worldview."

The language of worldview has become widespread among Christians in the past few years as a way for understanding both their own faith and the surrounding culture. There are "worldview academies," "worldview weekends" and "worldview ministries," like the one that aims "to equip Christians in understanding and defending the Christian worldview in the public square." There is even a site that bills itself as "the complete yellow pages of Christian Worldview Sites," with links to dozens of other "worldview resources."

One of the best expositions of the importance of worldview, Brian J. Walsh and J. Richard Middleton's *The Transforming Vision*, defines worldview this way:

> World views are perceptual frameworks. They are ways of seeing. . . . Our world view determines our values. It helps us interpret the world around us. It sorts out what is important from what is not, what is of highest value from what is least. A world view, then, provides a model *of the world* which guides its adherents *in the world.*

A worldview, Middleton and Walsh say, comprises a culture's answer to four crucial questions: *Who are we? Where are we? What's wrong? What's the remedy?*

Walsh and Middleton engagingly present the Christian answers to these questions. And those answers are intended to be, as the title puts it, a transforming vision. As the back cover of the book says, Walsh and Middleton "long to see Christianity penetrate the structures of society, reforming and remolding our culture. From scholarship in the universities to politics, business and family life, the Christian vision can transform our world."

Yet as Nicholas Wolterstorff observes in his foreword to Walsh and Middleton's book, the world seems strangely unaffected by the "transforming vision":

> Why doesn't it actually work this way? Why does the Christian world view remain so disembodied in spite of the fact that so many in our society count themselves as Christians? The answer that Walsh and Middleton develop is that Christians in general *fail to perceive the radical comprehensiveness of the biblical world view.*

Authors are not responsible either for forewords or for back covers, but I think both Wolterstorff and the anonymous copy writer accurately reflect the thrust of Walsh and Middleton's book and most of the Christian writing on "worldview." The emphasis is on *understanding* worldview. "Why does the Christian world view remain so disembodied?" Wolterstorff asks. His answer is telling—it remains disembodied because it is insufficiently understood, or to use Wolterstorff's verb, *perceived*. Christianity has not yet reformed and remolded our culture because of a lack of "vision." But this is a strange turn of thought from Wolterstorff's acute statement of the core problem, namely that Christianity is "disembodied." You would think that the solution to disembodiment would be embodiment—the living out in the flesh of the transforming vision. And indeed every Christian proponent of worldview thinking gestures enthusiastically in this direction. But the emphasis always somehow stays on perception and vision, on thinking, on analysis.

One of the leading proponents of worldview, Nancy Pearcey, wrote an ambitious book called *Total Truth*. It is engagingly written and well-sprinkled with anecdotes, but its preoccupation is with demonstrating the radical comprehensiveness of a Christian way of thinking. Indeed, for Pearcey, "worldview" and "worldview thinking" are all but synonymous. "The heart of worldview thinking lies in its practical and personal application," she writes, but the section of her book on that subject, titled "What Next? Living It Out," takes up 21 pages out of the book's 480. On the very last page we find the language of embodiment again, in a quote from theologian Lesslie Newbigin: "The gospel is not to meant to be 'a disembodied message,' Newbigin writes. It is meant to be fleshed out in a 'congregation of men and women who believe it and live by it.' . . . In one sense," Pearcey concludes, "this chapter should have been the first."

Yet embodiment may not flow as naturally from thinking as many books on worldview imply. The cartoonist Sidney Harris's most famous drawing shows two scientists standing in front of a blackboard covered with a series of equations. In the middle of the equations is written, "Then a miracle occurs." One scientist says to the other, "I think you need to be more explicit here in step two."

When we say, "The Christian vision can transform our world," something similar is happening. Is it really true that simply perceiving the radical comprehensiveness of the Christian worldview would "transform the world"? Or is there a middle step that is being skipped over all too lightly?

Indeed, apply Walsh and Middleton's questions to the worldview enterprise itself. *Who are we?* We are thinkers—academics, writers and readers. *What is wrong?* The problem is an ineffectual, "disembodied" Christianity, one that makes little difference in culture or even, all too often, in the life choices of its adherents. Yet this is subtly rewritten into a fundamentally intellectual problem, that of insufficient attention to or perception of the Christian worldview. *What is the remedy?* The remedy is further explication of, and sometimes defense of, the truth of the Christian worldview.

What is privileged above all in the world of worldview is *analysis*. Worldview is a concept drawn from the world of philosophy, and in the world of philosophy the philosopher is king. Perhaps inevitably, people with strong analytical and philosophical gifts look at the evident problem of Christian disembodiment and propose not a profound program of embodiment but more thinking as the solution. And after we have done a lot *more thinking*, how exactly does the world change? Well, "then a miracle occurs."

Worldviews are important. They lurk under our first two diagnostic questions—*What does culture assume about the way the world is? What does it assume about the way the world should be?* There is no doubt that underlying beliefs and values play an important part in human choices about what culture to make. Indeed, you could say that the second of our two senses of the phrase *what human beings make of the world*—the sense or meaning we make of the world—is all about worldview in exactly the way that Walsh and Middleton describe it.

But "worldview," when it means a set of philosophical presuppositions, is too limiting a way of analyzing culture. What is the worldview of an omelet? What is the worldview of the Navajo language? What is the worldview of a chair? The language of worldview is well suited to forms of culture that deal primarily with ideas and imagination—books like this one, poems, plays, paintings. Of all these artifacts we can easily ask what view of the world they presuppose. But it's not so easy or useful to ask that question about omelets or lasers. Omelets do not arise out of a worldview—they create a world.

The danger of reducing culture to worldview is that we may miss the most distinctive thing about culture, which is that *cultural goods have a life of their own.* They reshape the world in unpredictable ways. The interstate highway system was certainly based on a worldview (assumptions about the way the world is and ought to be), and it did have many of the effects that its proponents predicted. But it also had other effects that were equally if not more significant, effects that were unpredicted and unpredictable. The interstate highway system was not just the result of a worldview, it was the source of a new way of viewing the world.

The language of worldview tends to imply, to paraphrase the Catholic writer Richard Rohr, that we can think ourselves into new ways of behaving. But that is not the way culture works. Culture helps us behave ourselves into new ways of thinking. The risk in thinking "worldviewishly" is that we will start to think that the best way to change culture is to analyze it. We will start worldview academies, host worldview seminars, write worldview books. These may have some real value if they help us understand the horizons that our culture shapes, but they cannot substitute for the creation of real cultural goods. And they will subtly tend to produce philosophers rather than plumbers, abstract thinkers instead of artists and artisans. They can create a cultural niche in which "worldview thinkers" are privileged while other kinds of culture makers are shunted aside.

But culture is not changed simply by thinking.

4

CULTIVATION AND CREATION

Tonight I will cook dinner for my family. Over high heat I will sauté onions and green peppers until they begin to caramelize and turn golden brown. I will add coriander and chili powder, mixing up a fragrant and spicy paste, then—when the whole glorious mess is just short of smoking—pour chopped tomatoes into the pot. As steam rises from the rapidly cooling pan, I will deglaze it with a wooden spatula, then add red kidney beans, black beans, corn and bulgur wheat cooked in tomato juice. When the whole mixture has returned to a boil, I will turn down the heat to a barely visible simmering flame. I will have spent less than thirty minutes, a good thing on a busy weeknight in autumn.

Then I will light the candles on our table, the little votive lights and the lantern, and—if I'm in the mood—the six candles in the chandelier overhead. I will set out cloth napkins, plates, glasses and silverware. I will call the family from the corners of the house, we will sit down, and I will bring the pot to the table. We will say our prayer of thanks, adapted from a Jewish blessing that has served God's people for several millennia: "Blessed are you, Lord God, King of the Universe, who gives us this food to eat." And then we will have our chili.

Actually that is not quite right. Because my children do not like chili.

They particularly protest whenever they see a green pepper looming in the bowl, and they don't much care for the tomatoes, even though—as Catherine and I have pointed out to them over and over—they are perfectly happy when those same ingredients are served in spaghetti sauce.

In a few years, when my children are older, they will probably like chili, green peppers and all. But suppose they don't—suppose that this part of our family culture still strikes them as a violation of their taste buds and the Law of Not Combining Green and Red Things. What are their options?

They could protest more and more vociferously until Catherine and I give up on making chili altogether. The problem with this is that Catherine and I love, deeply love, our chili. When autumn comes around each year, we'll be making chili until we are too old to chop the onions. And we are not particularly indulgent parents—what is served for dinner is what's for dinner.

Instead of simply protesting, our children could increase the sophistication of their critique of the chili, explaining in more detail why the green peppers are too sour, why tomatoes are appealing when puréed but appalling when chunky.

Alternatively, our children could just give up, consuming whatever we serve. They might even grow to tolerate, if not like, the green peppers and chunky tomatoes. Or, at the other extreme, when they are old enough they could simply stop coming to dinner altogether. Once they leave the house they will be able to cook their chili any way they want.

For the moment, however, they are stuck—no chili, no dinner until tomorrow night. As far as my children are concerned, our dinner is the only game in town. And none of these strategies is likely to change the menu on a crisp fall night when time is short and we are looking for something hearty and filling to serve.

There is one thing our children could do, though, that could have a decisive effect on our family's culture of the table. If I come home on a Tuesday night a few years from now (when they are old enough that I can trust them with the knives) and find dinner already simmering on the stove, even if it's not chili, I will likely be delighted. Especially if the food being prepared is a substantial improvement on our usual fare, just as tasty and even more creative than I would have prepared myself.

Consider this a parable of cultural change, illustrating this fundamental rule: *The only way to change culture is to create more of it.* This simple but elusive reality follows from observations we've already made about culture. First, culture is the accumulation of very tangible things—the stuff people make of the world. This is obscured when people talk about culture as something vague and ethereal—such as the common comparison between human beings in culture and fish in water. The fish, we suppose, are completely unaware of the existence of water, let alone all the ways that water both enables and constrains their fishy lives. While it's certainly true that culture can have effects on us that we're not aware of, culture itself is anything but invisible. We hear it, we smell it, we taste it, we touch it, and we see it. Culture presents itself to our five senses—or it is not culture at all. If culture is to change, it will be because some new tangible (or audible or visible or olfactory) thing is presented to a wide enough public that it begins to reshape their world.

Second, as the philosopher Albert Borgmann has observed, human cultures have the strange yet fortunate property of always being full. No culture experiences itself as thin or incomplete. Consider language. No human language seems to its speakers to lack the capacity to describe everything they experience—or, at least, all our languages fail at the same limits of mystery. Even though our languages divide up the color spectrum very differently from one another, for example, every human language has a name for every color its speakers can see. No one is waiting for a new word to come along so they can begin talking about yellow. Consequently, cultural change will only happen when something new displaces, to some extent, existing culture in a very tangible way. Our family eats dinner every night and, if our country's prosperity continues, we will go on eating dinner every night. Our dinner-table culture will only change if someone offers us something sufficiently new and compelling to displace the current items on our menu.

So if we seek to change culture, we will have to create something new, something that will persuade our neighbors to set aside some existing set of cultural goods for our new proposal. And note well that there are a number of other possible strategies, none of which, by themselves, will have any effect on culture at all.

Condemning culture. Children turn up their noses at chili for many reasons, most of them childish. But adults can be disgusted by culture too, and often for very good reasons. However, if all we do is condemn culture—especially if we mostly just talk among ourselves, mutually agreeing on how bad things are becoming—we are very unlikely indeed to have any cultural effect, because human nature abhors a cultural vacuum. It is the very rare human being who will give up some set of cultural goods just because someone condemns them. They need something better, or their current set of cultural goods will have to do, as deficient as they may be.

Consider the movie industry. A long economic chain stretches from the writers, directors, actors and producers of movies through the distributors and movie theaters to the customers who show up on a Friday night. There are tremendous incentives at every link of the chain to keep the cycle of production, distribution and consumption going. Suppose we don't like what the local cinema is showing on a given weekend. No matter how much we may protest—condemning the cultural goods on offer—*unless we offer an alternative*, the show will go on.

Critiquing culture. What if we are a bit more subtle? We do not simply condemn the movies outright—we analyze them, critiquing them carefully to show how they are inadequate or misguided. Perhaps we even recognize that some movies have certain redeeming qualities, and we expend a great deal of energy tabulating the moments when they succeed. We may produce very sophisticated analyses of the cultural goods around us. And to be sure, if our analysis takes the form of words on paper, voices on a podcast or text on the Internet, the analysis itself is a cultural good. But the depressing truth—especially for those of us who make our living as cultural critics!—is that critique and analysis very rarely change culture at all. For several decades Hollywood's profits have been driven by blockbusters and sequels that are frequently panned by the best-respected critics. No matter how barbed (or beneficent) the reviews, year after year the summer blockbusters break records. The analysis of the critics has only the tiniest effect on what succeeds and fails, swamped by the simple word-of-mouth endorsements of ordinary folks looking for some entertainment on Friday night.

Critics who publish in popular newspapers and websites at least can hope that tens of thousands of readers will encounter their opinions. Yet the most prolific producers of cultural analysis are found in the world of academia, even though outside the rarefied world of the universities, learned critiques, whether positive or negative, rarely make contact with the culture as a whole. *Within* the cultural world of academia, works of analysis can be significant, making and breaking careers and even starting whole schools of interpretation, but these works are inert if they never leave the ivory tower. The academic fallacy is that once you have understood something—analyzed and critiqued it—you have changed it. But academic libraries are full of brilliant analyses of every facet of human culture that have made no difference at all in the world beyond the stacks.

To be sure, the best critics can change the framework in which creators do their work—setting the standard against which future creations are measured. But such analysis has lasting influence only when someone creates something new in the public realm.

Copying culture. Another, rather different approach to unsatisfactory culture is to imitate it, replacing the offensive bits with more palatable ones. A subculture within American society might decide that the best solution to the desultory state of the film industry is to start their own movie industry, complete with producers, directors, writers, actors and even theaters, and create a kind of parallel film industry that will fix the apparent problems in mainstream cinema. The new movies created and distributed by this system would certainly be cultural goods, of a sort. But if they were never shown in mainstream movie theaters—if, indeed, they were created and consumed entirely by members of a particular subculture—they would have no influence on the culture of mainstream movies at all.

Any cultural good, after all, only moves the horizons for the particular public who experience it. For the rest of the world, it is as if that piece of culture, no matter how excellent or significant it might be, never existed. Imitative culture might provide a safe haven from the mainstream—but those who never encountered it would keep going to the movies just as they did before. When we copy culture within our own private enclaves, the culture at large remains unchanged.

Consuming culture. Another possible approach, though, is simply to consume culture, perhaps selectively or even strategically. In a consumer soci-

ety the choices of consumers do have undeniable power in shaping what is
produced. What if enough consumers decided to vote with their dollars in
order to compel Hollywood to produce a different kind of movie?

Among Christians, easily the most controversial movie of 2006 was
The Da Vinci Code, the film version of Dan Brown's best-selling gnostic
detective thriller. Barbara Nicolosi, a screenwriter and Christian leader
in Hollywood, wrote a perceptive piece that was published on the widely
read website Christianity Today Movies. Nicolosi rejected the idea that
The Da Vinci Code (the movie or the book) could be constructively "engaged" or seen as a resource for "evangelism." "Is slander an opportunity?
Is angry superiority an opportunity? [*The Da Vinci Code*] represents all the
'opportunity' that the Roman persecutions offered the early Church." But
she also observed that a boycott, the usual last resort of Christians upset
with a cultural product and its producers, simply wouldn't work:

> Any publicity is good publicity. Protests not only fuel the box office, they
> make all Christians look like idiots. And protests and boycotts do nothing
> to help shape the decisions being made right now about what movies Hol-
> lywood will make in the next few years. (Or they convince Hollywood to
> make more movies that will provoke Christians to protest, which will drive
> the box office up.)
>
> Some suggest that we simply ignore the movie. But the problem with
> this option is that the box office is a ballot box. The only people whose votes
> are counted are those who buy tickets; if you stay home, you have thrown
> your vote away, and you do nothing to shape the Hollywood decision-
> making process regarding what movies will make it to the big screen.

Nicolosi offered an ingenious and (as far as I know) unprecedented alternative: an "othercott."

> On [*Da Vinci Code's*] opening weekend—May 19-21—you should go to the
> movies. Just go to another movie. That's your way of casting your vote, the
> only vote Hollywood recognizes: The power of cold hard cash laid down
> on a box office window on opening weekend. . . . The major studio movie
> scheduled for release against [*Da Vinci Code*] is the DreamWorks animated
> feature *Over the Hedge*. The trailers look fun, and you can take your kids.
> And your friends. And their friends. In fact, let's all go see it.
>
> Let's rock the box office in a way no one expects—without protests,

without boycotts, without arguments, without rancor. Let's show up at the box office ballot box and cast our votes. And buy some popcorn, too.

There are several things to note about Nicolosi's article. First, her article itself was a cultural good—and a creative one at that. She even coined a new word to describe the new cultural strategy she was proposing. Nicolosi was already far from simply condemning, critiquing or copying culture—she was doing her best to be creative in the face of a real (though also, as it turned out, stultifyingly dull) challenge to faith.

Second, her article, which began as a post on her own blog, "Church of the Masses," had significant success as a cultural good—that is, it was successfully *published*, in the literal sense: brought to the attention of a public who began to make something of it themselves. Not only did Christianity Today Movies pick it up and republish it, a Google search suggests that the word *othercott* was used on 1,860 websites in the weeks after Nicolosi's post first appeared.

But the third observation about Nicolosi's charming suggestion of an "othercott" is a rather deflating one. As a strategy for cultural change, it had almost no chance of success, as becomes clear when we run the numbers. An unauthorized peek into the Web statistics of my employer suggests that Nicolosi's article had somewhere between 30,000 and 40,000 readers during the month of May, and let's suppose that a similar number found her article through links elsewhere on the Web, for a total of 75,000 readers. The usual response rate for any kind of call to action—whether an invitation to click on a link on a page or to send a donation to a cause—is in the very low single-digit percentages, as publishers and politicians know all too well, and of course the numbers go down for a call to spend any significant amount of money and time. But let's be generous and suppose that Nicolosi's call generated an unprecedented response rate of 20 percent. Let's further optimistically suppose that each of those motivated and exceptionally influential readers did indeed bring their kids (2.54 of them, of course) and their friends (2 more) and their friends (2 more) to *Over the Hedge* on opening weekend. That would be a total of 113,100 people who shelled out, let's say, an average of $8 per ticket, bringing gross revenue of just over $900,000 to the studios—call it $1 million if you throw in some popcorn.

Well, it's not nothing. But the gross receipts of *Over the Hedge* on its opening weekend were $38.5 million—and the gross receipts of *Da Vinci Code* that same weekend were $77 million. Eventually *Over the Hedge* went on to gross $155 million in the United States and *Da Vinci Code* pulled in $218 million. (An eye-popping number only for someone outside of Hollywood, since that made it only the two-hundredth most successful movie in history.)

In other words, a stunningly enthusiastic response to Nicolosi's call to alternative consumption would have produced an effect of 0.9 percent on the opening weekend performance of the two major feature films (the number goes down to 0.6 percent if you count the top twelve films in wide release that weekend)—and a vanishingly small 0.3 percent on their overall gross. By comparison, good and bad weather (which are bad and good, respectively, for the movie business) are routinely blamed or credited for swings in box office receipts of up to 10 percent. A motivated group of Christian consumers on one of the most hyped weekends in faith-related movie history might have had the impact of a weak low-pressure system in the Upper Midwest.

The reality of life in a globalized culture is that individual consumers, or even large groups of consumers, can only very rarely consume their way into cultural change. Individual consumption decisions are made, as economists say, at the margin, at the edges of the huge effects of aggregated decisions of millions of other purchasers. It should not be too surprising that consumption is an ineffective way to bring cultural change, because consumption is completely dependent on the existence of cultural goods to consume in the first place. The only way to motivate a large enough bloc of consumers to act in a way that really shapes the horizons of possibility and impossibility, in Hollywood or any other massive cultural enterprise, is to create an alternative.

The remarkable fact, however, is that Hollywood is changing—and not because of condemnation, critique, copying or consumption. It is changing because a relatively small group of people—perhaps a few thousand at most, many of them directly or indirectly influenced by Nicolosi's screenwriters training program Act One—have invested their energy, creativity and money in feature films like *The Passion of the Christ* or Walden Media's *The Lion, the Witch, and the Wardrobe*, both of which easily beat *The Da Vinci Code* at the domestic box office. Of course, there were millions of consumers who made those movies commercial successes—but they did so because someone had created something worth seeing and worth bringing your friends to. Creativity is the only viable source of change.

THE ART OF CULTIVATION

There is a paradox here, however. Because culture is cumulative—because every cultural good builds on and incorporates elements of culture that have come before—cultural creativity never starts from scratch. Culture is *what we make of the world*—we start not with a blank slate but with all the richly encultured world that previous generations have handed to us.

So when I go to the kitchen to make dinner or when a screenwriter sits down to write a script, the first requirement of us is that we be sufficiently acquainted with our cultural world. To cook well I need to be familiar with the proper use of knives, the qualities of spices, the properties of stainless steel and cast iron pots. I need to understand something about the culinary tradition I am joining—am I making Italian or Chinese or Mexican food? Likewise, a screenwriter needs to understand the way Western visual storytellers approach their craft, ideally reaching back from Aristotle's *Poetics* through the history of the novel to the act structure of the movie *Chinatown*. She also needs to know the minutiae of the software Final Draft, with its universal standard of fifty-four lines per page, and the meaning of the terms *beat* and *POV*. When it comes to cultural creativity, innocence is not a virtue. The more each of us knows about our cultural domain, the more likely we are to create something new and worthwhile.

To be sure, from time to time throughout history would-be culture makers have tried to throw off traditions of culture altogether, declaring revolutions of various sorts. The high modernity of the twentieth century was perhaps the high watermark of culture making that was deliberately cut off from tradition. In his masterful book *Theology, Music, and Time*, Jeremy Begbie writes about the correspondence between two ultramodernist composers of the twentieth century, John Cage and Pierre Boulez. Cage sought to make music out of natural and random events. His most famous (or infamous) piece, "4' 33"," calls for a performer to come on stage and sit at the instrument, but to make no sound for a predetermined amount of time. Instead, "music" emerges from the random noise heard when a group of people sit quietly and listen: suppressed coughs, the shifting of bodies in seats, distant traffic, low-humming fans. Yet for all its notoriety at the time, Cage's "environmental" music is rarely performed. In the long run it will likely be remembered as an historical curiosity—a provocative but fruitless attempt to cut off the cultural tradition of music. And as Cage was well aware, even his nonmusical music requires a host of cultural traditions. "4' 33"" specifically calls for a performer. It presumes an audience gathered in a chamber. A bold attempt to escape the bonds of the culture of music, it does not quite succeed.

Boulez chose a different and opposite direction from Cage. Instead of eliminating musical tones and gestures altogether, he sought to regiment them through the use of mathematical formulas. But as Begbie points out, this experiment was arguably even less successful than Cage's was. Boulez's music is nearly unlistenable because it does not yield to the human need for variety and shape to sound, nor to the Western tradition's way of imparting that variety and shape.

Boulez and Cage each explored the possibility of culture without culture, culture that tried to escape the culture that preceded it. Yet culture has a way of sneaking in even when it is not wanted. The modern painter Jackson Pollock, who tried to completely eradicate the difference between culture and nature, artist and gravity, produced paintings that have an insistent figural quality to them. As abstract expressionist Makoto Fujimura writes of Pollock, when art students try to imitate Pollock's seemingly grade-schoolish splatters and drips, their work does not begin to compare: Pollock's work is imbued with a tradition of painting, no matter how insistently the artist tries to overthrow that tradition. It would not be great painting without the tradition in which Pollock was trained and shaped.

All culture making requires a choice, conscious or unconscious, to take our place in a cultural tradition. We cannot make culture without culture. And this means that *creation begins with cultivation*—taking care of the good things that culture has already handed on to us. The first responsibility of culture makers is not to make something new but to become fluent in the cultural tradition to which we are responsible. Before we can be culture makers, we must be culture keepers.

CULTIVATION AND DISCIPLINE

Cultivation is a somewhat less appealing word, I've found, than *creation*. *Creation* appeals to our insatiable modern but also simply human quest for the new and the unexpected. *Cultivation* has the ring of another generation, since postindustrial economies can afford to leave the literal cultivation of fields and gardens to a tiny minority of farmers and gardeners—less than 2 percent of the population in the United States in the twenty-first century are farmers, compared to 38 percent in 1900 and 58 percent in 1860. I am just two generations removed from working farmers, so I have vivid memories of hot summer afternoons with my grandparents on their dairy and cattle farms in Illinois and Georgia. Their work was dusty, dirty, sweaty and unending—starting for my dairy-farming grandfather at 5 a.m. every day most of his life. And year after year, with some variation for weather and seasons, they would do much the same thing. Milking a cow is pretty much the same process in January as in October, in 1935 as in 1975.

At the same time, farmers' work demanded great attention to the soil, plants and creatures in their care, and while it could be quite monotonous it also required sensitivity and attention to the fine changes in condition that could mark the beginning of an illness, the onset of a crop disease or an outbreak of weeds. In fact, our word *husband* seems to come from an Old Norse word for someone who lived on and cultivated the soil—suggesting that the intimacy and responsibility of marriage was once made most clear by comparing it to the life of a farmer.

Cultivation in the world of culture is not so different from cultivation in the world of nature. One who cultivates tries to create the most fertile conditions for good things to survive and thrive. Cultivating also requires weeding—sorting out what does and does not belong, what will bear fruit and what will choke it out. Cultivating natural things requires long and practiced familiarity with plants and their place; cultivating cultural things requires careful attention to the history of our culture and current threats and opportunities that surround it. Cultivation is conservation—ensuring that the world we leave behind, whether natural or cultural, contains at least as many possibilities and at least as much excellence as the one we inherited.

Often, whether the subject is chili for children or cinema for conservative Christians, our first instinct with culture is to figure out how to change it. And yet most human beings, most of the time, spend their lives cultivating—conserving—culture. As cultural animals our first task in life is simply to learn the culture we have been born into—a process that is so complex that adulthood is delayed longer for human beings than any other creature. In the West it is popular to imagine children as innately creative, since they lack the self-censoring self-awareness that plagues grownups. And children certainly do express their creative drive to make something new of the world from an early age. But childhood is much more fundamentally about *imitation* than *creation*. Learning language, learning our culture's vast store of stories and sayings and symbols, learning the meaning of street signs and stop lights, learning the rules of baseball, learning to jump a rope and dribble a basketball—none of these are, strictly speaking, acts of culture making. But they are indispensable acts of culture keeping, and they are necessary if the child is ever to grow up to contribute something to that cultural realm. We can only create where we have learned to cultivate.

The most demanding forms of cultivation are *disciplines*—long apprenticeships in the rudiments of a cultural form, small things done over and over that create new capacities in us over time. Nearly every cultural domain has its own disciplines, and it is intriguing that the domains we often consider the most "creative"—art and music, for example—require some of the most demanding disciplines: day after day of practice in the fundamentals of an instrument or exercises in developing the eye and the hand. Chefs practice their knife work; doctors continually read through medical journals. None of these activities, in themselves, is about culture making; all of them are essential to culture keeping.

It's difficult to think of anything more tedious than listening to a pianist playing scales in the privacy of her studio—and my ten-year-old assures me there is nothing more tedious than having to actually do it. He looks forward to the day when he will be able to stop playing scales and play "real music"—though I have warned him that the more serious about piano he becomes, the more scales he will play, since professional musicians can work through the rudiments of their instruments for half an hour or more daily. The discipline of playing scales is a prerequisite for forming the facility with the piano that equips a musician to create a new song or perform an old one with creativity and fidelity.

As small and seemingly insignificant as they are, disciplines can have powerful cultural effects. If I make dinner tonight for my family, nothing much will change in my family's culture. But if I make dinner tonight, tomorrow night, next Tuesday and for the next fifteen years of our children's lives, seeking to do so with creativity, skill and grace that grows over time—even if I never become an avant-garde chef and always follow the recipe—that discipline alone will indeed create a powerful family culture with horizons of possibility and impossibility that we may not even now be able to glimpse.

So underneath almost every act of culture making we find countless small acts of culture keeping. That is why the good screenwriter has first watched a thousand movies; why the surgeon who pioneers a new technique has first performed a thousand routine surgeries; and why the investor who provides funds to the next startup has first studied a thousand balance sheets. Cultural creativity requires cultural maturity. Someday my own children will undoubtedly cook me a wonderful meal—but by that time, they will also have learned to love chili. With any luck, they will be both culture keepers and culture makers—both cultivators and creators. And then they will be prepared to both conserve culture at its best and change it for the better by offering the world something new.

5

GESTURES AND POSTURES

How have Christians related to the vast and complex enterprise of culture? The answers are as varied as the times and places where Christians have lived. When Christians arrive in a new cultural setting, whether a village in the highlands of Thailand or a Thai fusion restaurant in the East Village, they encounter an already-rich heritage of world making. One of the remarkable things about culture, as we observed in chapter four, is that it is never thin or incomplete. Culture is always full. Human beings need culture too much—language, food, clothing, stories, art, meaning—to endure its absence. So from its first years taking root in Palestine to its astonishing dispersion into nations around the world, Christian faith has always had to contend with well-developed and, usually, stable and satisfying cultural systems.

What have Christians made of the world? Consider the four Gospels of the Bible, each one a cultural product designed to introduce the good news in a culturally relevant way. Matthew begins his Gospel this way: "An account of the genealogy of Jesus the Messiah, the son of David, the son of Abraham" (Mt 1:1). His story finds its place in the meaning-making system of Jewish symbolism and textual interpretation. Matthew's

Jesus correlates closely with major figures of Jewish history—Moses on the mountain, David the King—recapitulating familiar stories and fulfilling long-held expectations. Mark, while just as aware of Jesus' Jewish heritage, seems much more engaged with the cultural heritage of Rome. He begins: "The beginning of the good news of Jesus Christ, the Son of God" (Mk 1:1). The Greek word *euangelion*, here translated "good news" but commonly translated "gospel" (making Mark the only Gospel writer to actually call his work a "gospel"), referred to an official proclamation of good news, in particular the Roman practice of sending out heralds to declare victory over Rome's foes. But this *euangelion* is about a very different kind of victory, one that is paradoxically won at the very moment of apparent defeat by Rome itself. Mark's story, in distinction to Matthew's, is not about fulfilled expectations but confounded ones.

Luke, meanwhile, takes on the mantle of a Greek historian, beginning his stately and rhythmic account with the epistolary preface that Greek readers expected, addressing his reader, "most excellent Theophilus" (Lk 1:3). He is careful to note that he has consulted a wide variety of sources and pays close attention, in both his Gospel and its sequel, Acts, to details of medicine, business, politics and geography. John takes up the Jewish philosophical tradition of a thinker like Philo, blending in the first sentence of his Gospel the Hebrew creation story ("In the beginning . . .") with the rarefied vocabulary of Greek metaphysics (". . . was the *logos*").

And in the end each Gospel writer also adopts a different attitude toward the prevailing culture. Luke is broadly positive toward the righteous Gentiles who were probably his primary audience. He traces the apostle Paul's journey to Rome, the center of the dominant culture, with evident hope that this journey would spread the gospel to the ends of the earth. Matthew, Mark and John each seem less certain that the cultures they engage will be welcome homes for the message they are bringing. The world that "God so loved" in John 3:16 is by John 15:18 the world that "hated me before it hated you." The Jewish tradition that Matthew so reveres is also the source of the Pharisaism that his Jesus excoriates. The *euangelion* of Mark is an upside-down good news, in which the King goes willingly to defeat rather than bravely to victory, overturning the expectations of friend and foe alike.

So already in the four initial, inspired retellings of the story of Jesus, we start to see divergent approaches to culture. We can trace the divergences further still when we look at the two thousand years of the Christian faith in the Western world. In the first four centuries Christians lived in the midst of a powerful dominant culture, the Roman Empire, whose tremendous technological and political achievements belied increasing fragmentation and disintegration. Then, at the time of the Emperor Constantine, came the extraordinary breakthrough in which Christianity became the established religion of the empire. For nearly fifteen hundred years, both in Europe and in the Byzantine Empire to the east, Christianity and culture became synonymous in a way the earliest Christians could never have imagined. But fissures had begun to appear in this tidy fusion of Christianity and culture as early as 1054, when the one holy catholic church divided in two, and the fissures spread at the time of the Reformation, when competing expressions of Christian belief and practice rent the political fabric of Europe.

The Reformation and the Renaissance unleashed tremendous cultural energies. But much of this energy had the side effect, usually unintended, of separating the work of culture from Christian faith itself. The world that post-Reformation Europeans had to make something of was a world that no longer had a single unified belief. They also had to contend with the rise of science, a form of culture making that was more powerful in harnessing the natural world to human ends than anything humanity had ever experienced, and which seemed at times to contradict the stories of Scripture and the theology built upon them. But more profoundly, science seemed to promise that human culture could not just *make something of* but could *entirely dominate* the natural world. There seemed to be less and less need for the humility that came from the theology of a transcendent Creator, and also from the everyday human experience of smallness in the face of nature's overwhelming power.

AMERICAN CHRISTIANS AND CULTURE

At the turn of the twentieth century, when Europe, especially its elites, was well into the long decline of Christian faith that has marked that continent since the Enlightenment, America was just emerging from a period of exceptional cultural dominance by evangelical Protestant Christians. The religious right's emphasis on the "faith of the founders" has tended to obscure the fact that the golden age of faith in America was not the time of the founding but the era after the Civil War, when a wave of reform movements, institution-building and cultural creativity was energized by self-described evangelical faith. Aside from a few partially secularized bastions of post-Puritan liberalism in New England (plus Cornell, founded in 1865 as the nation's first explicitly nonsectarian university), the veritable deluge of colleges and universities that were founded in the second half of the nineteenth century were led by earnest Christians, or at the very least people who maintained the polite fiction of being such. As with most golden ages, this one's central figures had plenty of clay appendages, and it did not last long.

When the secularizing culture of Europe finally arrived, it recruited American elites with astonishing speed, driven by two intellectual movements in particular: the scientific movement of Darwinism and the theological-historical movement of biblical criticism. Providing the fuel for swift cultural change was the rise of technology, the application of newly rigorous scientific methods to ordinary life. Within less than a generation, institutions that had been securely in the hands of traditional Protestants were transferred to a new breed of Protestants who were much more accommodating of liberal modernity. From Duke in the South to Princeton in the North, to name two bellwether universities, traditional Protestants were ushered from their positions of cultural dominance, and the charters of the institutions were reinterpreted to express their vestigial Christian identity much more broadly and vaguely. The same forces were at work in hospitals, charities, voluntary associations like the YMCA and YWCA, and in individual churches, in a rapid taking of sides that is now remembered as the "fundamentalist-modernist split." On one side were Christians who were eager to embrace modern (and secularized) culture, sure that this culture too would advance the gospel of "the brotherhood of man under the fatherhood of God"; on the other side were Christians more willing to sacrifice cultural legitimacy than the particulars of their faith.

And thus began the cultural exile of the "fundamentalists," named after a series of pamphlets called *The Fundamentals* but probably made most famous in a stem-winding sermon by the eminent liberal Harry Emerson Fosdick at New York's Riverside Church in 1922: "Shall the Fundamentalists Win?" In Fosdick's lifetime, the fundamentalists certainly did not "win" by any usual measure of cultural influence. The great, grand churches of the mainline denominations—so christened at a time when that word connoted permanence and dominance rather than fading glory—were ceded overwhelmingly to more or less moderate versions of modernism. Indeed, aside from a few outspoken representatives, it is not at all clear that most fundamentalists were interested in "winning." Their understanding of the gospel, reacting in no small part against a "social gospel" that had seemed to sideline many of the traditional concerns of faith, made them more and more suspicious of cultural power. They were disinclined to engage in the sophisticated political maneuvering required to hold on to the large bureaucracies that an earlier generation of evangelicals had so lovingly constructed. By the time Fosdick preached his sermon, it really was all over but the shouting.

For mainline Christians, the chili was just fine. They retained the trappings of cultural power: perches at prestigious universities, beautiful buildings in downtown locations, connections to the wealthy and powerful. The price they paid was to accept that the Christian story would, at a minimum, need to be accommodated to the stories being told by emerging centers of cultural power, the physical sciences and their eager imitators in the newly formed "social sciences." At the time, that price seemed eminently worth paying, and the project of accommodating Christian faith to new cultural developments was exhilarating to a generation of liberal Protestant leaders and churchmen. As a student in a mainline seminary fifteen years ago, I had professors who remembered with awe being present when the theologian Paul Tillich delivered his famous 1948 sermon "You Are Accepted," a masterful reinterpretation of the Christian gospel in an age of privatized psychotherapy.

But the mainline Protestants placed too much confidence in the durability of a particular cultural moment. This was true at the level of ideas, but it was true in more concrete forms of culture as well, like concrete itself. Tremendous assets were invested in church buildings in urban locations that changed dramatically in the second half of the twentieth century. For several years I attended the Church of All Nations, a United Methodist congregation in downtown Boston that had once had a thriving ministry to European immigrants in Boston's South End. At the beginning of the twentieth century, the Church of All Nations had been a cultural powerhouse in its neighborhood, living out the "social gospel" through myriad social services (including the church ministry that eventually became Goodwill Industries). But its building and its neighborhood stood directly in the path of a master plan for so-called urban renewal: the extension of the Massachusetts Turnpike into downtown Boston. Church members, along with their neighbors, fought the Turnpike extension, but the logic of the freeway was irresistible. The lovely Gothic church building was razed to the ground, and the congregation was given a reasonable sum in compensation.

It was then that the church made a quintessentially mainline, and utterly doomed, cultural choice. The church's leaders retained an architectural firm that designed an ultramodern building, a pure two-story cylinder of dull brick, without a single window, set in the midst of a bricked-over plaza. The overwhelming impression of the building was that of a small but fiercely self-protective fortress in a hostile environment, a castle with its drawbridge permanently fixed in the up position, or perhaps a jail. The interior walls, constructed of extruded concrete, curved around a sanctuary that, thanks to wall-to-wall carpeting and a complete lack of parallel reflective surfaces, was nearly acoustically dead, except for the occasional bizarre echo from across the room. Lacking any natural light, daily life in the church required constant artificial light and consequently stratospheric electric bills.

A remarkably diverse and faithful congregation eked out an existence in that building for thirty-five more years, but the truth is that the church's fate was sealed with that single architectural decision in the late 1960s. The Church of All Nations was midcentury mainline Protestantism in a microcosm, steamrollered by a wider culture that was not in the least committed to its success, yet eager to imitate the worst and most transient features of that culture—its industrial hubris, its interstate architecture, its fear of the urban and the poor. It did not matter that, as with many urban mainline congregations, the faith preached from the pulpit was largely orthodox and evangelistic. The church was doomed not by theology or ideology, but by its captivity to a culture that was busy bulldozing down human communities in order to erect efficient facsimiles. Cultures have a powerful drive toward equilibrium, and Boston soon enough abandoned its fascination with modernistic architecture and the discredited rubrics of "urban renewal" and returned to its tremendous historical riches. But the Church of All Nations was too weak to recover and accompany the city surrounding it into renewed health. A few years ago, its doors closed for the last time.

Ninety years after Fosdick's sermon, when we approach the question of Christians and culture in America, we have to pay a great deal of attention to the fundamentalists, their children and their children's children. Far from fading into cultural irrelevance, Christians of traditional theological convictions have come to enjoy the greatest cultural prominence they have known since the nineteenth century—though true nineteenth-century-style dominance is well out of reach. The story of mainline Protestants' engagement with culture is largely unidirectional—greater and greater accommodation paradoxically accompanied by smaller and smaller influence. (There are a few interesting exceptions, most notably the Duke Divinity School ethicist Stanley Hauerwas and his disciples.) But the story of conservative Protestants' relationship to culture is a roller-coaster ride that compresses into one century all the postures I outlined in chapter four, and more.

CONDEMNING CULTURE:
FUNDAMENTALIST WITHDRAWAL

Our stereotype of the twentieth-century Christian fundamentalist surely includes a sweaty preacher decrying the cultural innovation *du jour*. And closely linked with the popular idea of fundamentalism is the idea of withdrawal from culture into a sanctified and safe world of fellow believers. Of course, the fundamentalists did not condemn cultural goods like sturdy church buildings or modest clothing. They were even innovators in the use of new communication technologies like radio and television. Likewise, it is not really true to say that the fundamentalists withdrew from culture.

To withdraw from culture is to wander naked into the rain forest or the desert and never be seen again. While a handful of human beings have done exactly that, the fundamentalists did not. They, like all of us, were cultural beings.

Yet there are several grains of truth in describing fundamentalists as withdrawn from or condemning culture. First, fundamentalist Christians did often, as an article of faith, withdraw from many of the institutions of American culture, from entertainment to politics. Whether their absence was voluntary or forced, lamented or welcome, by midcentury Christians of orthodox theological convictions were scarce indeed at institutions where in many cases they had been dominant two generations before: eastern universities, newspapers and publishers, even the YMCA and YWCA.

Second, "holiness" for fundamentalists came to be closely associated with negative choices—avoiding cultural activities like dancing or going to the movies. I did not grow up in or near fundamentalist Christianity, but friends who did remember plenty of sermons about the *danger* of the world, but none about the *delights* of the world. And fundamentalist Christians, like modernist ones, indulged in an attractive but specious distinction between the church and the culture. Their unspoken assumption was that "the culture" was something distinguishable from their own daily life and enterprises, something that could be withdrawn from, rejected and condemned. In this respect they were just as modern as everyone around them, in accepting too uncritically an easy distinction between the "sacred" and the "secular." This distinction, which served liberals by carving out a sphere of public life that did not have to entangle itself with religion and religious controversies, served fundamentalists by assuring them that it was possible to eschew "secular" pursuits altogether.

So while it is not strictly true to say that fundamentalists "condemned culture," full stop, perhaps it is fair to say that their attitude toward culture—their basic posture—was one of suspicion and condemnation toward any human activity not explicitly justified on biblical grounds and engaged in by fully converted Christians. While the fundamentalist movement is smaller than it was in the twentieth century, you don't have to travel far to encounter Christians for whom this suspicion is still second nature.

CRITIQUING CULTURE:
EVANGELICAL ENGAGEMENT

The second generation of fundamentalism quickly recognized the limitations of cultural condemnation. The "neo-evangelicals"—who chose that name to identify with the more culturally creative and engaged Protestants of the nineteenth century—began to call their fundamentalist communities back into relationship with the wider culture. After World War II a host of evangelical institutions arose that tried to strike a moderate stance between beating the world and joining it. The first editor of *Christianity Today*, Carl F. H. Henry, wrote a landmark book titled *The Uneasy Conscience of Modern Fundamentalism*, questioning the disengagement of many fundamentalist church leaders from social issues like the labor movement and the ethics of war. Significantly, Henry, like many others in his generation, was educated at a decidedly nonfundamentalist institution (Boston University). He engaged in dialogue with modernist Christians and ensured that *Christianity Today*'s coverage ranged beyond intrachurch theological debates.

But the movement that most signaled a change in conservative Christians' posture toward culture was started by an intellectually adventuresome evangelist named Francis Schaeffer, who along with his wife, Edith, formed in the mountains of Switzerland a community called L'Abri that attracted a generation of believing and unbelieving seekers. The posture the Schaeffers modeled toward culture was different from the fundamentalists': they sought to "engage" it, a term that would become a watchword for a whole evangelical generation. Schaeffer was especially interested in high-modern philosophy, art, music and cinema. He treated culture not as something to be condemned and avoided, but as a valuable dialogue partner that offered access to the reigning philosophical assumptions of the time, along with clues to the best way to convince skeptical moderns that the gospel was indeed the most compelling account of reality. Schaeffer and others appropriated the German idea of "worldview" to argue that cultural artifacts were expressions of deep-seated philosophical beliefs that were worth engaging rather than ignoring.

This was a dramatic and positive shift from fundamentalism's negativism. Yet as with all movements, L'Abri was both empowered by and limited by the temperament of its founding generation. The dominant posture toward culture the movement adopted was analysis—often impressively nuanced and learned analysis, to be sure. To "engage" the culture became, and is still today, a near-synonym for *thinking about* the culture. It was assumed, as we observed earlier, that action would follow from reflection, and transformation would follow from information. But the faculties that were most fully developed and valued were the ability to analyze and critique, not to actually sort out how to participate in the hurly-burly of cultural creativity in a pluralistic world. It is perhaps not unfair to say that to this day, evangelicalism, so deeply influenced by the Schaeffers and their many protégés, still produces better art critics than artists.

COPYING CULTURE:
THE JESUS MOVEMENT AND CCM

Of the thousand flowers that bloomed in the 1960s and 1970s, surely the Jesus Movement was one of the least expected. In the midst of the counterculture a widespread revival brought thousands of young people to embrace a very theologically traditional form of Christian faith. But the Jesus Movement was anything but culturally traditional. The taming of the counterculture is so far advanced in our day—when pastors of the most bourgeois of churches may wear Hawaiian shirts and jam with the worship band—that it is hard to remember just how vigorously conventional churches resisted young people's long hair, beads and, worst of all, electric guitars and drums. But in truth the gap between church culture and the wider culture, especially in matters of music and dress, was probably unsustainably wide even before the rise of a vigorous Christian counterculture forced the issue. Church music had remained resolutely classical, or at least classicalish, during one of the most fruitfully creative periods of American popular music, from swing to jazz to bebop and finally to rock 'n' roll. Even before the first Christian rocker played a power chord, American Christianity was cut off from cultural forms that were becoming the primary musical language.

The Jesus Movement changed all that, parrying condemnations of rock's allegedly demonic rhythms with a rallying cry borrowed, it was said, from Martin Luther: "Why should the devil have all the good music?" Christian rockers couldn't deny that the lifestyles and lyrics of rock 'n' roll were incompatible with Christianity, but they had a simple solution: change the content while adopting the form. Over the decade of the 1970s a musical movement that began with a few beleaguered bands touring in seriously beaten-down vans had grown to encompass an entire "industry" called Contemporary Christian Music (CCM).

The rise of CCM was a turning point in the shaping of evangelicalism as we know it today. No Christian movement in the twentieth century had so adroitly borrowed energy from the mainstream culture. Christians were no longer rowing grimly against the wind, as the fundamentalists had done, or tacking across the mainstream of modern culture to try to persuade modern seekers to go in a different direction, as Schaeffer had done so effectively. Now their sails were wide open, running downwind, as CCM producers and artists found a way to fit Jesus into any cultural form that was climbing the charts. All that was required was a keen ability to track the currents, and thanks to a steady influx of converts from "secular music" plus a generation of evangelical youth who had been primed for cultural critique, there was plenty of that to go around. Words could not describe my delight, as a thirteen-year-old just come to personal faith in Christ in the early 1980s, to discover a parallel universe of music that sounded just like the music that played on my clock radio every morning, replacing the sexual innuendo of mainstream pop with a kind of Christian innuendo of artfully expressed faith: "All over me, all over me / I've got the blood of an innocent man all over me."

CCM, along with the many other mini-industries it encouraged, embodied a dramatically different posture toward culture from either the fundamentalists' condemnation or the evangelicals' critique. It was essentially and often uncritically welcoming toward any cultural form that the wider culture might embrace. It shared with the best of evangelical cultural critics a crucial openness to the "common grace" that might be present in the unlikeliest places, but went further than they did to embrace active participation in those forms rather than merely arms-length investigation. But the flip side of this openness to form was a nearly puritanical approach to content, illustrated in the widely shared belief that to succeed in the CCM market, a recording had to meet a "Jesus quotient" in its lyrics.

Artists who attempted to convert from secular music to CCM were told
in no uncertain terms that they had to abandon their earlier repertoire,
which led to painful sights like the 1960s rocker Dion ("The Wanderer")
earnestly performing half-baked anthems in church sanctuaries.

CONSUMING CULTURE:
EVANGELICALISM'S PRESENT TENSE

Perhaps because of discomfort with this lingering sacred-secular split, but
probably also because of CCM's tremendous commercial success, which
has included a fair number of "crossover" acts that have successfully abandoned their Jesus quotient and gone mainstream, it has become fashionable
in many Christian circles to make fun of CCM. The truth is that like critique and even condemnation, copying culture is a posture toward culture
that is alive and well in American conservative Christianity. But it has been
superseded by a simpler approach: simply cutting out the Christian middle-
men who repackaged cultural forms for Christian consumption and going
straight to the source, "secular" culture itself. The dominant posture among
self-described evangelicals today toward culture is neither condemnation
nor critique, nor even CCM's imitation, but simply consumption.

The fundamentalists said, *Don't go to the movies.* The evangelicals said,
*Go to the movies—especially black and white movies by Ingmar Bergman—and
probe their worldview.* Experimenters in CCM-style film would say, *Go to
movies like* Joshua, *soft-focused retellings of the gospel message using cinematic
form.* But most evangelicals today no longer forbid going to the movies,
nor do we engage in earnest Francis Schaeffer-style critiques of the films
we see—we simply go to the movies and, in the immortal word of Keanu
Reeves, say, "Whoa." We walk out of the movie theater amused, titillated,
distracted or thrilled, just like our fellow consumers who do not share our
faith. If anything, when I am among evangelical Christians I find that
they seem to be more avidly consuming the latest offerings of commercial
culture, whether *Pirates of the Caribbean* or *The Simpsons* or *The Sopranos,*
than many of my non-Christian neighbors. They are content to be just like
their fellow Americans, or perhaps, driven by a lingering sense of shame at
their uncool forebears, just slightly more like their fellow Americans than
everyone else.

POSTURES AND GESTURES

I've found that a helpful word for these various responses is *postures*. Our posture is our learned but unconscious default position, our natural stance. It is the position our body assumes when we aren't paying attention, the basic attitude we carry through life. Often it's difficult for us to discern our own posture—as an awkward, gangly teenager I subconsciously slumped to minimize my height, something I would never have noticed if my mother hadn't pointed it out. Only by a fair amount of conscious effort did my posture become less self-effacing and more confident.

Now, in the course of a day I may need any number of bodily *gestures*. I will stoop down to pick up the envelopes that came through the mail slot. I will curl up in our oversized chair with my daughter to read a story. I will reach up to the top of my shelves to grab a book. If I am fortunate I will embrace my wife; if I am unfortunate I will have to throw up my hands to ward off an attack from an assailant. All these gestures can be part of the repertoire of daily living.

Over time, certain gestures may become habit—that is, become part of our posture. I've met former Navy SEALs who walk through life in a half-articulated crouch, ready to pounce or defend. I've met models and actors who carry themselves, even in their own home, as if they are on a stage. I've met soccer players who bounce on the balls of their feet wherever they go, agile and swift. And I've met teenage video-game addicts whose thumbs are always restless and whose shoulders betray a perpetual hunch toward an invisible screen. What began as an occasional gesture, appropriate for particular opportunities and challenges, has become a basic part of their approach to the world.

Something similar, it seems to me, has happened at each stage of American Christians' engagement with culture. Appropriate gestures toward particular cultural goods can become, over time, part of the posture Christians unconsciously adopt toward every cultural situation and setting. Indeed, the appeal of the various postures of condemning, critiquing, copying and consuming—the reason that all of them are still very much with us—is that each of these responses to culture is, at certain times and with specific cultural goods, a necessary gesture.

Condemning culture. Some cultural artifacts can only be condemned.

The international web of violence and lawlessness that sustains the global sex trade is culture, but there is nothing to do with it but eradicate it as quickly and effectively as we can. The only Christian thing to do is to reject it. Likewise, Nazism, a self-conscious attempt to enthrone a particular culture and destroy others, was another wide-ranging cultural phenomenon that demanded Christian condemnation, as Karl Barth, Dietrich Bonhoeffer and other courageous Christians saw in the 1930s. It would not have been enough to form a "Nazi Christian Fellowship" designed to serve the spiritual needs of up-and-comers within the Nazi party. Instead, Barth and Bonhoeffer authored the Barmen Declaration, an unequivocal rejection of the entire cultural apparatus that was Nazi Germany.

Among cultural artifacts around us right now, there are no doubt some that merit condemnation. Pornography is an astonishingly large and powerful industry that creates nothing good and destroys many lives. Our economy has become dangerously dependent on factories in far-off countries where workers are exploited and all but enslaved. Our nation permits the murder of vulnerable unborn children and often turns a blind eye as industrial plants near our poorest citizens pollute the environment of born children. The proper gesture toward such egregious destruction of the good human life is an emphatic *Stop!* backed with all the legitimate force we can muster.

Critiquing culture. Some cultural artifacts deserve to be critiqued. Perhaps the clearest example is the fine arts, which exist almost entirely to spark conversation about ideas and ideals, to raise questions about our cultural moment, and to prompt new ways of seeing the natural and cultural world. At least since the Renaissance, artists in the Western tradition want the rest of us to critique their work, to make something of what they have made, and to make the connections between their work and the traditions of art making as well as the broader streams of change in their culture as a whole. The proper thing to do with art, as Christians or indeed simply as human beings, is to critique it. Indeed, the better the art, the more it drives us to critique. We may watch a formulaic blockbuster for pure escapism, laugh ourselves silly and never say a word about it after we leave the theater. But the more careful and honest the filmmaking, the more we will want to ask one another, "What did you make of that?" Critique is the gesture that corresponds to the particular calling of art and artists.

By the same token, other "gestures" toward art are almost always beside the point. Serious works of art are not made to be consumed—slotted unthinkingly into our daily lives—nor, by law in fact, may they be simply copied and appropriated for Christian use. Of all the possible gestures toward culture, condemnation, in particular, almost always ends up sounding shrill and silly when applied to art. If an attention-starved contemporary artist spatters dung on a portrait of the Madonna or slices up an embalmed shark, what harm is really done? These works are safely ensconced inside the walls of museums with hefty admission prices, not on the street or in the air endangering our children. Furthermore, it is difficult to think of a single instance where condemnation of a work of art has produced any result other than heightened notoriety for the work and the artist.

Consuming culture. There are many cultural goods for which by far the most appropriate response is to consume. When I make a pot of tea or bake a loaf of bread, I do not condemn it as a worldly distraction from spiritual things, nor do I examine it for its worldview and assumptions about reality. I drink the tea and eat the bread, enjoying them in their ephemeral goodness, knowing that tomorrow the tea will be bitter and the bread will be stale. The only appropriate thing to do with these cultural goods is to consume them.

Copying culture. Even the practice of copying cultural goods, borrowing their form from the mainstream culture and infusing them with Christian content, has its place. When we set out to communicate or live the gospel, we never start from scratch. Even before church buildings became completely indistinguishable from warehouse stores, church architects were borrowing from "secular" architects. Long before the Contemporary Christian Music industry developed its uncanny ability to echo any mainstream music trend, church musicians from Bach to the Wesleys were borrowing well-known tunes and reworking them for liturgical use. Why shouldn't the church borrow from any and every cultural form for the purposes of worship and discipleship? The church, after all, is a culture-making enterprise itself, concerned with making something of the world in the light of the story that has taken us by surprise and upended our assumptions about that world. Copying culture can even be, at its best, a way of honoring culture, demonstrating the lesson of Pentecost that every human language, every human cultural form, is capable of bearing the good news.

WHEN GESTURES BECOME POSTURES

The problem is not with any of these gestures—condemning, critiquing, consuming, copying. All of them can be appropriate responses to particular cultural goods. Indeed, each of them may be the only appropriate response to a particular cultural good. But the problem comes when these gestures become too familiar, become the only way we know how to respond to culture, become etched into our unconscious stance toward the world and become postures.

Because while there is much to be condemned in human culture, the posture of condemnation leaves us closed off from the beauty and possibility as well as the grace and mercy in many forms of culture. It also makes us into hypocrites, since we are hardly free of culture ourselves. The culture of our churches and Christian communities is often just as lamentable as the "secular" culture we complain about, something our neighbors can see perfectly well. The posture of condemnation leaves us with nothing to offer even when we manage to persuade our neighbors that a particular cultural good should be discarded. And most fundamentally, having condemnation as our posture makes it almost impossible for us to reflect the image of a God who called the creation "very good" and, even in the wake of the profound cultural breakdown that led to the Flood, promised never to utterly destroy humankind and human culture again. If we are known mostly for our ability to poke holes in every human project, we will probably not be known as people who bear the hope and mercy of God.

Similarly, there is much to be said for critiquing particular cultural goods. But when critique becomes a posture, we end up strangely passive, waiting for culture to deliver us some new item to talk about. Critique as a posture, while an improvement over condemnation as a posture, can leave us strangely unable simply to *enjoy* cultural goods, preoccupied with our interrogation of their "worldview" and "presuppositions." The posture of critique also tempts us toward the academic fallacy of believing that once we have analyzed something, we have understood it. Often true under-standing, of a person or a cultural good, requires participation—throwing ourselves fully into the enjoyment and experience of someone or some-thing without reserving an intellectual, analytical part of ourselves outside of the experience like a suspicious and watchful librarian.

Cultural copying, too, is a good gesture and a poor posture. It is good to honor the many excellences of our cultures by bringing them into the life of the Christian community, whether that is a group of Korean Amer-ican chefs serving up a sumptuous church supper of bulgogi and *ssamjang* or a dreadlocked electric guitarist articulating lament and hope through a vintage tube amp.

But when copying becomes our posture, a whole host of unwanted consequences follows. Like the critics, we become passive, waiting to see what interesting cultural good will be served up next for our imitation and appropriation. In fast-changing cultural domains those whose posture is imitation will find themselves constantly slightly behind the times, so that church worship music tends to be dominated by styles that disappeared from the scene several years before. Any embarrassment about being cul-tural laggards is mitigated by the fact that like a private highway that is only open to cars with fish emblems, our copy-culture by definition will never be seen by the vast majority of the mainstream culture. And in this way, when *all* we do is copy culture for our own Christian ends, cultural copying fails to love or serve our neighbors.

The greatest danger of copying culture, as a posture, is that it may well become all too successful. We end up creating an entire subcultural world within which Christians comfortably move and have their being without ever encountering the broader cultural world they are imitating. We breed a generation that prefers facsimile to reality, simplicity to complexity (for cultural copying, almost by definition, ends up sanding off the rough and surprising edges of any cultural good it appropriates), and familiarity to novelty. Not only is this a generation incapable of genuine creative partici-pation in the ongoing drama of human culture making, it is dangerously detached from a God who is anything but predictable and safe.

For a lesson in the dangers of adopting the posture of cultural copying, Christians might do well to look to Hollywood in the 1990s and 2000s, when major studios seemed mired in an endless series of sequels and adaptations, paralyzed by a dearth of original storytelling. Even movies beloved by Christians—perhaps *especially* movies beloved by Christians—fell prey to this temptation. The original Chronicles of Narnia were the creation of an Oxford don whose posture toward culture was anything but imitative. But movies based on the Chronicles of Narnia are almost required to be slavish imitations of the original, precisely because the original stories were so successful in carving out new horizons of possibility and impossibility. This is not to say that they are not impressive cultural artifacts, achievements of technology, performance and direction. But their very charter is to faithfully transfer an original work in one medium to a derivative work in another. As gestures, the Narnia movies are delightful; but if they reflect and perpetuate a posture of imitation, they only reinforce the poverty of a culture that has forgotten how to tell new stories.

Finally, consumption is the posture of cultural denizens who simply take advantage of all that is offered up by the ever-busy purveyors of novelty, risk-free excitement and pain avoidance. It would not be entirely true to say that consumers are undiscerning in their attitude toward culture, because discernment of a kind is at the very heart of consumer culture. Consumer culture teaches us to pay exquisite attention to our own preferences and desires. Someone whose posture is consumption can spend hours researching the most fashionable and feature-laden cell phone; can know exactly what combination of espresso shots, regular and decaf, whole and skim, amaretto and chocolate, makes for their perfect latte; can take on extraordinary commitments of debt and commuting time in order to live in the right community. But while all of this involves care and work—we might even say "cultural engagement"—it never deviates from the core premise of consumer culture: we are most human when we are purchasing something someone else has made.

Of all the possible postures toward culture, consumption is the one that lives most unthinkingly within a culture's preexisting horizons of possibility and impossibility. The person who condemns culture does so in the name of some other set of values and possibilities. The whole point of critique is becoming aware of the horizons that a given culture creates, for better or worse. Even copying culture and bringing it into the life of the Christian community puts culture to work in the service of something believed to be more true and lasting. But consumption, as a posture, is capitulation: letting the culture set the terms, assuming that the culture knows best and that even our deepest longings (for beauty, truth, love) and fears (of loneliness, loss, death) have some solution that fits comfortably within our culture's horizons, if only we can afford to purchase it.

ARTISTS AND GARDENERS

For a while my own posture toward much of the culture around me was suspicion. I would walk through a mall taking notes on crass commercialism. Upon learning that someone had achieved a certain amount of cultural influence I would begin probing for signs of idolatry, egoism and vanity. I scanned the newspaper looking for obituaries on not just the obituary page but the front page—signs of cultural decay and decline. Of course, in every case there was plenty for me to find, since our malls are full of commercialism, our cultural heroes are often astonishingly full of themselves, and our newspapers never fail to deliver bad news.

But the more I adopted a *posture* of suspicion and critique, the more I felt I was missing something. I had trouble accounting for my own consumption—was my delight in my Apple laptop simply a sign that I had surrendered to the siren song of consumer culture? Disturbingly often I encountered people of tremendous cultural creativity who seemed to be enjoying themselves too sincerely and faithfully to be mere idolaters. And the same newspaper that delivered news of yet another cultural meltdown also brought reasons for hope: an artist working to create beauty in a war zone, tens of thousands of spring-break volunteers descending on a hurricane-ravaged coast, and a big-box retailer that actually paid its workers well, covered their health insurance and sold fine wine to boot.

I thought back to my years serving with a campus ministry at the world's most prestigious university. For many years we were adept at deconstructing the pretensions of Harvard and calling students to a countercultural kingdom life that would undermine (or, to use one of our favorite words, *subvert*) Harvard's power. Our specialty in Harvard critique certainly attracted a certain kind of student, those disaffected from Harvard for one reason or another. But we had a very hard time accounting, in the language of faith, for the delights of a place like Harvard: the thrill of research in a well-equipped laboratory, the ineffable joys of the library stacks, the exhaustion and exhilaration of rowing in a six-man boat on the Charles at 5:30 in the morning. I suspect that many students who visited our fellowship, oriented as it was toward critiquing the culture, simply moved on, puzzled at our diffidence or even annoyed at our apparent hypocrisy. If Harvard was so bad, why didn't we just counsel students to leave and give their tuition money to the poor?

What was missing, I've come to believe, were the two postures that are most characteristically biblical—the two postures that have been least explored by Christians in the last century. They are found at the very beginning of the human story, according to Genesis: like our first parents, we are to be creators and cultivators. Or to put it more poetically, we are artists and gardeners.

The postures of the artist and the gardener have a lot in common. Both begin with contemplation, paying close attention to what is already there. The gardener looks carefully at the landscape; the existing plants, both flowers and weeds; the way the sun falls on the land. The artist regards her subject, her canvas, her paints with care to discern what she can make with them.

And then, after contemplation, the artist and the gardener both adopt a posture of purposeful work. They bring their creativity and effort to their calling. The gardener tends what has gone before, making the most of what is beautiful and weeding out what is distracting or useless. The artist can be more daring: she starts with a blank canvas or a solid piece of stone and gradually brings something out of it that was never there before. They are acting in the image of One who spoke a world into being and stooped down to form creatures from the dust. They are creaturely creators, tending and shaping the world that original Creator made.

I wonder what we Christians are known for in the world outside our churches. Are we known as critics, consumers, copiers, condemners of culture? I'm afraid so. Why aren't we known as cultivators—people who tend and nourish what is best in human culture, who do the hard and painstaking work to preserve the best of what people before us have done? Why aren't we known as creators—people who dare to think and do something that has never been thought or done before, something that makes the world more welcoming and thrilling and beautiful?

THE POSTURES OF FREEDOM

The remarkable thing about having good posture (as my mother never ceased to tell me when I was growing up) is that if you have good posture, you are free to make any number of gestures. As we're reminded when we encounter a skilled dancer or athlete, good posture preserves our body's basic freedom, allowing us to respond to the changing environment with fluidity and grace. But poor posture—being bent into a particular position from which we can never quite escape—leaves us unable to exercise a full range of motion. With good posture, all gestures are available to us; over time, with poor posture, all we can do is a variation of what we have done before.

And the simple truth is that in the mainstream of culture, cultivation and creativity are the postures that confer legitimacy for the other gestures. People who consider themselves stewards of culture—guardians of what is best in a neighborhood, an institution or a field of cultural practice—gain the respect of their peers. Even more so, those who go beyond being mere custodians to creating new cultural goods are the ones who have the world's attention. Indeed, those who have cultivated and created are precisely the ones who have the legitimacy to condemn—whose denunciations, rare and carefully chosen, carry outsize weight. Cultivators and creators are the ones who are invited to critique and whose critiques are often the most telling and fruitful. Cultivators and creators can even copy without becoming mere imitators, drawing on the work of others yet extending it in new and exciting ways—think of the best of hip-hop's culture of sampling, which does not settle for merely reproducing the legends of jazz and R & B but places their work in new sonic contexts. And when they consume, cultivators and creators do so without becoming mere consumers. They do not derive their identity from what they consume but what they create.

If there is a constructive way forward for Christians in the midst of our broken but also beautiful cultures, it will require us to recover these two biblical postures of cultivation and creation. And that recovery will involve revisiting the biblical story itself, where we discover that God is more intimately and eternally concerned with culture than we have yet come to believe.

PART TWO

GOSPEL

6

THE GARDEN AND THE CITY

At this point I need to invite you to take what may seem to be a sharp turn, from culture in all its manifold and changing forms to one particular cultural good: the Bible. The Bible is itself a manifold collection of cultural artifacts—poetry, history, proverbs, letters and songs—written and compiled over one thousand years, and like all the most influential cultural goods it has in turn spurred endless human creativity. It is daunting indeed to try to add to the voices of commentary on this complex and sometimes perplexing book, but if we are going to be oriented to culture in any distinctively Christian way, we need to consider whether the Bible offers us some distinctive approach to the subject. And indeed it does—although many Christians haven't yet realized how radical and wonderful the biblical vision of culture is. So in the next chapters I will try to share some of the discoveries—few or none of them original with me, but many of them unfamiliar to Christians even now—that have energized my reading and rereading of Scripture.

And when considering the Bible's perspective on culture, the Bible's beginning is, as Maria sings in *The Sound of Music*, a very good place to start.

What do we find when we look at the beginning of Scripture for clues about culture? If culture is *what human beings make of the world*, we'd expect to find our first clues when human beings take their place in the world's unfolding drama. And this is exactly what we find in the first mention of humankind on the sixth day of creation in Genesis 1:

> Then God said, "Let us make humankind in our image, according to our likeness; and let them have dominion over the fish of the sea, and over the birds of the air, and over the cattle, and over all the wild animals of the earth, and over every creeping thing that creeps upon the earth."
>
> So God created humankind in his image,
>> in the image of God he created them;
>> male and female he created them.
>
> God blessed them, and God said to them, "Be fruitful and multiply, and fill the earth and subdue it; and have dominion over the fish of the sea and over the birds of the air and over every living thing that moves upon the earth. (Gen 1:26-28)

Even in translation from the original Hebrew, we can see culture at work in the way this story is told. In an age without bold face, capital letters or even written vowels, how would you convey to readers that one section of your text, more than another, was of special importance? In an age long before the invention of paper, when papyrus and parchment were precious, repetition was not something a writer engaged in lightly. The biblical writers, and the oral traditions on which they drew, lavished space, time and breath on the most important parts of their stories. Up until this point each "day" of creation has taken a carefully measured amount of words. But the sixth day stretches out on the first page of my Bible for nearly as long as the previous five days together, and here at the climax in verses 26-28 two key ideas are repeated.

First we are told twice, once as intention and once as instruction, that humans' likeness to God will equip them to "have dominion" over animals in sky, sea and land. We shouldn't pass over this three-part taxonomy too quickly. The author clearly intends us to grasp the extent of human beings' responsibility—they are made to rule not just a few easily domesticated animals like cattle, chickens and goldfish, but the whole panoply of the animal kingdom. It's extraordinary that a biblical author who had seen neither airplanes nor submarines, and for whom boats were small and rudimentary affairs, could anticipate humankind being able to "rule" over fish and birds in any meaningful way. Either the author's conception of rule and dominion is much less about the naked exertion of power than we might imagine, or this text anticipates millennia of cultural developments that would eventually bring us to the point where we truly have the power to shape the destiny of most species on the planet. Perhaps both. In any event, the repetition and comprehensiveness of description makes it plain: human beings will be responsible for the creation in its totality, not just for their immediate neighborhood.

But the double description of the animal kingdom is matched by a quadruple repetition: No less than four times we are told that human beings are made in God's "image" and "likeness." Similar to the language of dominion, the language of likeness is repeated in two contexts: first as God's intention, then as a summary of the results of his work. In each context the language of image or likeness appears twice in a row. At no point before this moment has there been any sense that the created world bears a resemblance to the Creator. God has hovered over it, formed it, rejoiced in its goodness—but he has never seen himself in it. Now, at the climax of creation, he sets out to create a new kind of creature that bears his image.

But what exactly is meant by these words *image* and *likeness?* Generations of readers have offered suggestions ranging from the exegetical to the fanciful. In closest proximity to the summary of the image-bearers' creation, we find humanity created "male and female," suggesting that God's image could only be borne by creatures who embodied both similarity and difference—echoing both the "us" of Genesis 1:26 and the later Christian conviction that God himself is more than a singularity. Less anchored in the text, Augustine suggested that the *imago Dei* is summed up in human beings' rational faculty: our ability to reason logically. Biblical scholar Richard Middleton has drawn the ancient Near Eastern parallel to "viceroys" who would rule in the name of a distant king, and who were said to bear his image. Surely the biblical text is carefully enough crafted that all these insights bear some truth.

But what has been most abundantly clear about God in Genesis 1?

What have we seen of his character over and over, six breathtaking days'
worth? Of course, what we have seen most clearly is that "In the beginning, God created." There may or may not be a hint of trinitarian
diversity, a sense of reason and deliberation, or an echo of Near Eastern
empire, but splashed all over the page is God's purposeful and energetic
desire to create.

So when the human beings, male and female, are created "in God's
image," surely the primary implication is that they will reflect the creative
character of their Maker. Genesis 1 suggests several marks of that character that the divine image-bearers might reflect.

Creation brings being out of nothing. It's customary for Christian writers
to demur that while God truly does bring stuff out of nothing at all, mere
human beings exercise a more limited creativity, working with the world
that God has given. Of course this is true, to a point—the Hebrew word
bara, translated "create," is used exclusively with God as its subject in the
Hebrew Bible. There is a kind of creation that only God can do. For God
to bring something into being required nothing other than his eternal,
loving reality as a starting point. We, on the other hand, always start in
the middle of things, working with the raw materials given us by God
and by the generations before us. Culture is what we *make of the world*, not
what we make out of pure imagination. The Hebrew word *asah*, used of
both human beings and God in the first pages of Genesis, means "make"
in this sense.

And yet there is an *ex nihilo*, "out of nothing," quality to human creativity as well. Human language is so marvelously fruitful, linguists have
asserted, that every human being who has acquired a rudimentary facility
with language has uttered a completely original sentence: a combination
of words that no one else has created. Creativity is not something just for
"creatives"—we all have given being to some sentence the world had never
heard before, and may never hear again. In all likelihood, unless we are
stuck in a dull job and have dull friends, we have done so this very day.
Where did that sentence come from? It was potentially present in the
grammar and vocabulary of our language; it may well bear a resemblance
to words we and others have thought and said before, but it did not exist
before and does now. Had we not spoken it, it would have gone unsaid.

Creation is relational. Not only does God speak in the plural in Genesis 1:26, probably reflecting the ancient idea of a heavenly court as well as foreshadowing the Christian recognition of God as three persons in one, the various elements of creation are created *for one another.* After the first two days, once the most basic element, light—which encompasses heat, energy and information—has been created, and once a space has been created "in the midst of the waters" where creativity can flourish, everything else is created with a view to what comes before and after it. The land created on the third day is immediately followed by the creation of plants and trees that will take root in the land. The land is for the plants, and their seed and fruit fall onto the land, begetting another generation—a tightly integrated web of life in which no one part can stand alone. The "lights in the dome of the sky" are not simply created to exist independently, they are created to shed light on the unfolding story on the land and sea, "to give light upon the earth." The seas become the habitat for the fish; the birds are commanded to multiply to fill the sky. The vegetation is food for the "living creatures of every kind." The human beings likewise do not exist independently of the rest of creation but in profound dependence on it and with great responsibility for parts of it. And in the climax of creation, it becomes plain that the whole world, both those parts that humans can control with relative ease (livestock and plants) and those parts on which they are completely dependent but unable to control (the sun, moon and the waters that lie restrained above the earthly firmament—in modern terms, the fragile skin of atmosphere that makes life possible) is designed for the flourishing of exquisitely relational creatures, male and female, who themselves are very good because they bear the image of a relational God.

Human creativity, then, images God's creativity when it emerges from a lively, loving community of persons and, perhaps more important, when it participates in unlocking the full potential of what has gone before and creating possibilities for what will come later. When human creativity is defective and falls short of God's intention, as with environmental pollution that lays waste to ecosystems or exploitative use of resources like clear-cut logging, it neither honors what has come before nor creates fruitful space for the creatures, human and otherwise, who will come later.

The music of Cage and Boulez was ultimately not relational enough to be satisfying—concerned with escaping what had come before and unable to create space for future composers and musicians to fruitfully inhabit. The same could be said of brutalist architecture, the concrete structures briefly popular in the twentieth century, that seem to begrudge rather than serve their human residents. None of these cultural forms are motivated by the sense of grateful and graceful interdependence that we find woven through the Genesis creation accounts.

From the beginning, *creation requires cultivation*, in the sense of paying attention to ordering and dividing what already exists into fruitful spaces. On the very first day God not only brings light into being, he "separates" light from darkness; on the second and third day, the waters, which left undifferentiated would drown out future life, are separated into the sky and the oceans, carving out a space of dry land. Throughout the creation, the author attends to the distinctions between fish and birds, "cattle and creeping things and wild animals of the earth of every kind." God does not simply create randomly or willy-nilly, but according to a cultivated plan, with the keen attention of a horticulturist or zoologist to species and their proper place in the created order. Indeed, for this Creator, order is itself a gift, a fruitful space.

This is an important point at a time in history when "creativity" often is associated with the rejection of order and when artists in particular can seem to be trying to outdo one another in provocative acts of chaos making. To be sure, there is a place for messy art like the unmade bed that Tracey Emin submitted to the Whitney Biennial several years ago. And no one can read about teeming "swarms of living creatures," let alone contemplate the glorious diversity of our world, and imagine that the world's Creator is primarily interested in neat rank-and-file grids. Yet an essential part of the creative process is in fact the work of sorting, separating and even excluding some alternatives in favor of others. In the text of Genesis the "waters," which seemed endlessly deep and wide to the ancients, are the symbol of limitlessness, of infinity. God's task on the second day is to set limits for the waters, to create sky and land where more creatures can flourish.

If even the divine Creator paints on a limited canvas, then this is much more true for us. We can only introduce so many products, write so many laws, paint so many pictures. The best creativity involves discarding that which is less than best, making room for the cultural goods that are the very best we can do with the world that has been given to us.

Creation leads to celebration. Creation at its best leaves us joyful, not jaded. It prompts delight and wonder, even in the creators themselves, who marvel at the fruitfulness of their small efforts. Creating culture certainly can leave us tired, even exhausted. If the divine Creator chooses to rest, we human creators must rest from our work in order to sustain creativity. The biblical record suggests that we need to rest not just one day a week but for longer times at longer intervals, up to the forty-nine-year cycle called the "jubilee" that allowed both land and farmers to be rejuvenated. But if the work of creating consistently leaves us depressed or drained, it is likely that we have somehow missed the path. Creation, even on a human scale, is meant to end with the glad exclamation, "It is very good."

GENESIS 2: DIRT AND GARDEN

After the first chapter's majestic and stately account, full of sweeping wide-angle shots and soaring vistas, Genesis 2 is an ultratight shot of a hand digging into the ground, a whisper of breath.

> The LORD God formed man from the dust of the ground, and breathed into his nostrils the breath of life; and the man became a living being. And the LORD God planted a garden in Eden, in the east; and there he put the man whom he had formed. . . . The LORD God took the man and put him in the garden of Eden to till it and keep it. (Gen 2:7-8, 15)

If Genesis 1 was about humanity's amazingly dignified position in the cosmos, Genesis 2 is about humanity's call to culture. Indeed, if Genesis 1 is the prologue—the grand scene-setting vision of the goodness of God's creativity and the central place of his image-bearers in the whole great process—Genesis 2 is where the story properly begins. For here we find humankind not just ushered onto a universe-wide, six-day stage of cosmic beginnings but placed in a human-scale environment. We begin with a single, vulnerable individual (Hebrew *adamah*, as yet undifferentiated into male and female) in a garden. And a garden, of course, is not just nature: it is nature *plus culture*.

One of my southern relatives used to like to tell the old story of a city slicker (I think he had me in mind) who visited a farm far out in the country and remarked with awe, "Isn't God's creation beautiful?" The farmer looked at him skeptically and said, "Well, you should have seen it when God had it all to himself."

Yet in Genesis 2, God has already gotten his hands dirty—forming not just the man but also his initial cultural environment. God has seeded the world, as it were, with cultural goods. Adam is not set to work carving a non-existent garden out of wilderness. From the very beginning he benefits from the Creator's own cultural initiative. Here we get a crucial correction to a potential misunderstanding of our definition of culture as *what we make of the world* (and a gentle rebuke to the farmer's understandable skepticism): it is not just nature that is God's gift to humanity. Culture is a gift as well. In the biblical view culture is not simply something we have made up on our own—God was the first gardener, the first culture maker. As in Genesis 1 he asks us not to do something fundamentally different but rather to imitate him—in Genesis 1, to imitate his creativity and gracious dominion over the creation, and here in Genesis 2, to imitate him by cultivating the initial gift of a well-arranged garden, a world where intelligence, skill and imagination have already begun to make something of the world.

Genesis 1 is above all about the Creator's creativity and humankind's creativity in God's image—with a secondary emphasis on the role of cultivation in taking proper care of creation. But in Genesis 2 the primary emphasis is on *cultivation*. The Creator is also a Cultivator, "planting" a garden in the east and arranging its contents. "Out of the ground the Lord God made to grow every tree that is pleasant to the sight and good for food" (Gen 2:9)—notice the emphasis, as in a well-tended garden, on the combination of the beautiful and the useful. He has carefully chosen its location, adjacent to a river and near deposits of precious minerals and the aromatic gum tree that produced a pearl-like substance called bdellium: "the gold of that land is good; bdellium and onyx stone are there" (Gen 2:12). This is not *ex nihilo* creativity—it is paying attention to what already exists and what will be the most fruitful and beautiful use of it; most of all, what will most contribute to the flourishing of the human beings he is about to create.

Yet just as cultivation was a minor theme in the first chapter's symphony of creation, so too here in Genesis 2, where the dominant note is cultivating the garden, there is still a clear thread of creativity. If we focus too narrowly on the phrase "to till and keep it," we might think that the essential cultural task is simply not to mess anything up. We can almost imagine God saying, "All right, Adam, I've laid out this garden very carefully—don't change anything! Just keep it the way it is. And watch out for snakes."

Yet Genesis 2 includes a remarkable scene that suggests that God has much more in mind for Adam's cultural activity than merely being a dutiful conservationist. For when God creates the animals in preparation for completing Adam's humanity with a woman as his companion and partner, we read this extraordinary statement:

> So out of the ground the LORD God formed every animal of the field and every bird of the air, and brought them to the man to see what he would call them; and whatever the man called every living creature, that was its name. (Gen 2:19)

Here again we find the biblical author, heedless of wasted papyrus, stopping to repeat an important idea—and this time it's hard not to detect a hint of a smile in the narrator's words. There's something absurd about the Lord God, who only lately breathed life into a muddy clay figure, patiently bringing every one of the vast panoply of animals and birds to his own creation and waiting "to see what he would call them." Is it possible that the Lord God does not know that a camel is, well, a camel? Does he really need the man to instruct him in the names of cockatiels, cockroaches and crawdads? And yet, just in case we missed the point, "Whatever the man called every living creature"—here the teller of the tale shrugs his shoulders—"that was its name."

What is happening here? What is happening is, in fact, central to the whole of Genesis 2, which depicts God *making room* for his image-bearers to begin to grow into the vast cosmic purpose that was disclosed in Genesis 1. God is perfectly capable of naming every animal and giving Adam a dictionary—but he does not. He makes room for Adam's creativity—not just waiting for Adam to give a preexisting right answer to a quiz but genuinely allowing Adam to be the one who speaks something out of nothing, a name where there had been none, and allowing that name to have its own being. To be sure, God has provided the raw material—the garden, the animals themselves and Adam's very breath. But now the Creator graciously steps back just enough to allow humankind to begin to discover what it means to be a creator. Adam, like his Maker, will be both gardener and poet, both creator and cultivator. The Creator simply watches and listens, and it is good.

And this is what we see, subtly in Genesis 2 and more clearly in Genesis 3: In order for humankind to flourish in their role as cultivators and creators, God will have to voluntarily withdraw, in certain ways, from his own creation. He makes space for the man to name the animals; he makes room for the man and the woman to know one another and explore the garden. He even gives them freedom, tragically but necessarily, to misuse their creative and cultivating capacities. God is always willing to be present, walking in the garden in the cool of the day, but he is also willing to grant humankind their own cultural presence. Without this gracious carving out of space, they would never be able to fulfill their destiny as divine image-bearers; without the gift of a garden protected from the full wild wonder of the teeming earth and waters, they would be overwhelmed. God's first and best gift to humanity is culture, the realm in which human beings themselves will be the cultivators and creators, ultimately contributing to the cosmic purposes of the Cultivator and Creator of the natural world.

BETWEEN THE WILDERNESS AND THE THEME PARK

Before we go on to Genesis 3, it is worth pondering a bit more the significance of the garden as the place where the Creator intends human culture to flourish.

Wilderness is hard to find these days in North America. Still, you can get a taste of it even on a day hike in Wyoming's Grand Teton National Park, where Catherine and I spent our honeymoon. In our ten days there we shared trails with bear, deer and moose; we walked through fields of brilliant flowers that no one had planted or tended, fields that would have flourished in all their glory even if no human being ever found their way to them; we panted in the thin air and shielded our eyes from the strong high-altitude sun.

And then we hiked down the mountain, drove back to our cozy room at the lodge, and enjoyed nice hot showers. I've always been a sucker for hot showers, and it was our honeymoon, after all. Friends of ours spent a two-week honeymoon in the backcountry without a shower in sight. At the time I thought it sounded crazy—though after a decade of marriage, I have to admit it sounds like a good preparation for life together.

But while I can survive, and have even enjoyed, more rigorous adventures, I know this: we would have enjoyed our hikes in the Tetons considerably less if we'd had to survive through even a few summer days and nights there with just our strength and our wits. That would have been closer to hell than honeymoon. The wilderness, by definition, is not a place where human beings can thrive for very long.

Indeed, history suggests that one of culture's first jobs was to domesticate the wilderness—to bring the wildness of nature down to a human scale. I am writing these words on a winter afternoon in front of our fireplace, where logs glow and flicker with comforting heat. Even in our age of central heating, when an open fire is a luxury rather than a necessity, building and tending a fire is a wonderfully human act. I love watching the flames on the logs and the pulsating embers. But of course I enjoy this fire only because it is in its place—a fire*place*. Should a spark jump from the fireplace to a fire-not-place, like our wood floor, fire could change from luxury to disaster in an instant. Only when it is contained is fire a comforting presence. No sane person warms himself innocently at a forest fire.

The journey from fire to fireplace is the journey from wilderness to garden, from nature to culture. Likewise the journeys—some of them thousands of years in the making—from wolves to dogs, waterfalls to dams, or lightning to electric lights.

Yet for many of us, most of the time, this journey out of the wilderness into culture seems as remote as the days of covered wagons wending their perilous way over the Rocky Mountains. Thanks to the explosion of technology in the last century, modern Westerners live in unprecedented isolation from the wildness of the world. Humankind tamed fire millennia ago, keeping the cold at bay; but only in the past hundred years have we figured out how to beat the heat with air conditioning. Nearsighted people like me have had access to lenses for a few hundred years, but only in the past fifty years have contact lenses become ubiquitous. There have been roads as long as there have been communities of people who sought to trade with or conquer one another, but only in the last century, after the invention of hot mix asphalt pavement, have we had roads on which we can glide effortlessly from the Atlantic to the Pacific without feeling more than a few transient bumps. Human beings have cobbled together medicines as best they could to deal with the germs that thrive in the microscopic wilderness all around us, but only in the past century have we had antibiotics that could stop the germs in their tracks.

This extraordinary isolation from wildness deserves a name. It is what makes our generation's moment in history so different from our ancestors', and quite possibly from our descendants'. Let's name it after Walt Disney's masterfully modern cultural invention: the theme park.

In the theme park, culture's triumph over nature seems to be complete. Indeed, the *theme* is more powerful than the *park:* Even the shrubs at Disney World look like Disney characters. All the vestiges of wildness have been carefully pruned. You have no more to fear from the Shark Tank than the Tower of Terror—you may get a thrill from each, but the theme park is carefully designed to eliminate all real risk.

The theme park is a much safer place to be a human being than the wilderness. Or is it? It may be harder to be a human being, as Genesis understands a human being, in a theme park than anywhere else. For if human beings are made in the image of God, creative cultivators of God's creation, the theme park gives them precious little space for such image bearing. There is nothing for me to create or even to tend at a theme park—employees (or to use Disney's term, "cast members") do the creating or tending for me. Unlike the Garden, the theme park is not a place where you can get hurt—or if you do, it's not your fault, and you can sue. And to keep you from getting hurt, in the theme park, you are never alone. Not only are you accompanied by throngs of other park guests but by omnipresent representatives of the theme park corporation, there to ensure and (if necessary) enforce enjoyment of the theme park on the owners' terms.

The Garden, though it is indeed sheltered, is a place of ultimate moral seriousness because it is a place where the Creator himself, having provided all the essentials of the good life yet also having allowed risk and choice (how else can we explain the presence of the serpent?), withdraws for a time to allow the divine image bearers to fulfill their calling to culture, returning only to walk in the garden "in the cool of the day." Only because of this gracious and terribly risky withdrawal does the serpent have the opportunity to tempt the man and the woman. And only in the provisional absence of the Creator do the human beings have the opportunity to twist and degrade their divine image by reaching for what the serpent craftily and deceitfully describes as "be[ing] like God, knowing good and evil" (Gen 3:5)—as if creativity and cultural responsibility were not much more deeply "like God" than mere knowledge.

If we take this story seriously, we will conclude that neither wilderness nor theme parks are good places to be human. Both may be enjoyable places to visit (though I have my doubts about theme parks), but our ability to enjoy them actually requires qualities that only culture, the garden of humanity, can provide. Woe to the traveler who ventures into the wilderness without taking advantage of cultural resources like maps, compasses, hiking boots, tents and accumulated millennia of wisdom about ways to survive in the trackless world. Woe to the tourist parents who have developed no capacities for creativity and cultivation in their own children—they will wander through Disney's surgically sculpted paradise fending off endless complaints of boredom.

Our world is unevenly divided, to say the least, between wilderness and theme parks. Most of humanity lives all too close to wilderness, at the mercy of a creation whose original good wildness has been made implacably hostile to human flourishing by the Fall. A privileged billion or so can choose to live in theme parks, where neither the dangers nor the beauty of the created, fallen world intrude on a manufactured environment of amusement. But we were made for neither theme parks nor wilderness—we were made for the place where we are challenged to become creators and cultivators. We began as gardeners.

FRUIT, FALL AND FIG LEAVES

The serpent too lurks in the Garden, ready to take advantage of the Creator's voluntary withdrawal. Notably, his temptation to them takes the form not of an invitation to create but to consume—and in doing so, to abrogate their role as cultivators who know the proper and improper uses of the trees in the Garden. We know that the primordial humans' creative freedom could be distorted—as we'll see, within a few chapters in Genesis, human creativity would go badly awry. Presumably the serpent could have challenged head-on their task as cultivators as well. But instead he goes for the all-but-passive, minimal disobedience of consumption—the easiest way to breach the trust between humankind and God. And he throws in a bit of critique as well: "Did God really say . . . ?" God had forbidden neither critique nor consumption in general, but here the serpent invites Adam and Eve to warp these gestures into postures, to become critics of God (and another) and to begin seeking wisdom in a quince. We can only sigh with disappointment as Adam and Eve swallow, so to speak, the idea that a fruit could bring "wisdom," even as we recognize how adroitly contemporary advertisers persuade us of equally unlikely results if we will just consume their cosmetics, cars or cigarettes.

But what happens next, for the purposes of our study, is most significant. Once their posture is deformed, once they have broken their relationship of trust with God, they also lose their trust with one another. "Then the eyes of both were opened, and they knew that they were naked; and they sewed fig leaves together and made loincloths for themselves" (Gen 3:7).

They sewed fig leaves together—the first human act after the consumption of the fruit is *cultural*, the creation of that basic cultural good called clothing. They make something of the world. They are no longer freely and spontaneously naming God's good creation; they are no longer cultivating the good Garden; now they are protecting themselves from the sudden alienation they feel from one another and their own bodies. But what they are doing is culture—creating and cultivating—all the same.

This is how deeply culture is embedded in the human character: it is the first response to sin, the first place where the inward alienation from God finds its outward expression. The coming chapters of Genesis will show this kind of culture making at its worst. To be sure, human beings will continue to make something of the world in more or less good ways. They will domesticate livestock and till the ground (Abel and Cain [Gen 4:2]), they will play stringed instruments and pipes (Jubal [Gen 4:21]) and forge tools (Tubal-cain [Gen 4:22]). But the first murder will take place "in the [cultivated] field," and along with the tools will come weapons and violence. After the judgment of the flood, Noah, the one man considered "righteous . . . in this generation" (Gen 7:1) will plant a vineyard, restoring a semblance of the memory of Eden, but he will become drunk on the wine from that very vineyard, and in his drunkenness—consumption that oversteps simple enjoyment into idolatrous use—he will expose his nakedness to his own shame and that of his sons. From the fig leaves onward, culture becomes entwined with sin—indeed, it is the place where humanity acts out their rebellion from God and their alienation from one another. From Genesis 3 to 11, the narrative of culture is a steady descent—from the creativity and the cultivation of Eden to desperate and violent perversions of culture, slathered with self-justification, shame and recrimination.

THE REBELLIOUS CITY

The low point in the arc of Genesis's primordial story is Genesis 11. Human beings arrive in the plain of Shinar in Genesis 11 and systematically put their most advanced culture to work in cementing their alienation from God.

> Now the whole earth had one language and the same words. And as they migrated from the east, they came upon a plain in the land of Shinar and settled there. And they said to one another, "Come, let us make bricks, and burn them thoroughly." And they had brick for stone, and bitumen for mortar. Then they said, "Come, let us build ourselves a city, and a tower with its top in the heavens, and let us make a name for ourselves; otherwise we shall be scattered abroad upon the face of the whole earth." The Lord came down to see the city and the tower, which mortals had built. And the Lord said, "Look, they are one people, and they have all one language; and this is only the beginning of what they will do; nothing that they propose to do will now be impossible for them. Come, let us go down, and confuse their language there, so that they will not understand one another's speech." So the Lord scattered them abroad from there over the face of all the earth, and they left

off building the city. Therefore it was called Babel, because there the LORD
confused the language of all the earth; and from there the LORD scattered
them abroad over the face of all the earth. (Gen 11:1-9)

This justly famous story is packed with culture, for it is the first biblical
story about a city, and cities are the place where culture reaches critical
mass—where culture overtakes nature as the dominant reality that human beings must make something of. A town and a city both have streets,
but when you follow the streets in a town you quickly arrive in the countryside; most city streets lead only to more city. Even in a place like San
Francisco, the city's dramatic hills are of less consequence for daily life
than the grid of streets and trolley routes.

Babel is built on technology: mortar, well-dried bricks and sophisticated architecture. Mortar, bricks and city buildings have a different relationship to nature than a garden. Whereas the garden essentially arranges
the given goods of nature, the city is built on cultural goods like bricks
that are dramatic departures from nature, fundamental reinventions of the
underlying clay and bitumen. So the primordial story of Genesis begins in
a garden and ends in a city—begins with the shaping of nature and ends
with the supplanting of nature.

More significant than this cultural progression, though, is the comprehensive way that culture, for the people of Babel, has supplanted all traces
of dependence on God. Their aim is not just to "build ourselves a city"—it
is to build "a tower with its top in the heavens." Undoubtedly the author
and first readers of Genesis would remember here the Babylonian ziggu-
rat, a massive pyramid-shaped structure with its steps leading to heaven.
The separation between earth and heaven had been a good gift of God
in creation on the second day; but such a separation made human beings
dependent on God "coming down." The completed tower of Babel, on
the other hand, would enable the leaders of Babel to take over the function of communication with the heavens (or so they imagined)—to enter
themselves into the heavenly court envisioned in Genesis 1 rather than to
wait for the Lord to come to them. And this massive cultural project—not
just the tower, it seems, but the city itself—would enable them to "make a
name for ourselves, lest we be scattered abroad upon the face of the whole
earth": to control their own identity and security.

So the city of Babel amounts to a massive declaration of independence from God: a defiantly human effort to deal with the world in its wonder and terror—and to put distance between humans and God in all his wonder and terror. Babel and its tower are the logical end point of the process that began when the man and woman made fig leaves in their first moments of self- and sin-consciousness—a completed cultural project, a city, whose entire purpose is to cover, protect and shield its people from other human beings and from their Creator.

This, then, is one of the arcs of the story of Genesis 1–11, from the fig leaves to the tower. Culture attempts to deal with the consequences of sin. But this is a vain attempt, in all the senses of the word *vain:* prideful, self-regarding and futile. What human beings make of the world only deepens their alienation and independence from their maker. This is the germ of truth in all condemnations of culture. For all its moments of beauty and ingenuity, culture can easily be Babel: a fist-shaking attempt to take over God's roles for ourselves.

And this kind of culture meets with swift judgment. God had barred the way back to Eden lest the man "might reach out his hand and take also from the tree of life, and eat, and live forever" (Gen 3:22)—a merciful gesture to prevent Adam and Eve from living eternally in the futility of their vain attempt to "be like God, knowing good and evil," not realizing that knowing good and evil was very different from being able to *choose* good and reject evil. So at Babel, wryly observing that "nothing that they propose to do will now be impossible for them"—surely not because the Lord is threatened by their ambition but because he recognizes the havoc that such cultural vanity could wreak—God intervenes, scattering humanity into many linguistic-cultural groups, saving them from the worst of their tremendous creative capacity (now turned to creative captivity) and making their mutually incomprehensible languages a sign of their alienation from one another and from God. Now language, the primal cultural gift that most closely mirrored the creative word of the Creator himself, will always also be a sign and reminder of sin.

But the story of culture, which in Genesis 11 already seems to have reached the point of exhaustion and futility, is actually, miraculously, just beginning.

INTERLUDE
The Primordial Story

It is hard to reconcile the definiteness of the Genesis creation stories, where the first human beings are birthed with the same suddenness as a human baby, with the story told by archaeologists and anthropologists. Genesis 1 certainly doesn't require us to think in terms of twenty-four-hour "days," since the first two "days" are completed before the sun or earth are even created. But it is hard to read Genesis 2, where the Creator bends down one day and forms a man in his own image from the clay, without feeling some dissonance with the archaeological record, in which human history seems to fade in, ever so gradually, from the shadows of time. When and where was there an Adam and an Eve? Isn't the history of human culture both more complicated and less sudden than Genesis would have us believe?

I am not personally persuaded by the valiant efforts Bible-believing Christians have made to fit every detail of the Genesis creation stories into the story told by modern cosmology and archaeology. Yet I am not sure the biblical writers would have been terribly troubled by the failings of Genesis 1–11 as literal cosmological history. The Garden of Eden, after all, is described as being at an intersection of four rivers that ancient people knew had no intersection. Genesis's "primordial story"—the arc from Garden to Babel—needs to be read not in the context of modern judgments of archaeological evidence that the biblical writers knew nothing of, but in the context of ancient creation myths that the biblical writers were keen to counter with their own version of the story.

Even so, the stories in Genesis 1–11 strike me and many well-informed readers as much more compatible with our modern understandings of cosmic and human beginnings than most of the creation myths that were circulating in the ancient Near East at the same time. There are rough parallels between the sequence of days in Genesis 1 and our best guess at the gradual evolution in the universe of light, planets, plants and more complex creatures, with humanity coming very late in the game. Genesis 2 does not claim, like some other ancient religions, that humanity is a separate kind of being from the rest of creation, the offspring of the gods. Instead, we are made from dust—made of the same stuff as the world around us. This too turns out to be surprisingly and, for many ancient people, counterintuitively true.

For its part, archaeology cannot answer an equally compelling question: what is it that makes human beings distinctive, and when and how did that happen? Archaeology and anthropology can document the omnivorous human appetite for culture, but they cannot explain where that appetite comes from. Even our closest biological relatives, the orangutans and chimpanzees that are capable of rudimentary language and toolmaking, show no sign of the relentless drive to extend culture beyond what they have inherited, to constantly create and reshape the world. Chimpanzees, like collies, do show curiosity about the world. But they never give any signs of pondering the meaning of the world. Nor do they ever attempt to interpret the world in the complex and beautiful way the painters of Lascaux did, so early in humanity's cultural story.

There is something in us that cannot be reduced to dust—a creative spirit that has the capacity for speech and meaning, in short, for culture. Genesis suggests that this cultural creativity, by which we recognize human beings wherever in time or space we find their traces, is rooted in something just as real as our material being. From Genesis 1 we learn that the world is the work of a Creator, already part of a creative society ("Let us make humankind in our image") that seeks to bring into being a beautiful, ordered, meaningful world. From Genesis 2 we learn that our creative spirit did not simply emerge from the dust but was breathed into us by the same Spirit that originally hovered over the dark, informationless chaos, speaking a sudden and decisive word that set creation in motion.

To be sure, we don't "learn" these things from Genesis 1 or 2 in the same way that we can "learn" about the big bang from studying data produced by radio telescopes. Then again, there are many things we cannot "learn" in that way. The most important things in our life are learned by trust, not by deduction from experiment.

With their primordial story, the chapters of Genesis 1–11 already stand apart from what follows in Genesis 12 and beyond in their form, style and content. They are less a finely documented history than a story that invites our trust. In this way they are very much like the other bookend of the Bible, the book of Revelation—also a story that stands outside recorded human history, offering us a possible vision of the cosmos's ultimate destination, something we will never be able to attain through investigation alone. Are these two bookend stories about beginnings and endings to be trusted? I believe they are. If there is some way, in the new heavens and new earth, to have access to the whole story of this wonderful broken universe, I will not be surprised if I find that the biblical authors missed some of the details about how God created the universe and the human race. But I am confident I will not feel in any way deceived by them—indeed, I believe I will be unspeakably grateful that, prompted by the Holy Spirit, they told stories that made the best possible sense of the world.

And my reason for extending this level of trust has much to do with the books between the bookends—the much more historically accessible and verifiable story of the people of Israel, their exodus from bondage from Egypt, and the eventual arrival of a man who claimed to fulfill all of Israel's original promise. This story, which makes a central claim to history especially at its most radical point, the resurrection of Jesus from the dead, can be tested; it has proven it can be trusted; and it gives me confidence that the bookends, no less than the book, say something uniquely true about our beginnings, and our ending.

7

THE LEAST OF THE NATIONS

Every good story has a twist. Midway through Jane Austen's novel *Pride and Prejudice*, Elizabeth Bennet coldly informs Mr. Darcy that he is "the last man in the world whom I could ever be prevailed on to marry." But as high-school juniors the world over know—whether because they saw the movie, read the Cliff's Notes or breezed past the "spoiler alert" on Wikipedia—Mr. Darcy is the very man who ends up winning Elizabeth's heart. Turn from the first pages of *Pride and Prejudice* to the last, and you'll find out how the story ends—but you won't know *how*. What overcomes Elizabeth's suspicions of the aloof and possibly dishonorable (if appealingly wealthy) Darcy? To find out, you have to read the book—or at least the entry in Wikipedia.

Sometimes it's not enough just to know the ending of the story. The pleasure and the plausibility of a good story lie in the way it gets from the beginning to the ending: the surprising upending of the characters' prejudices and pride, not to mention the reader's. We celebrate novelists like Jane Austen, filmmakers like Alfred Hitchcock and Brad Bird, and composers like Ludwig van Beethoven, Igor Stravinsky and Miles Davis not just for the satisfying endings in their work but the satisfying middles:

the way they get from the beginning to the end in a way that defies prediction and yet, in retrospect, seems inevitable.

But no novel, film or free jazz improvisation can surpass the surprise that greets us if we turn directly from Scripture's beginning to its end. As we've seen, Genesis 1–11 lays out culture as, on the whole, a downward trajectory from the Garden to the city: from God's original good intention to a wholesale human rebellion against the world's maker. Suppose you knew nothing of the middle of the story—suppose your only Bible lacked everything between Genesis 12 and Revelation 20. After reading about the scattering of humanity at Babel and then turning to the back of the book, you'd find this good-news twist: "Then I saw a new heaven and a new earth; for the first heaven and the first earth had passed away, and the sea was no more" (Rev 21:1). Ah! you'd think. God is starting over again, just as he was tempted to do at the time of the flood. But this is not simply destruction, which God promised never to do again. This is re-creation. Surely this remade world will once again have a good Garden at its center, a place where redeemed humanity can reclaim their role as cultivators and creators in intimate relationship with God.

You'd be so close to right.

But then you'd read Revelation 21:2: "And I saw the holy city, the new Jerusalem, coming down out of heaven from God, prepared as a bride adorned for her husband."

The *what?* The holy *city?*

Revelation 21:2 is the last thing a careful reader of Genesis 1–11 would expect: in the remade world, the center of God's creative delight is not a garden but a city. And a city is, almost by definition, a place where culture reaches critical mass—a place where culture eclipses the natural world as the most important feature we must make something of. Somehow the city, the embodiment of concentrated human culture, has been transformed from the site of sin and judgment to the ultimate expression of grace, a gift coming "down out of heaven from God."

American Christian culture is full of nostalgic agrarian images, from the softly lit snug cottages that emerge from the brush of "The Painter of Light"™ to the old hymn, "I come to the garden alone, while the dew is still on the roses." But when God walks among redeemed humanity at the end of the Bible's story, he walks not just on garden paths but also on city streets.

We'll come back to Revelation's extraordinary portrait of redeemed culture in chapter ten. But just as any moderately curious person would want to know what happened to change Elizabeth Bennet's opinion of Mr. Darcy, the surprise ending of Revelation 21 drives us back to the middle of the story: the chapters between Genesis 11 and Revelation 21 that disclose how God will manage to rescue not just human beings but the entire project of human culture from the vanity of Babel. And as it turns out, to get our first clue we don't have to look very far. In fact, as in the best stories, our first clue to the story's crucial plot twist comes almost at the beginning—though we probably didn't realize it was a clue at all.

LEATHER FOR FIG LEAVES

Genesis 3, the story of the Fall, is full of bad news, including cultural bad news. Not only do the man and woman immediately turn to culture— loincloths made of leaves—to protect themselves from the sudden alienation brought on by sin, God also serves notice that in the wake of the Fall both nature and culture will be corrupted as a sign of judgment. God warns the woman that the natural process of childbearing will become unnaturally painful. The cultural institution of the family, meanwhile, will never be as whole as it had been: "your desire shall be for your husband, / and he shall rule over you" (Gen 3:16). The rule that human beings had properly exercised over the creatures of the sky, land and sea will now be turned upon one another, especially between men and women.

To the man, God pronounces another natural and cultural judgment. Nature itself will turn against humanity. "Cursed is the ground because of you; / in toil you shall eat of it all the days of your life" (Gen 3:17). The field will turn against the gardener, and making something of the world will cease to have the ease of Eden: "By the sweat of your face / you shall eat bread / until you return to the ground" (Gen 3:19).

And yet something remarkable happens just after judgment is pronounced on serpent, woman and man alike. Before he sends them into exile from the garden, God replaces the fig leaves that have been humanity's pitiable first attempt at clothing. "The LORD God made garments of skins for the man and for his wife, and clothed them" (Gen 3:21). The fig leaves would not take them far in a wilderness of thorns and thistles. Mercifully, God improves their culture. He gives them leather for fig leaves—durable clothes that will protect them from the real perils they are about to face, not just from a harsh environment but from the distorted relationship that makes nakedness a source of vulnerability and shame.

Once again, as in Genesis 2, God becomes a culture maker. Culture, even in Genesis 3, is not just the site of human rebellion against God, not just the site of God's judgment against sin, it is also the site of God's mercy.

And when we begin to look, we find this cultural mercy woven like a bright thread through the gloomy narrative of Genesis 3–11. After judging Cain, God also places a "mark" on Cain to protect him from revenge—a cultural gesture of mercy. As he prepares to flood the earth and wash away its worst iniquities, God gives instructions to Noah for the building of a boat—a cultural artifact that will carry the human race through the worst that God's wrath can do. In fact, at every point in Genesis 3–11, human culture's darkest moments provoke not just God's explicit and sorrowful judgment, they also prompt a cultural countermove, a new cultural artifact introduced by God into the story to protect human beings from the worst consequences of their choices. God never allows human culture to become solely the site of rebellion and judgment; human culture is always, from the very beginning, also marked by grace.

So perhaps it is not surprising that after he brings humanity's most sophisticated, most rebellious culture-making project to an abrupt halt in Genesis 11, God unveils his most daring experiment in cultural mercy: the experiment that turns out to be the key to understanding why, in Revelation 21, the best gift God can give a redeemed world is not a garden but a city.

THE BLESSING OF A NATION

It was one thing to supply leather as a substitute for fig leaves—a simple solution for a fairly simple problem, human culture just beginning to show its inadequacy. But Babel shows the full extent of human hubris and folly. What is a commensurate act of cultural mercy to the rebellion and judgment of Genesis 11? The answer comes in Genesis 12—after a lengthy interruption for that most characteristic of biblical cultural expressions, the genealogy. Just after the high drama of Babel, we get this:

> These are the descendants of Shem. When Shem was one hundred years old, he became the father of Arpachshad two years after the flood; and Shem lived after the birth of Arpachshad five hundred years, and had other sons and daughters.
>
> When Arpachshad had lived thirty-five years, he became the father of Shelah. (Gen 11:10-12)

And on it goes.

To a modern reader these detailed yet strangely incomplete lineages are like the dietary fiber of Bible reading—dutifully swallowed at best, if we don't simply skip over them for the juicy bits. What possible use are they? Yet, even today, members of less thoroughly modernized societies listen to the genealogies with rapt attention. Genealogies assert that the story being told is not simply a timeless myth—it is anchored in a particular group of people in a particular place.

In Genesis 12 God singles out one of the scattered lineages spreading out from the desolation of Babel: the line of Terah, whose large extended family, settled in a town called Haran, includes a man named Abram.

> Now the LORD said to Abram, "Go from your country and your kindred and your father's house to the land that I will show you. I will make of you a great nation, and I will bless you, and make your name great, so that you will be a blessing. I will bless those who bless you, and the one who curses you I will curse; and in you all the families of the earth shall be blessed." (Gen 12:1-3)

What is at the center of God's call and promise to Abram? "I will make of you a great nation." The biblical term *nation* is less bound up with political and geographic concerns than our modern word suggests: the Kurds of the Middle East do not have their own nation-state at this writing, but to the biblical mind their people, with their own language and distinctive culture that has lasted for centuries, would certainly qualify as a "nation." A nation is, fundamentally, culture plus time: a culture extensive enough and complex enough to be passed on through multiple generations and retain its distinctive identity.

After the scattering of Babel, the world will fill with ethnolinguistic groups, "nations," all heirs of Babel's rebellion and judgment. In a world full of nations, God seeks to provide a different and better nation through Abram: a nation through whom "all the families of the earth shall be blessed." Just as God provided leather in place of fig leaves, again God chooses culture, on a vastly grander and longer scale, to show his mercy. And what form will this mercy take? How will the nations of the earth be blessed by God's chosen nation? The family of Abram will demonstrate, in the midst of the world and all its cultures, what Babel forgot: how to be a nation that depends for its identity, security and very existence on the Creator of the world. Just as Babel was the cultural embodiment of independence from God, so Israel will be the embodiment of dependence on God. In its history and culture, Israel will enact over and over the encounter Abraham's grandson Jacob has by the river in Genesis 32 when he is about to face Esau, his estranged brother and perhaps his mortal enemy. When faced with the most severe dangers to its existence, this nation will grapple with God, saying, "I will not let you go, unless you bless me" (Gen 32:26). It will be the people whose very culture is defined by their wrestling matches with God—the ones they win and the ones they lose. In the midst of the nations, Israel will be a sign that it is possible to be a nation whose key characteristic is trust in the world's invisible Maker—to use the biblical word, a culture defined by *faith*.

So God's response to the ultimate cultural problem—a world full of mutually antagonistic nations entrenched in the self-provision and self-justification seen in Babel—is a fully cultural solution. Which is to say, it is fundamentally a *creative* solution. To be sure, over Israel's history God himself will employ the full range of possible gestures toward culture. At times, there will be *condemnation*, including the wholesale deliverance of Israel into the hands of its enemies, Assyria and Babylon. The prophets will bring word of God's *critique* to Israel and its neighbors. In constructing a cultural identity Israel will be led by the Spirit to *copy* many features of surrounding culture—over its history it will borrow Semitic linguistic forms for its national language, Egyptian wisdom literature for its court poetry, Lebanese woodworking for its worship spaces, and Mesopotamian treaties for its international relations and even its understanding of its relationship with God. At the height of its power Israel's ability to *consume* the cultural products of its neighbors will be a sign of God's blessing, as when the psalmist celebrates a royal wedding that features imported Ophirian gold (Ps 45:9).

But the heart of God's agenda with Israel is to create something that has never existed: a nation that belongs in a special way to the Creator of the heavens and the earth. Seen from this perspective a number of features of the biblical story become clear in a new way.

TIME

First, this extraordinary cultural project will need to unfold over centuries, because it will need to be sufficiently complex, deep and rich to bear true witness to the world's Creator among the great human civilizations, the incredibly complex aggregations of culture that represent the full flowering of the human ability to make something of the world.

There is no such thing as instant culture. To create a new "nation"—a new cultural tradition—will require time: time for many generations to absorb, reflect on and respond to God's intervention in the life of a single nomadic Middle Eastern family. Only a nation with the cultural depth acquired through many generations of history will be able to offer a compelling response to the variety of human experience, the many different features of the world that human beings must make something of. How does a nation faithfully celebrate? mourn? plant seed? harvest grain? conquer? be conquered? "For everything there is a season," Qoheleth writes in Ecclesiastes, "and a time for every matter under heaven" (Eccles 3:1)—developing a cultural tradition rich enough to do justice to every season and every "matter under heaven" is a project for ages, not generations, let alone single lifetimes. What God promises Abram—a great nation equipped to be a blessing to every nation—will take a while, especially after Babel, when fallenness is so deeply entrenched in the cultural project.

Seen from this vantage point, some parts of the Hebrew Bible that initially seem superfluous to us take on new significance. The genealogies that bore many a modern reader are evidence of God's faithfulness over many generations of cultural formation—and they are simply a sign that

God does indeed work in the midst of history, rather than outside it in some spiritualized or ahistorical fashion.

The book of Numbers, with its census of every tribe and its seemingly picayune recitation of details about the Israelites, is a bit like the baby photographs that eager parents pass around: documentation of the earliest days of Israel's formation as a nation. To someone who has never been a parent, all baby pictures look roughly the same, but to those indebted to the cultural project of Israel these beginnings are important and fascinating—just as the average baby picture, while not tremendously interesting in itself, is significant because it documents the beginning of a human person, however much they may have changed and grown.

The book of Leviticus, graveyard of so many good intentions to read straight through the Bible, is in fact an instruction manual for the creation of a distinct people in the context of the ancient Near East. By observing its commands and prohibitions—both the broadly ethical, such as "you shall love your neighbor as yourself," and the narrowly specific, such as keeping meat and milk separate in Israel's diet—Abram's descendants will be shaping their own distinctive cultural identity. Even the most puzzling and seemingly arbitrary features of the Levitical code require Israel to consciously depend on the God who revealed them rather than simply absorbing and imitating the cultures that surround them.

PLACE

The location God chooses for his chosen people is of tremendous historical significance. The valley of the Jordan River, in ancient times and even today, lies at the intersection of major trade routes and strategic corridors between major powers. This central location, at the strategic heart of the ancient Near East, was the bane of Israel's existence—a tiny nation constantly attracting all-too-keen interest over the centuries from the empires of Egypt, Assyria, Babylon and Rome, who regularly sent their armies barreling through Israel's territory en route to greater conquests.

Yet Israel's location also ensured that its unique cultural vocation would be lived out in "public," we might say, among the great nations of its day. As much as Israel might have been tempted to withdraw from the larger cultural currents over the centuries of its history, it simply never had that option. And because Israel's neighbors were so often technologically more advanced, economically more prosperous and militarily more sophisticated, Israel's faith was repeatedly put to the test. Would Israel borrow the perceived clout of neighboring gods to hedge its bets on political and economic survival (1 Kings 18)? Would Israel, forged in the experience of deliverance from slavery in Egypt, return to Egypt for a military alliance against the encroaching Assyrian Empire (Is 31)? Above all, how would Israel respond to the crushing experience of being conquered by Assyria and Babylon?

All of these tests of faith could have been avoided by placing God's chosen redemptive nation well out of the way: say, in the Swiss Alps, the mountains of Nepal or the rainforests of Brazil. An isolated location might have spared Israel the worst moments of its history—the ignominious compromises of even its successful kings, the forced march of its leaders into the city whose very name echoed Babel's. But in such a location, neither would have Israel's extraordinary claim to worship not just its own local god, but the world's very Maker and Lord, made much of a difference in the wider course of history.

It was only in "public," in the context of tremendous political and economic pressure, that Israel's cultural creativity could be made available to the neighboring nations big and small: its legal code with its keen sense of justice and responsibility toward the weak; its poetry of praise, thanksgiving and lament; its Scriptures bearing witness to the character of the one true God. Indeed, without those cultural pressures Israel's culture might have been substantially less creative in the first place. The exile into Babylon was the most devastating blow Israel suffered, an attempt at cultural eradication comparable to the Holocaust of the twentieth century. But the exile forced Israel to grapple with the implications of its faith beyond its borders, to ask what faithfulness looked like in a diaspora where neither kings nor priests had majority power, to cry, "How could we sing the LORD's song / in a foreign land?" (Ps 137:4) and begin to find an answer.

SIZE

There is one other remarkable aspect of God's cultural creativity in Israel that bears mentioning. In Deuteronomy 7 Moses is warning the Hebrews

not to culturally assimilate to the surrounding nations. He clearly anticipates that the apparent cultural superiority of the Canaanite tribes will
tempt Israel to religious syncretism and intermarriage. Faced with a thriving pagan culture, Israel's confidence in their invisible God, who has no
reassuring idol or pillars on the high places to confirm his presence and
provision, may easily waver.

But Moses assures them: "It was not because you were more numerous
than any other people that the LORD set his heart on you and chose you—
for you were the fewest of all peoples" (Deut 7:7, emphasis added). There was
no shortage of existing nations, tribes and clans when God singled out
Abram—and compared to any of these existing cultural entities, Abram
and his elderly wife, Sarai, were indeed "the fewest of all" nations. The
Hebrew slaves departing Egypt in ragtag flight from the era's greatest
army were similarly overmatched and outmanned. Yet God has chosen
the smallest "nation" for his cultural creativity. His culture making does
not begin with the mighty and powerful; it begins with "the fewest of all
peoples," in the most unlikely place.

God's cultural project in Israel, then, anticipates what Paul would say
about the ministry, death and resurrection of Jesus: "God chose what is
foolish in the world to shame the wise; God chose what is weak in the
world to shame the strong; God chose what is low and despised in the
world, things that are not, to reduce to nothing things that are, so that no
one might boast in the presence of God" (1 Cor 1:27-29). This is not just
a "spiritual" principle detached from history: it accurately describes God's
cultural project from Genesis 12 onward. Israel, beleaguered, weak, low
and despised among the great empires around the Mediterranean Sea, is
God's choice of nation—precisely "so that no one might boast," including
Israel itself.

God's intervention in human culture will be unmistakably marked by
grace—it will not be the inevitable working out of the world's way of
cultural change, the logical unfolding of preexisting power and privilege.
Wherever God steps into human history, the mountains will be leveled
and the valleys will be raised up. "Then the glory of the LORD shall be
revealed" (Is 40:5)—the glory of a God who confounds even his own people's expectations of how culture changes. In culture as in every human

life, God begins with the small and humble so that the full dimensions of his grace can be seen—or to put it another way, all divine creativity starts *ex nihilo*, from nothing, bursting into goodness that could never have been anticipated or simply extrapolated from preexisting conditions. Nothing less than creation beginning with the smallest, the weakest and the seemingly least promising can do justice to the infinite creativity of God.

ISRAEL IN HISTORY

So the whole of the Hebrew Bible, from Genesis 12 to Malachi 4, can be seen as a record of Israel's education in faith—not "faith" as a purely spiritual or religious enterprise, but as a cultural practice of dependence on the world's Creator that encompasses everything from military strategy to songwriting. At times the record is forthrightly inspiring. Israel brings into history some of the most captivating poetry ever written alongside one of the most demanding moral codes ever embraced by a society. Smallest among the nations, Israel at its best embodies God's concern for the small and seemingly insignificant; having been strangers and wanderers themselves, the people of Israel learn how to welcome wanderers and strangers. Above all, Israel's singular gift to the world is its transition from henotheism to monotheism—from worshiping one national god to proclaiming that there is only one God, "the Creator of the ends of the earth," in Isaiah's phrase, who loves the world not in addition to or in spite of his special relationship to Israel, but *through* that relationship.

Other aspects of Israel's history are harder for us to readily accept. Israel's conquest of Canaan is marked at times by daring acts of trust in God—as when Joshua relies on musicians, not weapons, to bring down the walls of Jericho, or when Gideon obeys God's command to shrink his expeditionary force by 99 percent. Yet God is recorded as ordering the destruction of entire people groups in what we today would call genocide—and our horror is inspired in no small part by the biblical ethic itself. It is difficult to reconcile some of these stories with the promise in Genesis 12 that all nations would be blessed through Abram's family. Even the less shocking passages in Israel's history, like the rise of David's line to kingship, are a bewildering mixture of grace and sin, faith and folly. The institution of kingship, as the prophet Samuel knows, is very much like a fig leaf, an accommodation to faithlessness: after telling Samuel that the demand for a human king amounts to a rejection of his own lordship, God nonetheless says, "Listen to their voice and set a king over them" (1 Sam 8:22). Indeed, the story of David's line is told twice, in 1–2 Samuel and in 1–2 Chronicles, by authors who have distinctly different perspectives on the same events. And the Hebrew Bible ends inconclusively, with Jerusalem half rebuilt and another empire, Rome, looming on history's horizon.

There is nothing tidy about the cultural project of Israel. When we read it as a whole, rather than plucking selected passages to justify our culture wars or cultural withdrawal, the story is profoundly humbling. If God's chosen people experienced such frustration and failure in creating and cultivating culture, how can followers of Christ, scattered among the nations, expect to do better?

And yet the Hebrew Bible itself contains the beginnings of a hopeful answer to this perplexity. The postexilic prophets are more acutely aware than we could ever be of Israel's failure to create and cultivate a culture of faithfulness, and yet they return from their encounters with Israel's God bearing a message of hope. They can gaze on the rubble of Jerusalem and the decrepit state of its worship and still envision a time when "the sun of righteousness shall rise, with healing in its wings," and when God's curse will be averted (Mal 4:2). After all of Jerusalem's failures, all the ways that it concentrates just as much of Israel's rebellion and God's judgment as God's mercy and Israel's faithfulness, the prophets are convinced that God has not abandoned his plan to sustain a redeeming nation, a nation through whom all the nations will be blessed. Though he vividly foretells the exile of Israel into Babylon, Isaiah also envisions a time when

> the mountain of the LORD's house / shall be established as the highest of the mountains, / and shall be raised above the hills; / all the nations shall stream to it. / Many peoples shall come and say, / "Come, let us go up to the mountain of the LORD, / to the house of the God of Jacob; / that he may teach us his ways / and that we may walk in his paths." (Is 2:2-3)

The story of God's original chosen people is complex to this very day, when a political entity called Israel occupies much of the land given to

God's chosen people yet also dwells uneasily with its neighbors and deals harshly with the foreigners in its land. In one sense Isaiah's prediction clearly has yet to be fulfilled. And yet two remarkable things have happened in the 2,600 years since that prophecy. First, against all odds, Abraham's children have survived repeated attempts at eradicating their culture. Indeed, their culture has influenced nearly every culture on earth, including two successor religions, Christianity and Islam. And second, the followers of one of Abraham's descendants, Jesus of Nazareth, have indeed gone, figuratively if not literally, "to the house of the God of Jacob," so that the particular cultural story of Israel now leavens countless cultures with its stories, its rhythms of life, its songs and its laws. Indeed, Christians see Jesus as the turning point of history, the fulfillment of God's original intentions in singling out Israel and the breaking out of God's original intentions from a single "peculiar people" to a people drawn from every language, tribe and nation. Jesus of Nazareth, as we shall see, turns out to be the most significant culture maker of all.

8

JESUS AS CULTURE MAKER

The first thing to notice about Jesus is the hardest thing for many Christians to notice about him. It helps if we back away for a moment from our Anglicized version of his name and call him Yeshua; better yet, Yeshua bar-Yosef, and do our best to envision him, a bronze-skinned young Middle Eastern man, lying down next to a low table to enjoy a meal with his friends. (The idea of a Jesus who is so un-Western that he has never used a chair was sufficiently striking to filmmaker Mel Gibson that he had the young carpenter invent the chair during one of the flashbacks in *The Passion of the Christ*.) He speaks Aramaic at home, a language we have never heard, and reads biblical Hebrew in the synagogue. Even through layers of biography and translation (Aramaic to Greek to English) we can hear him say things we would never say and do things we would never do, like addressing his mother cursorily as "woman" (Jn 2:4) in a way that might earn a Western son a rebuke.

Two of Jesus' four biographers include a genealogy—Matthew tracing his line back to Abraham, Luke going all the way back to Adam. As we saw in chapter seven, genealogies were precious signs of cultural continuity to the biblical authors and readers. Matthew states his agenda up front in the very first verse of his Gospel, which begins abruptly: "An account of the genealogy of Jesus the Messiah, the son of David, the son of Abraham"—highlighting Jesus' continuity with both Israel's royal house and Israel's founding ancestor himself. Luke's genealogy, which unlike Matthew's is postponed until after all the stories of Jesus' conception, birth and childhood have been told, begins with a striking statement: "He was the son (as was thought) of Joseph son of Heli, son of Matthat, son of Levi." And on it goes until the punch line: "son of Adam, son of God" (Lk 3:23, 38).

"He was the son *(as was thought)* of Joseph"? It's a very strange way to begin a genealogy. Luke himself has told us in great detail about the miraculous conception of Jesus without Joseph's involvement. If we believe his account—and whether we believe it or not, Luke certainly believed it—Jesus is the one person in human history for whom a patrilineal genealogy makes no sense. Why would Luke include it at all?

Clearly Luke, although he writes supple Greek and has been influenced by Greek culture, has also absorbed the Hebrew Bible's concern with the continuity of culture. Luke's genealogy of Jesus does not just make the point that Jesus is ultimately the "son of God"—it also makes the point that he is fully and completely human. To be human is to have a cultural inheritance, to be part of a tradition of making something of the world. To be human is to have a father—even in the uniquely miraculous circumstance of not having a biological father. Jesus, like every human being since Adam, arrives in the midst of not just "culture" but a culture, a specific cultural tradition of a family, a language, a people, a nation. He is not Jesus, full stop—he is not Jesus the Son of God or even just Jesus the Messiah. He is Yeshua bar-Yosef, Jesus Joseph's son. "As was thought"—but as to his culture, the horizons of possibility and impossibility that shaped his life from its first days, not just as was thought. He was the son of Yosef and Miriam. He was a cultural being. If he had not been, he would not have been a human being at all.

JESUS AS CULTIVATOR

For the first thirty years of his life—in spite of the dramatic events of his infancy and one precocious scene at age twelve in the temple at Jerusalem—

Jesus is just Yeshua bar-Yosef. It's not entirely surprising that the biblical writers pass over these years mostly in silence—papyrus is expensive—and given their silence it's not surprising that you rarely hear sermons on Jesus' first thirty years. But for our purposes, paying careful attention to the traces of culture in the biblical story, they are worth noticing.

What would have happened in those thirty years? As a child Jesus would have acquired language. He would have studied the Hebrew Bible, immersing himself in his nation's cultural project and Israel's sense of special vocation from the world's Creator. He would have attended weddings and funerals, learned the trade of carpentry (if not chair making) from his father ("as was thought"), savored food and watched his mother sweep the house clean of leaven before Passover.

And he would have done all these things not just as a child but as a young man. Jesus at twenty-five or twenty-eight would have seemed to his contemporaries like no more and no less than a faithful student of Scripture and a tradesman (with one notable exception: it seems surpassingly unlikely that Jesus ever married).

Jesus was a cultivator of culture. He did not just acquire enough maturity to get about his real, "spiritual" business of saving the world and then wash his hands of responsibility to tend and conserve his cultural heritage. He spent prime years simply absorbing, practicing and passing on his culture—not preaching, not healing, not introducing the dramatic innovations that would bring him into conflict with the nation's leaders. A few decades later one of his followers would write, "He is the image of the invisible God, the firstborn of all creation; for in him all things in heaven and on earth were created, things visible and invisible, whether thrones or dominions or rulers or powers—all things have been created through him and for him" (Col 1:15-16). And yet in his twenties, all that extraordinary divinity was manifested—not concealed but lived out—in the life of a superficially ordinary person. To turn from the exalted language of Colossians to our best guess about the daily life of the twenty-five-year-old Yeshua of Nazareth is like going from Genesis 1 to Genesis 2—from a cosmic drama to a divine hand in the dust. When the image of the invisible God arrived, he took on not just flesh but culture as well.

One of the contributions of contemporary New Testament scholar

N. T. Wright has been to recover for us just how thoroughly Jesus of Nazareth was embedded in his cultural context. Wright's monumental series Christian Origins and the Question of God, especially the volume *Jesus and the Victory of God*, places Jesus firmly in a first-century Jewish environment—so much so that a typical Protestant reader encountering Wright's work can feel quite disoriented. Jesus, Wright demonstrates, was preoccupied with the questions—cultural and historical—that preoccupied all Jews living in first-century Palestine. He, like his contemporaries, had to confront the continuing occupation of the land of Israel, with all the depressing implications about the limits of the power of Israel's God; he visited the temple, with its distasteful compromises between worship and appeasement of the Roman overlords; he was immersed in speculation about the coming, or the delay, of Israel's Messiah, who would deliver Israel from their oppressors once and for all. Jesus' ministry was oriented not toward addressing some universal set of "spiritual" issues but toward addressing these very particular, history-bound questions of his time and place. Jesus was first of all a culture cultivator.

JESUS AS CREATOR

Yet obviously Jesus did not simply preserve and pass on his culture's inheritance. Instead, whenever Jesus touched part of Israel's cultural inheritance, he brought something new to it. All four Gospel writers stress Jesus' innovative teaching. "They were astounded at his teaching, for he taught them as one having authority, and not as the scribes" (Mk 1:22). Jesus' opening sermon in Matthew begins, "Blessed are the poor in spirit, for theirs is the kingdom of heaven" (Mt 5:3)—a teaching that echoed the prophetic record of God's concern for the poor, yet recast it in a radically new way. In Luke Jesus takes a commonplace rabbinic story of an injured man on the road to Jericho being ignored by religious leaders, but creatively retells it with a Samaritan rather than an ordinary pious Jew in the starring role.

Jesus' cultural creativity encompassed much more than words and texts. He dramatically altered the practice of *meals*, which were culturally central not just for nourishment but for delineating social boundaries, horizons of possibility and impossibility that demonstrated who was "in" and who was "out" of a person's social circle. Jesus moved the horizons with abandon, inviting himself over to sinners' houses for dinner and even welcoming them into Pharisees' homes. He stretched the horizons of traditional *rituals*, not just healing but allowing his disciples to gather food on the sabbath. When he reclined for dinner on the fateful night before his death, he took the Passover rituals and boldly reinterpreted them, taking the cup of the covenant and saying, "This cup is the covenant in my blood."

Perhaps most fatefully, Jesus confronted head-on the most powerful cultural institution of first-century Judaism, the temple in Jerusalem, lashing out at the commerce in its outer courts. Indeed, when we look for signs of the criticisms of Jesus, they often have more to do with his deeds than his words. As innovative as his teachings were, his adversaries seem to have been most provoked by his actions. And this should not be surprising to us: it is the embodied practices of a culture that most powerfully enforce what that culture makes of the world. Jesus did not just teach creatively; he lived creatively, and the guardians of the horizons were unsettled by him.

Jesus had a profoundly cultural phrase for his mission: *the kingdom of God*. It is hard to recapture the concept of *kingdom* in an age where monarchs are often no more than ornamental fixtures in their societies, if they exist at all. But for Jews of that time and place, the idea of a kingdom would have meant much more. In announcing that the kingdom of God was near, in telling parables of the kingdom, Jesus was not just delivering "good news," as if his only concern was to impart some new information. His good news foretold a comprehensive restructuring of social life comparable to that experienced by a people when one monarch was succeeded by another. The kingdom of God would touch every sphere and every scale of culture. It would reshape marriage and mealtimes, resistance to the Roman occupiers and prayer in the temple, the social standing of prostitutes and the piety of Pharisees, the meaning of cleanliness and the interpretation of illness, integrity in business and honesty in prayer.

For as Jesus saw it, Israel's horizons were misplaced. The Sermon on the Mount is a case study in Jesus' moving the horizons of possibility and impossibility, especially his refrain, "you have heard that it was said . . . but I say to you." In each case, "you have heard that it was said" identifies misplaced horizons:

You have heard that it was said to those of ancient times, "You shall not murder"; and "whoever murders shall be liable to judgment." But I say to you that if you are angry with a brother or sister, you will be liable to judgment; and if you insult a brother or sister, you will be liable to the council; and if you say, "You fool," you will be liable to the hell of fire. So when you are offering your gift at the altar, if you remember that your brother or sister has something against you, leave your gift there before the altar and go; first be reconciled to your brother or sister, and then come and offer your gift. Come to terms quickly with your accuser while you are on the way to court with him, or your accuser may hand you over to the judge, and the judge to the guard, and you will be thrown into prison. Truly I tell you, you will never get out until you have paid the last penny. (Mt 5:21-26)

The law's prohibition against murder, and the social structures that had been put in place to enforce that prohibition—to move murder as far as possible to the edge of possibility—had not addressed the deeper issue of anger and insults, which remained all too possible. Jesus' response is not just to offer a different set of horizons—one in which judgment will eventually be meted out to the angry as well as the violent—but to offer a cultural solution, a new set of practices embedded in the life of worship and the courts. It is often observed that in the Sermon on the Mount Jesus takes the commandments of the law, which applied to external behavior, and applies them to the internal state of human hearts—but his prescription for changing the heart involves changes in *culture*. Prayer will no longer take place primarily on street corners but in quiet rooms. Divorce and remarriage will no longer be blithely tolerated as long as the divorcing party follows the letter of the law. The cultural practice of swearing oaths will be eliminated. The language and the look of prayer and fasting will change. The followers of Jesus will begin to demonstrate a new set of horizons for human life to their neighbors and even to their enemies—the horizons of shalom, the horizons of true humanity living in dependence on God.

Jesus' greatest innovation, of course, was not merely the alternative culture he proposed. He made—and lived out—the astonishingly bold claim that Israel's original vocation, to demonstrate complete dependence upon God in the sight of the nations, had come to rest on himself. Rather than offering shalom to the nations, Israel had been cowed into compromise with them—but Jesus would turn the other cheek to the soldiers of Rome without ever endorsing Rome's brutal hegemony. Rather than demonstrating God's compassion to their neighbors, the Israelites kept a sanctimonious distance from them—but Jesus, after feeding five thousand Israelites, crossed over to Gentile territory and fed four thousand "unclean" people as well. Rather than making room for the nations to come to the house of God, as Isaiah had predicted, Israel had filled the temple's outer courts with commerce—but Jesus would clear out the merchants and offer healing, teaching and welcome to a Syrophoenician mother and a Roman centurion as well as synagogue leaders. His calling was to be everything Israel had been called to be, but had forgotten (or never quite learned) to be: a light to the nations, a sign of the one true God's horizons of possibility.

But Jesus' calling went even deeper than this—far deeper than simply being a good example of what Israel should have been all along. His calling was to take upon himself all of Israel's failure, all of its cultural dead ends, the accumulated history of independence from God that had led to a seemingly inescapable, permanent state of exile. In order for the culturally creative movement Jesus sought to unleash to flourish, the brokenness of culture had to be faced head on. And so Jesus accepted the calling of the cross.

CULTURE AND THE CROSS

There were crosses long before there was *the* cross. The cultural artifact called a cross was an attempt to make something of the world as the Romans saw it, a world in which rebellion against the empire's peace needed to be brutally and publicly punished. And yet what began, in its inventors' minds, as a grim necessity was perverted in the case of Jesus (and no doubt many others) into an instrument of senseless violence against the innocent. Likewise, the crazy quilt of miscarried justice that led to Jesus' condemnation implicated two sets of ruling elites, Roman and Jewish, both guardians of potentially good cultural institutions that became agents of the most profound injustice.

On the cross, we believe, Jesus did the one thing no human being has been able adequately to do before or since. He suffered the full weight of the human story of rebellion against God. He was literally impaled on the worst that culture can do—an instrument of torture that stood for all the other cultural dead ends of history, from spears to bombs, gas chambers to waterboards. Like other instruments of violence, a cross is cultural folly and futility at its most horrible. There is nothing to cultivate about a cross, nothing good that can be affirmed or tended there, and it is designed to extinguish life itself, ruling out creativity with inexorable gasps of suffocation. Not only does the cross represent an all too literal dead end for its victim—it represents the dead end of culture, the perversion and exhaustion of our calling to make something of the world.

The cross is the culmination of the mordant story which began in Genesis 3—the story of culture gone wrong. The cross, more than anything else, is what prevents us from any sort of cultural triumphalism, as if we can merrily cultivate and create our way back to the Garden or on toward the heavenly city. The cross refutes progressivism, the idea that human beings can steadily improve their way into blessedness. Who else had ever been a more faithful steward of cultural cultivation than Jesus of Nazareth? Who demonstrated more extraordinary cultural creativity, more ability to turn even severely misplaced horizons toward God's shalom? And yet the active connivance of elites and the passivity of the crowds to whom he had appealed led to his execution. In the final minutes of Jesus' life, according to John, the original darkness of uncreation returns. If "the hopes and fears of all the years" met in Bethlehem at Jesus' birth, according to Phillips Brooks's beloved hymn, at the cross the concentric hopes of his disciples, his nation and of humanity itself are dealt a shattering blow.

What is more, we have solid evidence that Jesus' vocation, his sense of his role in the story of God's epic intervention in human culture, had included the cross from early on. The Gospels, as Martin Kähler noted, are essentially "passion narratives with an extended introduction"—each evangelist devotes a vastly disproportionate amount of space to Jesus' last week in Jerusalem. So in Jesus' own teaching, in his choice not to avoid confrontation with the temple leaders and their Roman overseers, we find that his most definitive calling is neither to cultivate nor create—though, as we have seen, he did both extensively. The core calling of his life is not something he does at all in an active sense—it is something he suffers. The strangest and most wonderful paradox of the biblical story is that its most consequential moment is not an action but a passion—not a doing but a suffering.

THE AFTERSHOCKS OF THE RESURRECTION

The first Christians were struck by the remarkable parallels and divergences between the story of the "first Adam" in the primordial Garden and the "second Adam" in the garden of Gethsemane. The first Adam acted on his own behalf, rashly and disobediently, to consume the fruit, to attempt to overcome his limitations and creatureliness; the second Adam chose deliberately and obediently *not* to act on his own behalf, to *be* consumed, to be overcome by the consequences of the first Adam's choice. The first Adam took his God-given freedom to make something of the world and chose a course that distorted and disfigured the world; the second Adam laid aside both his human and divine creative powers.

And yet in being crucified, the first Christians recognized, the second Adam did precisely what the first Adam had failed to do. Luke records Jesus' last words as, "Father, into your hands I commend my spirit" (Lk 23:46). The first Adam had declared independence of God, seeking godlikeness by his own means and wit; the second Adam, "who . . . was in the form of God" (Phil 2:6), declared his ultimate dependence on God in and by his death. As C. S. Lewis vividly put it, "he staked it all on one throw." If Jesus' Father was not able or willing to rescue him from death, if the lament of Psalm 22:1—"My God, my God, why have you forsaken me?"—was not followed by the praise of Psalm 22:24—"he did not hide his face from me, but heard when I cried to him"—then Jesus, and all his cultivation and creativity, would return to dust. The fear of the people of Babel would come true for the small movement of disciples from Galilee, who would soon be "scattered over the face of the earth," the name of their beloved rabbi forgotten to all except perhaps a few scholars of first-century Judaism. Everything was at stake on the cross; everything depended on God, the one Jesus trusted intimately enough to call Father.

The extraordinary Christian belief is that Jesus' trust was rewarded.

God the Father did not abandon Jesus to death. From Jesus' first followers to the present, Christians have celebrated the resurrection as God's vindication of Jesus as his "well-beloved Son," as the assurance that Jesus really did win the victory over sin, including our own, and as the down payment on our own future life beyond death. All of these are obviously central to the meaning of the resurrection.

But what has not been so widely commented on is the way that the resurrection was a culture-*shaping* event—in fact, arguably the most culturally significant event in history. This is not primarily a "religious" matter. It is fundamentally a statement of bald historical fact: the resurrection, if indeed it happened as Jesus' followers proclaimed, changed more of subsequent human history, for more people and more cultures, than any other event we can name. And if the resurrection did not happen, then something else of extraordinary historical power happened in an amazingly short span of time in Judea and Palestine in the 30s and 40s of the common era.

In his book *The Resurrection of the Son of God* N. T. Wright examines the resurrection using the tools of historical investigation, building up a remarkably strong case along the way that something happened three days after Jesus' crucifixion that was quite extraordinary, quite like what Jesus is said to have foretold and quite like what his disciples are said to have witnessed. Some of his evidence is familiar to most Christians: it is exceedingly difficult to explain the sudden rise of the early church, led by Galilean tradesmen who had by their own account been scared out of their wits after Jesus' crucifixion, without the encounter with the risen Lord that they were boldly proclaiming within a few years (at most) after that death. Apologists for Christianity have long noted that most of Jesus' inner circle of disciples died martyrs' deaths they could easily have avoided by recanting the improbable story of a risen rabbi who walked through walls.

Wright explores all these avenues of thought in great detail. But perhaps the most culturally salient observation he makes comes toward the end of the book, when he comments briefly on "the remarkable transfer of the special day of the week from the last day to the first day":

There is very early evidence of the Christians meeting on the first day of the week. . . . The seventh-day sabbath was so firmly rooted in Judaism as a major social, cultural, religious and political landmark that to make any adjustment in it was not like a modern western person deciding to play tennis on Tuesdays instead of Wednesdays, but like persuading the most devout medieval Roman Catholic to fast on Thursdays instead of Fridays, or the most devout member of the Free Church of Scotland to organize worship on Mondays instead of Sundays.

If anything, Wright understates the case. Of all the things cultures conserve most carefully—of all that they are most committed to cultivating—among the most important are *ritual* and *time*. For several thousand years, in the midst of a bewildering variety of geographic locations and civilizations—even as their own language and cultural practices changed in myriad ways—the Jews have never forgotten which day is the sabbath. The observance of the sabbath is written into the Ten Commandments and the story of creation itself, and was sustained in Jesus' time, as it is now, as a profoundly countercultural act with little or no support from the surrounding society. And yet, within a few years of Jesus' death, we have clear evidence (from Luke, Paul and John in the biblical canon, and from writers like Ignatius just a few decades later) of a group of largely or exclusively Jewish believers, living within sight of the temple no less, who have shifted their primary day of worship from the seventh to the first.

To grasp the cultural significance of this, imagine leaving the United States for a decade or so and returning to find that while the wider society continued to get up on Monday and go to work and school, a substantial number of churches left their buildings dark on Sunday and gathered for worship on Monday instead—perhaps getting up before dawn to do so, perhaps gathering after the work day was done, perhaps skipping work altogether—and, for good measure, now called Monday "the Lord's day." You would conclude that something absolutely extraordinary must have happened—or at least that they *believed* something extraordinary had happened.

As evidence that something extraordinary did indeed happen on the Sunday after Jesus' execution, the shift in worship from the seventh day to the first is arresting. But it is also, for those of us who believe the first disciples' report of Easter, perhaps the most vivid and indisputable sign of the cultural power of the resurrection. For through a complex and far-reaching chain of events, that tectonic shift from Saturday to Sunday directly shapes the lives of the great majority of the population of earth—even though many of them are Christian only nominally or not at all.

The latte-sipping customer at Starbucks on the Upper West Side of Manhattan is taking her time with the Sunday *Times*—why? Because in much of the world, the *first day* of the week has become the closest thing we have to a day of rest. Even when "blue laws" restricting business on Sundays have largely been repealed, the manager of the local department store who has to fill in schedules starting at 10 a.m. instead of 9 a.m. is still, however vestigially, touched by the resurrection. The resurrection of Jesus is like a cultural earthquake, its epicenter located in Jerusalem in the early 30s, whose aftershocks are still being felt in the cultural practices of people all over the world, many of whom have never heard of, and many more of whom have never believed in, its origins. Except the metaphor of an earthquake doesn't capture the slow-moving power of the resurrection—its invisibility to many closest to it, and its ongoing effects far away. Perhaps a better metaphor for the resurrection's cultural power is one of Jesus' most vivid images of the kingdom: it is like a mustard seed, almost imperceptible at first, but flowering into a living plant that grows, flourishes and provides shelter for the "birds of the air," shaping the life of the world around it.

The resurrection is the hinge of history—still after two thousand years as culturally far-reaching in its effects as anything that has come since. And it began with an act of trust, of supreme faith in the world's Creator. Of all the creators and cultivators who have ever lived, Jesus was the most capable of shaping culture through his own talents and power—and yet the most culture-shaping event of his life is the result of his choice to abandon his talents and power. The resurrection shows us the pattern for culture making in the image of God. Not power, but trust. Not independence, but dependence. The second Adam's influence on culture comes through his greatest act of dependence; the fulfillment of Israel's calling to demonstrate faith in the face of the great powers that threatened its existence comes in the willing submission of Jesus to a Roman cross, broken by but also breaking forever its power.

Indeed, one of the most dramatic cultural effects of the resurrection is the transformation of that heinous cultural artifact known as a cross. An instrument of domination and condemnation becomes a symbol of the kingdom that Jesus proclaimed: an alternative culture where grace and forgiveness are the last word. So Jesus, crucified and risen, is the culmination of God's culture-rescuing project that began in Genesis 12: he faces the worst that human powers can do and rises, not just with some merely "spiritual" triumph over those powers, but with a *cultural* triumph—an answer, right in the midst of human history, to all the fears of Israel in the face of its enemies.

So just as we can say that culture is what we make of the world, in both senses, we can say that the gospel is the proclamation of Jesus, in both senses. It is the proclamation *announced* by Jesus—the arrival of God's realm of possibility (his "kingdom") in the midst of human structures of possibility. But it is also the proclamation *about* Jesus—the good news that in dying and rising, Jesus has made the kingdom he proclaimed available to us.

In the kingdom of God a new kind of life and a new kind of culture becomes possible—not by abandoning the old but by transforming it. Even the cross, the worst that culture can do, is transformed into a sign of the kingdom of God—the realm of forgiveness, mercy, love and indestructible life.

9

FROM PENTECOST . . .

The book of Acts is a book of cities. Its story begins in Jerusalem, ends in Rome and along the way visits nearly every commercial and political center around the Mediterranean: Antioch, Lystra, Iconium, Corinth, Philippi, Thessalonica, Ephesus and Athens. Quite unlike the Gospels, much of whose activity takes place in relatively rural Galilee, the "action" in Acts takes place almost entirely in urban centers. (One notable exception, Philip's conversation with an Ethiopian court official, takes place in the desert—but the Ethiopian is on his way back to the queen's court.)

Which means that Acts is about culture. Cities, as we see in Genesis 11, are the place where culture reaches critical mass. And Acts is about *cultures* (plural), for the cities of the Roman world, no less than our own, were heterogeneous and frequently turbulent mixtures of people from many nations, brought together by economic opportunity and held together in uneasy peace by Rome's far-flung power.

And so, when the aftershocks of Jesus' resurrection began to be felt, when the mustard seed of his resurrection life began to emerge green from the ground, it did so at the place where culture, and cultures, were most tangibly felt—where the many languages of the scattered people of Babel rang in the marketplace and humanity's myriad ways of making something of the world clanged, clashed and sometimes collided.

Under the nose of the Roman guardians and the Jewish religious leaders, a small group of Galileans took up residence in the city of Jerusalem, probably attracting little enough notice now that their messianic hopes had been discredited by their leader's crucifixion. Yet amazingly enough, Luke reports that for over a month after the crucifixion and the strange events of the following Sunday, Jesus "presented himself alive to them by many convincing proofs, appearing to them during forty days and speaking about the kingdom of God" (Acts 1:3). His last words to them explicitly invoked the cultural geography of their surroundings: "You will be my witnesses in Jerusalem, in all Judea and Samaria, and to the ends of the earth" (Acts 1:8). And ten days later, on the minor festival day called Pentecost, their public testimony began.

Luke goes out of his way to note the cultural diversity of the crowd that gathers around the newly Spirit-filled apostles. "Now there were devout Jews *from every nation under heaven* living in Jerusalem." Surely most of them would have spoken one or more of the lingua francas of the city, whether the priests' Hebrew, the occupiers' Latin or the merchants' Greek. Yet the essence of the ensuing miracle is one of simultaneous translation into the cultural form closest to each listener's heart, the mother tongue that they learned as children. The litany of nations is worth dwelling on for a moment:

> Amazed and astonished, they asked, "Are not all these who are speaking Galileans? And how is it that we hear, each of us, in our own native language? Parthians, Medes, Elamites, and residents of Mesopotamia, Judea and Cappadocia, Pontus and Asia, Phrygia and Pamphylia, Egypt and the parts of Libya belonging to Cyrene, and visitors from Rome, both Jews and proselytes, Cretans and Arabs—in our own languages we hear them speaking about God's deeds of power." All were amazed and perplexed, saying to one another, "What does this mean?" (Acts 2:7-12)

Even though he is speaking to an exclusively Jewish audience, Peter's answer to their question hints that the eventual meaning of Pentecost will go far beyond the nation of Israel. He quotes the prophet Joel: "In the last days it will be, God declares, / that I will pour out my Spirit upon all flesh" (Acts 2:17). "For the promise is for you, for your children, *and for all who are far away,* everyone whom the Lord our God calls to him" (Acts 2:39, emphasis added)—suggesting that the benefits of Jesus' resurrection and the coming of the Holy Spirit will go far beyond the borders of Israel.

At Pentecost, as commentators both ancient and modern have observed, the curse of Babel is miraculously undone. In the wake of Babel, God chose a single ethnolinguistic group to be his people in order to be a blessing to the nations; Pentecost is the beginning, as Peter declares, of the "last days" in which that blessing will be broken open and poured out upon every cultural group, every "nation." And just as the curse on the citizens of Babel was a dramatic divine intervention in human affairs, so its reversal comes as a gift—a supernatural (or more to the point, supercultural) overcoming of separation. God is on the move in history, and his work will no longer be contained within the story of just one cultural group. Indeed, the challenge to faith and dependence will be posed and will be available to every cultural group. "Everyone who calls on the name of the Lord shall be saved" (Acts 2:21), and the promise is for "everyone whom the Lord our God calls to him" (Acts 2:39)—faith's call in both directions, from human beings to God and from God to humanity, will no longer be for Abraham's descendants alone.

THE PROBLEM OF THE GENTILES

Many movies begin with a dramatic sequence of events that sets the plot in motion and sets up the key characters, conflicts and themes that will drive the rest of the story. Pentecost serves that function in Acts: a telling, tantalizing beginning that makes us realize that for all the drama of the resurrection, even more extraordinary events are still to come. But strangely, few modern Christians have paid close attention to Acts' dramatic structure. It's as if someone had seen a thrilling chase sequence from the beginning of a James Bond film but neglected to keep watching, unaware that an even more dramatic chase scene occurs near the end. The story of Pentecost is widely known, but in fact it just sets in motion a series of developments that culminate in the first and most important crisis of the early church. And that crisis has everything to do with culture—

indeed, it might be said to be the place where the issue of faith and culture is most directly raised in the entire New Testament.

In spite of their many adopted cultural and linguistic backgrounds, the entire audience at Pentecost is Jewish, still closely identified with the cultural project of Israel. But the unfolding drama of Acts soon brings the apostles and other early Christians into contact with Gentiles, called in Greek *ta ethnē*—the "nations"—both religiously and culturally distinct from Israel. The story unfolds in a quite specific order. After the stoning of Stephen in Acts 7, Luke tells us that "a severe persecution began against the church in Jerusalem, and all except the apostles were scattered throughout the countryside of Judea and Samaria" (Acts 8:1). One of the scattered ones, Philip, goes to Samaria, a borderland of dubious legitimacy to purity-conscious Jews from Jerusalem, where he encounters the distinctly unorthodox practice of magic—and sees both people and magician come to faith. Next comes Philip's encounter with the Ethiopian eunuch, almost certainly not a member of the nation of Israel (both because of his nationality and because the cultural practice of making eunuchs of important officials was specifically forbidden in the Jewish law) but also clearly a regular visitor to Jerusalem and student of the Hebrew Scriptures.

Not long afterward Peter finds himself staying at the house of Simon, "a tanner" (Acts 9:43)—an occupation that was widely considered unclean by Jews, suggesting that Peter had already begun to relax his practices of cultural purity—when he is called to the house of the Roman centurion Cornelius, an unmistakable Gentile, though also "a devout man who feared God with all his household" (Acts 10:2). This invitation prompts Peter's anguished lunchtime conversation with Jesus himself in a vision, where Jesus asks Peter to set aside the laws of kosher food, one of the most central boundary markers of Israel's cultural identity, in order to proclaim the gospel in Cornelius's house. Standing in a Gentile's house, a place he has probably never been before in his life, Peter utters these astonished (and to a Jew, astonishing) words: "I truly understand that God shows no partiality, but *in every nation* anyone who fears him and does what is right is acceptable to him" (Acts 10:34-35, emphasis added).

When Peter steps over Cornelius's threshold, the mission of Jesus' followers decisively breaks free of the cultural specificity of Israel. After

Acts 10 the pace of change quickens, and tension within the church begins to mount. Peter, returning to Jerusalem, has to explain his actions to the "circumcised believers," and their response is telling: "Then God has given even to the Gentiles the repentance that leads to life" (Acts 11:18). *Even* to the Gentiles—the surprise and lingering suspicion are palpable.

Meanwhile, the word is spreading, reaching Antioch, the third-largest city in the ancient world, a city whose diverse population included a fair number of Greek-speaking Jews who had already assimilated to some extent to Greek culture (the "Hellenists"). When the leadership of the church at Antioch is named in Acts 13, they display significant cultural diversity: Barnabas, a Jew originally from Cyprus; "Simeon who was called Niger," whose nickname suggests that he had dark skin; "Lucius from Cyrene," who had a Roman name and origins on the north coast of Africa; "Manaen a member of the court of Herod the ruler"; and Saul, also known as Paul, the former persecutor of the church and student of the rabbi Gamaliel, who we discover has both a Roman cognomen and Roman citizenship.

It is this culturally varied community that sends Barnabas and Saul out on their mission around the Mediterranean. On their very first stop in Salamis, their bicultural capacities are put to use, when no less a personage than the Roman proconsul, Sergius Paulus, summons them and in short order becomes a believer (Acts 13:4-12). On their next stop, in another town named Antioch in the region of Pisidia, the Jewish community, alarmed by widespread Gentile interest in Barnabas and Saul's message, turns against them, leading them to publicly declare that their ministry will be focused on Gentiles—and indeed many Gentiles become believers (Acts 13:14-52).

After Pisidian Antioch, while Barnabas and Paul never neglect opportunities to meet Jews and invite them to faith in Jesus, the focus shifts more and more to "the nations." In Lystra, Paul and Barnabas are so deep into pagan territory that a single healing causes the crowds to mistake them for Hermes and Zeus! The apostles' response is a surprisingly good summary of a Christian view of culture, even if it is shouted over the clamor of the crowd:

"Friends, why are you doing this? We are mortals just like you, and we bring you good news, that you should turn from these worthless things to the living God, who made the heaven and the earth and the sea and all that is in them. In past generations he allowed all the nations to follow their own ways; yet he has not left himself without a witness in doing good— giving you rains from heaven and fruitful seasons, and filling you with food and your hearts with joy." Even with these words, they scarcely restrained the crowds from offering sacrifice to them. (Acts 14:15-18)

"In past generations he allowed all the nations to follow their own ways"—each nation has tried to make something of the world. And no matter how far these nations have fallen from the Creator's original intention, they have experienced something of his goodness in the bounty of the earth and the witness of their hearts. But the news Barnabas and Paul bring is that it is now possible for every nation to "turn from these worthless things"—the hopeless inadequacy of humanly constructed cult and culture—"to the living God."

When the apostles return to their community in Antioch, Luke reports, "they called the church together and related all that God had done with them, and how he had opened a door of faith for the Gentiles" (Acts 14:27). *A door of faith*—in the wake of the resurrection, as Paul and Barnabas are discovering with the rest of the first Christians, the opportunity to place trust in the living God rather than poor creaturely substitutes has been opened up to every nation scattered after Babel.

THE CUSTOM OF MOSES

But at this point in the story the tension that has been simmering in one way or another since the early chapters of Acts (or indeed, since Jesus set out in a boat to the Gentile side of the Sea of Galilee) breaks out into the open.

Then certain individuals came down from Judea and were teaching the brothers, "Unless you are circumcised according to the custom of Moses, you cannot be saved." And after Paul and Barnabas had no small dissension and debate with them, Paul and Barnabas and some of the others were appointed to go up to Jerusalem to discuss this question with the apostles and the elders. (Acts 15:1-2)

Acts 15 is the dramatic hinge of Acts: the decisive moment that was foreshadowed by the dramatic events of Pentecost. Like most dramatic moments, it is a conflict—as Luke puts it, using the rhetorical technique called litotes, "no small dissension and debate," which means, of course, a very great deal of dissension and debate. The debate is fierce enough to send Paul, Barnabas and others on a four-hundred-mile journey to determine how the followers of Jesus will deal with culture.

On one side were "believers who belonged to the sect of the Pharisees," whose concern was with the "custom" of Moses—the Greek word *ethos*, whose similarity to *ethnos* did not escape ancient people. Every *ethnos* had an *ethos*—every people had a custom, a distinctive way of making something of the world. The Pharisees, far from being simply legalists, were in fact passionately committed to preserving Israel's distinctiveness in the midst of the world. And for them God's purposes in history could not be separated from his chosen people, and his chosen people could not be separated from their *ethos*, marked (literally) by circumcision. If Gentiles were going to join God's purposes, that would mean taking on all the cultural marks of Israel: "It is necessary for them to be circumcised and ordered to keep the law of Moses" (Acts 15:5).

On the other side were Barnabas and Paul, who had been traveling in places like Antioch and Salamis. In these cities the presence of Jews who were willing to mingle to some extent with their Gentile neighbors had made it possible, as in Pisidian Antioch, for the Gentiles to seek to know more of the God of Israel. But it was in these cities as well that the Jews had refused to hear the apostles' message, while the nations had walked through the door of faith. These two Jerusalem-educated Jews were finding that *ethos* and *ethnos* were no longer a barrier to grace, while even the provision of Moses' law was not enough to ensure that Israel would respond to God in their very midst. Barnabas and Paul were not the last missionaries to come back to their home culture more aware of its flaws and more awed by the potential in every culture for people to respond to the message of the living God.

Luke surely does not report the full extent of the debate at what we now call the Council of Jerusalem. It was an unprecedented event in the life of the first Christians—a vastly more complex and freighted decision than the squabbles that had arisen, also on cultural grounds, between Greek- and Hebrew-speaking Jewish widows in Acts 6. When the dust had settled and the crucial voices of Peter and James, the brother of Jesus, had been heard, something extraordinary had happened. A group of Jews who spent every day in the temple, celebrating the return of the Messiah to fulfill the promise of Israel, determined that *ethos* and *ethnos*, as central as they had been in sustaining a witness to the world's Creator for over a thousand years, would now be less important than faith in the Lord Jesus. And, conversely, faith in the Lord Jesus could now be proclaimed and demonstrated in every cultural setting.

To be sure, the Council did not simply baptize every aspect of Gentile culture. "It has seemed good to the Holy Spirit and to us," they wrote to the believers of Gentile origin, "to impose on you no further burden than these essentials: that you abstain from what has been sacrificed to idols and from blood and from what is strangled and from fornication" (Acts 15:28-29). The Council's letter discerned features of Gentile culture that were not merely *ethos*, just "custom," but that made a dead end of the world: the cult of idolatry that worshiped the creation in place of the Creator; the consumption of animals that, in the ancient worldview, still had the blood of life in them rather than being humanely slaughtered; and sexual practices that fell short of God's intention for human beings. But the myriad smaller matters that made Israel a people, while still a good gift from God, were no longer the markers of faith.

And so Paul and his companions were set free on a mission to the nations, a mission that would ultimately take Paul from Jerusalem to Rome—from the center of Jewish identity to the center of pagan culture and power, along the way finding and founding churches with both Gentiles and Jews worshiping Jesus side by side. A movement that began in Galilee, at the very edges of the empire, would reach by the end of Paul's life to Caesar's household. From the garden to the city, the mustard seed of the gospel was being spread fast and far indeed.

LESSONS FROM ACTS

The events of Acts marked a dramatic turning point in the way biblical people think about culture. The essence of Israel was to be a singular and distinctive culture. But suddenly, faithful Jews, disciples of a Galilean Messiah, were traveling throughout the Roman Empire, taking advantage of that empire's notable cultural accomplishments in transport and trade to invite members of any and all cultures into their community. Indeed, if the legends of churches in Egypt and India are true, Christ's original apostles, Galilean Jews all, journeyed not just beyond their homeland but beyond the imperial borders as well. They would have grown up referring to "the nations," *ta ethnē,* with disdain. But now "the nations" in all their variety were to be offered the same message of faith and repentance as Israel. *Nations* was now a word of inclusion, not exclusion.

And behind this momentous shift in thinking was the experience of Pentecost and its aftermath, when the Holy Spirit given by Jesus made it possible for each person to hear "the mighty works of God" in their own language—translated into their own cultural idiom. As the scholar Lamin Sanneh has pointed out, this translatability sharply differentiates Christianity from Islam, which requires the Qur'an to be read in its original language. The gospel, even though it is deeply embedded in Jewish cultural history, is available in the "mother tongue" of every human being. There is no culture beyond its reach—because the very specific cultural story of Israel was never anything other than a rescue mission for all the cultures of the world, initiated by the world's Creator.

This sudden explosion of cultural diversity within the people of God does not mean that all cultures, and all cultural artifacts and traditions, are simply baptized and declared good. Instead, what Acts sets off is a vast and lengthy process of cultural discernment, of which the letter from the Jewish Christians in Jerusalem to their Gentile counterparts in Antioch was just the beginning. God had told Peter, "What God has made clean, you must not call profane" (Acts 10:15). But what exactly had God made clean? Clearly Jewish restrictions on food, however valuable and indeed divinely commanded, were not a crosscultural mandate. But the council in Acts discerned that certain features of Gentile cultures were permanently outside the horizons God had intended for humanity. In the wake of Pentecost the value of any given cultural artifact or tradition is not determined simply by its relationship to the Torah given to Israel; it is determined by everything Israel had learned about shalom, the all-encompassing peace in which the horizons of possible and impossible are in their proper place. Within those horizons there is no space for idolatry, irreverent exploitation of animals or sexual immorality—even though each of these practices were central to various cultures then and now. As the gospel was preached and embodied in various cultures, in fact, it would begin to call into question cultural traditions that had seemed unremarkable. But many other features of culture, like the language that was used to declare God's mighty acts in Acts 2, would prove to be completely capable of being put to use in faithfulness and dependence on God.

ACTS 29

Indeed, what the Holy Spirit unleashed through the first Christians was nothing less than a cultural revolution—a far-reaching wave of cultural creativity that reshaped the Roman Empire. One of the best accounts of the cultural effects of the early church is sociologist Rodney Stark's book *The Rise of Christianity*. Stark—not himself a Christian believer at the time— set out to try to understand in purely secular terms, with quantitative rigor, how the early church grew rapidly enough to become a powerful force in the empire by the time of Constantine, whose Edict of Milan made Christianity legal in 313. "In an empire having a population of at least 60 million, there might well have been 33 million Christians by [A.D.] 350—for by then some contemporary Christian writers were claiming a majority." How did a movement with a few thousand adherents at most in the first century become half the population of the empire by the fourth century?

The answer, which Stark unfolds in a series of chapters that read like professorial detective stories, comes down to culture. In feature after feature of Roman culture, Christians, animated by a powerfully different story from their pagan neighbors, were boldly creative. Their lives simply did not look like their neighbors'. But they were not cut off from their neighbors—the culture they created was public and accessible to all.

The most compelling chapter of Stark's book, "Epidemics, Networks, Conversion," examines how Christians responded to the epidemics that swept through Roman cities. At least two major epidemics claimed up to a third of the population of the Roman Empire in the first centuries of the Christian era. In the face of terrible conditions, pagan elites and their

priests simply fled the cities. The only functioning social network left behind was the church, which provided basic nursing care to Christians and
non-Christians alike, along with a hope that transcended death. "Many,
in nursing and curing others, transferred their death to themselves and
died in their stead," the bishop Dionysius wrote. "The best of our brothers
lost their lives in this manner, a number of presbyters, deacons, and laymen winning high commendation so that death in this form . . . seems in
every way the equal of martyrdom."

The church had no magic or medicine to cure the plague, but it turns
out that survival even of a terrible disease has a lot to do with one's access
to the most basic elements of life. Simply by providing food, water and
friendship to their neighbors, Christians enabled many to remain strong
enough that their own immune systems could mount an effective defense.
Stark engages in some rather macabre algebra to calculate the "differen-
tial mortality" of Christians and their neighbors compared to pagans who
were not fortunate enough to have the same kind of care—and concludes
that "conscientious nursing *without any medications* could cut the mortality
rate by two-thirds or even more." The result was that after consecutive epidemics had swept through a city, a very disproportionate number of those
remaining would either have been Christians or pagans who had been
nursed through their sickness by Christian neighbors. And with their
family and friends decimated by the plague, it is no wonder that many of
these neighbors, seeking new friends and family, would naturally convert
to Christian faith. The church would grow not just because it proclaimed
hope in the face of horror but because of the cultural effects of a new approach to the sick and dying, a willingness to care for the sick even at risk
of death.

In the succeeding chapters Stark examines a series of equally concrete
cultural issues. The first Christians lived in cities plagued by poor sanita-
tion and ethnic tension; they lived in a culture that radically constrained
the freedom and dignity of women; they lived in a society that exposed
or drowned unwanted infants. In each case the Christians were culturally creative, innovating new ways of solving challenges that they shared
with their neighbors. And their cultural creativity was not hidden away,
inaccessible to the wider public. Partly because their number included not

just the poor but also the culturally powerful (as Stark, following other scholars, argues in some detail), their innovations were able to permeate Roman society as a genuine alternative to the dominant culture.

After the book of Acts, with its miracles, prayers and evangelistic sermons, Stark's book can initially seem dry or even off-putting to a Christian reader looking for signs of God's work in history. Isn't something lost by subjecting the apparently miraculous growth of the Christian movement to the disciplines of statistics and demography?

However, we do not have to read Stark's rigorously scientific analysis of death and birth rates in isolation. We can read it alongside the writings of the Christians of the very eras he is studying—and when we do, we find them suffused with the same confidence in the presence and work of the Holy Spirit, the same awe at God's miraculous works in the midst of the Christian community, as we find in the pages of Acts.

Indeed, it would have been a dramatic and depressing turn of events if the Spirit's work suddenly disappeared from history into the realm of the merely and purely "religious" matter of private worship and inward sensations. God's plan for history had never been to escape from history. Our word *spirit* has acquired connotations of bodilessness, leaving modern Christians with the impression that the Spirit is some vague and largely psychological phenomenon. But both the Hebrew word *ruach* and the Greek word *pneuma* meant "wind" and "breath" much more than they meant "ghost." As Jesus told Nicodemus, the wind is in some ways ineffable and unpredictable—but when the wind blows, branches bend, grass ripples and waves rise. The same Spirit who brought the creation into existence has measurable, visible cultural effects, no matter how difficult it may be to tell exactly "where it comes from or where it is going." In Acts, in the first centuries of the Christian era, and today, especially when Pentecostal faith is reshaping vast swaths of our globe, there is no contradiction between divine power and cultural effects that can be measured by even the most irreligious scientist.

Stark himself acknowledges the limits of traditional sociological methods in accounting for the cultural change he documents. In an important postscript to *The Rise of Christianity*, he observes that modern historians "are more than willing to discuss how social factors shaped religious doctrines. Unfortunately, at the same time they have become somewhat reluctant to discuss how doctrines may have shaped social factors." But in this case, Stark believes, the church's doctrines were *the ultimate factor* in the rise of Christianity. . . . *Central doctrines of Christianity prompted and sustained attractive, liberating, and effective social relations and organizations.*" In simpler terms, Christian belief was neither just the product of social forces in Roman culture; nor was it a culturally inert "private" matter. The belief of Christians that Jesus of Nazareth had been raised from the dead made them culture makers, and the culture they created was so attractive that by the fourth century A.D., an entire empire was on the verge of faith.

10

. . . TO REVELATION

When we turn the page at the end of Acts, we are at the end of the biblical history that began with the call of Abram in Genesis 12. Of course there are pages of letters to come, but if we were to arrange them chronologically we would find nearly all of them had been written during the events that Acts describes or very shortly after its end, in the time between Paul's arrival in Rome and (not long after, according to Christian tradition) his execution by the agents of the empire. Genesis 12 through the final letters of the New Testament narrates the story of God's chosen people, starting from one man and ending with his spiritual descendants already multiplying throughout the Roman Empire.

The last book in the New Testament, however, stands outside of that history, telling an epic, mythic story that puts the whole sweep of human experience into perspective—just as the primordial history of Genesis 1–11 stands outside of the detailed narrative of God's covenant with Abraham. The aging apostle in exile on the dusty, distant island of Patmos writes to strengthen the wavering churches around the Mediterranean rim as they begin to face persecution. But Revelation is a quite different kind of exhortation from Paul's practical and detailed letters, even different from the affectionate short epistles also ascribed to John. "I was in the Spirit on the Lord's day," he reports:

> and I heard behind me a loud voice like a trumpet saying, "Write in a book what you see and send it to the seven churches, to Ephesus, to Smyrna, to Pergamum, to Thyatira, to Sardis, to Philadelphia, and to Laodicea."
>
> Then I turned to see whose voice it was that spoke to me, and on turning I saw seven golden lampstands, and in the midst of the lampstands I saw one like the Son of Man, clothed with a long robe and with a golden sash across his chest. His head and his hair were white as white wool, white as snow; his eyes were like a flame of fire, his feet were like burnished bronze, refined as in a furnace, and his voice was like the sound of many waters. In his right hand he held seven stars, and from his mouth came a sharp, two-edged sword, and his face was like the sun shining with full force.
>
> When I saw him, I fell at his feet as though dead. But he placed his right hand on me, saying, "Do not be afraid; I am the first and the last, and the living one. I was dead, and see, I am alive forever and ever; and I have the keys of Death and of Hades. Now write what you have seen, what is, and what is to take place after this." (Rev 1:10-19)

John's readers would have immediately recognized that this was no ordinary epistle. They would have heard the echoes of the vision recounted by another faithful seer who lived at the zenith of another empire: "I looked up and saw a man clothed in linen, with a belt of gold from Uphaz around his waist. His body was like beryl, his face like lightning, his eyes like flaming torches, his arms and legs like the gleam of burnished bronze, and the sound of his words like the roar of a multitude" (Dan 10:5-6). And they would have immediately recognized this "Son of Man" as the same one that Daniel had seen hundreds of years earlier:

> In my vision at night I looked, and there before me was one like a son of man, coming with the clouds of heaven. He approached the Ancient of Days and was led into his presence. He was given authority, glory and sovereign power; all peoples, nations and men of every language worshiped him. His dominion is an everlasting dominion that will not pass away, and his kingdom is one that will never be destroyed. (Dan 7:13-14 NIV)

The "Ancient of Days" had "clothing . . . as white as snow; / the hair of his head was white like wool" (Dan 7:9 NIV).

John was meeting the very One who summed up all of Daniel's visions, the Son of Man who is also the Son of God and bears the indelible likeness of his Father—woolly white hair and all. And in the following chapters of Revelation John recounts the visions he is privileged to see, setting the persecution of Jesus' scattered churches in a wider and more hopeful story than they could possibly have hoped. Revelation is a book of apocalypse, a Greek word that originally meant not *catastrophe* or *the end of the world*, but simply *disclosure*. In Revelation John offers a divine disclosure of the meaning of current and future events, setting them all in a distinctively Jewish language of cosmic drama.

Oceans of ink have been spilled trying to make sense of John's revelation for later historical eras. Some of what he wrote may have been unclear to his first readers and very possibly to the writer himself—certainly Daniel confessed that he did not understand much of what he wrote (Dan 12:8). But I am persuaded that much of the early chapters of Revelation would have been comprehensible to John's readers as coded commentary on the very real historical circumstances that surrounded them. For all its cosmic scope and sweep, the vivid language of apocalyptic was almost always tied to current events and their capacity for sudden reversals, certainly about "the end of the world as we know it" but not necessarily about "the end of the world."

But toward the end of Revelation, John does arrive at a truly cosmic turning point. Just as Genesis 1–11 recount the beginnings that led up to the calling of Abram, the last chapters of Revelation peer forward toward the ending of the whole vast project that began with a divine word in the darkness and a divine hand in the dust. The end of the story, after "the earth and heaven [have] fled from his presence" (Rev 20:11), is terrifying to the presently comfortable—and comforting to anyone who has suffered under human cultures at their worst. A final, honest and true judgment is rendered on every human being's works. Nothing finally escapes God's notice, and nothing wrong escapes his wrath. Every cry for justice is heard and accounted for. Then another book is read, the "book of life," a book based not on works but on faith. This book is terrifying for anyone who has resisted the life offered by God—and comforting for all who know how poorly they would fare in a brutally honest retelling of their life's work. All "whose name was not found written in the book of life" are cast into a sulfurous lake of fire (Rev 20:15). But those who survive that severe and gracious census pass into an astonishing new beginning.

And at the very end of Revelation, just as at the very beginning of Genesis, we find culture in a prominent role.

THE HOLY CITY

Revelation's end is a beginning, but as we've already observed, this beginning has some surprising differences from Genesis. The "new heaven and new earth" begins with "the holy city, the new Jerusalem, coming down out of heaven from God, prepared as a bride adorned for her husband" (Rev 21:2). Jerusalem, the city that summed up Israel's hopes, triumphs and failures, has somehow survived the cataclysmic judgment of the ages. The new Jerusalem is everything the old Jerusalem was ever imagined or intended to be, and more, and John describes it in a long passage that can either make our eyes widen with expectation or glaze over with boredom. But nearly every sentence of this description has implications for the way we think about the ultimate destiny of culture, and it is worth reading carefully.

> In the spirit [the angel] carried me away to a great, high mountain and showed me the holy city Jerusalem coming down out of heaven from God. It has the glory of God and a radiance like a very rare jewel, like jasper, clear as crystal. It has a great, high wall with twelve gates, and at the gates twelve angels, and on the gates are inscribed the names of the twelve tribes of the Israelites; on the east three gates, on the north three gates, on the south three gates, and on the west three gates. And the wall of the city has twelve foundations, and on them are the twelve names of the twelve apostles of the Lamb. (Rev 21:10-14)

This city comes "down out of heaven from God"—a phrase John emphasizes twice, in verses 2 and 10. Completely unlike Babel, with its attempt to reach the heavens by building upward toward heaven, this city is not a human achievement. It is a gift, just as the first creation was a gift. Its glory is God's glory, because God is its "architect and builder" (Heb 11:10). Very much like the primeval Garden, this is God's own cultural work.

The city at the heart of the new creation preserves much in continuity with the past. Represented here are both the nation of Israel (its tribes' names inscribed on the gates) and the church (its apostles' names inscribed on the twelve foundations—whatever exactly those are!). The story of God's saving intervention into human history is not forgotten here nor swept aside to make way for some better "spiritual" reality. Indeed, the only purely "spiritual" creatures in sight, the twelve angels that guard the gates, play a purely supporting role. Human beings' names mark the city's gates and foundation stones—twelve Hebrew brothers and twelve Galileans, none of them remembered in Scripture as anything other than the sometimes quarreling, sometimes courageous people they were. Human history, represented by human names, is here resurrected in its lasting significance.

> The wall is built of jasper, while the city is pure gold, clear as glass. The foundations of the wall of the city are adorned with every jewel; the first was jasper, the second sapphire, the third agate, the fourth emerald, the fifth onyx, the sixth carnelian, the seventh chrysolite, the eighth beryl, the ninth topaz, the tenth chrysoprase, the eleventh jacinth, the twelfth amethyst. And the twelve gates are twelve pearls, each of the gates is a single pearl, and the street of the city is pure gold, transparent as glass. (Rev 21:18-21)

I had always assumed that John's twice-mentioned vision of "gold, clear as glass" was an example of ecstatic spiritualizing, a metaphor for the unimaginable elements of the new creation. But then I became acquainted with the work of New York artist Makoto Fujimura, who draws on the Japanese artistic tradition of *nihonga*, a centuries-old art form that begins with pure minerals rather than already-mixed paints and pigments. One of Fujimura's primary materials is gold leaf, beaten until it is just micrometers thin. It turns out that when gold is beaten carefully this way, it does indeed become translucent, so that objects behind it become visible while still being bathed in a golden essence.

Gold, in its *natural* state, is not at all translucent, let alone transparent. But when worked by a skilled craftsman, gold acquires glasslike qualities. So when John speaks of gold as "clear as glass"—even though such gold is beyond the skill of any artist in this world—he almost certainly intends us to imagine gold that has been reworked by a cultural process, by a master Artist. And in fact this is true of all the elements listed by John as the adornments of the city. The foundations of the wall are adorned not with minerals but with jewels. And while jewels are made of minerals, they are minerals plus culture: minerals that have been selected by a discerning eye and polished and cut to bring out their most striking and beautiful qualities.

Indeed, readers with a keen and long memory will note that the natural resources that were nearby the original Garden in Genesis 2 are here in the new Jerusalem as well. "The gold of that land is good; bdellium and onyx stone are there," the author of Genesis reported in a seemingly tangential aside. Here the gold has been put to use; the onyx is one of the many jewels that make up the city's foundations; and the bdellium, a tree gum, like myrrh, that hardened into translucent white balls that were prized as jewelry as well as perfume, is echoed in the twelve pearls that form the gates to the city. The natural riches that surrounded the Garden have been cultivated and brought to their most striking expression for the city's adornment.

> I saw no temple in the city, for its temple is the Lord God the Almighty and the Lamb. And the city has no need of sun or moon to shine on it, for the glory of God is its light, and its lamp is the Lamb. The nations will walk by its light, and the kings of the earth will bring their glory into it. Its gates will never be shut by day—and there will be no night there. People will bring into it the glory and the honor of the nations. But nothing unclean will enter it, nor anyone who practices abomination or falsehood, but only those who are written in the Lamb's book of life. (Rev 21:22-27)

The new creation, while bearing some resemblance to the old, is not a carbon copy. The cultural artifact called a temple—the place where human beings sought to make something of their relationship to God—is no longer necessary. Neither are the natural bodies of sun and moon needed (John does not say whether or not there are other celestial bodies in the new creation, just that their light is not needed), for their functions of illumination have been superseded by the immediate presence of the glory

of God, who is in residence in the city day and night. And the very imme-
diacy of the divine presence means that many other things, all too familiar
from the old creation, cannot enter the city—things and people that were
unclean and false. Only those who have been given life, by the Lamb's
gracious gift, enter the city.

THE KINGS AND THEIR GLORY

And here we arrive at the heart of Revelation's cultural vision. The city is
already a cultural artifact, the work of a master Architect and Artist. The
citizens themselves are the redeemed people of the Lamb, drawn from
"every tribe and language and people and nation" (Rev 5:9). But God's
handiwork, artifacts and people alike, are not all that is found in the city.
Also in the city are "the glory and the honor of the nations"—brought into
the city by none other than "the kings of the earth."

Here, and throughout Revelation 21, John is recovering and recapitulating an ancient vision recorded by the prophet Isaiah. Isaiah too had
seen a future city where the sun and moon would no longer be necessary,
"but the LORD will be your everlasting light, / and your God will be your
glory" (Is 60:19). And Isaiah had already foretold the arrival of kings and
nations in the streets of the redeemed city:

> A multitude of camels shall cover you,
>   the young camels of Midian and Ephah;
>   all those from Sheba shall come.
> They shall bring gold and frankincense,
>   and shall proclaim the praise of the LORD.
> All the flocks of Kedar shall be gathered to you,
>   the rams of Nebaioth shall minister to you;
> they shall be acceptable on my altar,
>   and I will glorify my glorious house. . . .
>
> For the coastlands shall wait for me,
>   the ships of Tarshish first,
> to bring your children from far away,
>   their silver and gold with them,
> for the name of the LORD your God,
>   and for the Holy One of Israel,

because he has glorified you. . . .

Your gates shall always be open;
  day and night they shall not be shut,
so that nations shall bring you their wealth,
  with their kings led in procession. . . .
The glory of Lebanon shall come to you,
  the cypress, the plane, and the pine,
to beautify the place of my sanctuary;
  and I will glorify where my feet rest. (Is 60:6-7, 9, 11, 13)

The parallels between John's vision and Isaiah's are clear. Once again we have a city whose gates are never shut, upon which night never falls. And the streets of Isaiah's city too are teeming with cultural goods— not just from Israel's culture but from the nations that surrounded her. Domesticated animals, ships, precious minerals and jewels, and timber all appear in the city "to beautify the place of my sanctuary." (The one significant difference between Isaiah and John is that Isaiah clearly cannot imagine that the new Jerusalem would lack a temple—but John sees that in the new creation the city and the temple will all be one undivided sanctuary.)

In his marvelous short book *When the Kings Come Marching In*, Richard Mouw explores the implications of Isaiah's vision for the way biblical people think about both culture and the new creation:

> The contents of the City will be more akin to our present cultural patterns than is usually acknowledged in discussions of the afterlife. Isaiah pictures the Holy City as a center of commerce, a place that receives the vessels, goods, and currency of commercial activity. . . . Isaiah is, in contemporary jargon, interested in the future of "corporate structures" and "cultural patterns." And his vision leads him to what are for many of us very surprising observations about the future destiny of many items of "pagan culture." He sees these items as being gathered into the Holy City to be put to good use there.

So when John echoes Isaiah's vision of the new Jerusalem being filled with the "glory of the nations," he is not picturing simply "Christian" cultural artifacts—items made by and for people of faith. Just as the king of a nation, in the biblical mind, is the representative of an entire *ethnos* or people, the glory of a nation is simply its greatest and most distinctive cultural achievement—the camels of desert merchants, the carefully cultivated timber of Lebanon, the large and sturdy ships of Tarshish. It is precisely these very non-Israelite, non-Christian cultural goods that will be the furniture of the new Jerusalem.

Mouw properly asks how this can be, given that both Isaiah and John in Revelation specifically prophesy God's condemnation of pagan cultural goods, not least the ships of Tarshish (which God promises to "shatter" in Psalm 48:7). But this condemnation is a matter not of their intrinsic value but of the idolatrous function that they have come to play in the life of pagan societies (and all too often in Israel's life as well):

> There is no need to read the negative passages as insisting that these pagan entities as such will be destroyed. . . . My own impression is that the judgment that will visit the ships of Tarshish is of a purifying sort. We might think here of the "breaking" of the ships of Tarshish as more like the breaking of a horse rather than the breaking of a vase. The judgment here is meant to tame, not destroy. . . . When these ships are thus stripped of the haughtiness and rebellion with which they are presently associated, they are freed for service to the Lord and his people. They become vessels for ministry in the transformed City.

> When the kings come marching in, then, they bring the best of their nations—even the cultural goods that had been deployed against God and his people. The final vision of the City is one filled, not just with God's glory and presence, not just with his own stunningly beautiful architectural designs, not just with redeemed persons from every cultural background—but with redeemed human culture too.

Will all human culture find a lasting place in the new Jerusalem? Clearly not. The ships of Tarshish, broad-sailed and wide-keeled, may find a place once they have been "broken." But swords whose only purpose was to take life will have no place in a creation where there is no war or death. They will have to be turned into plowshares (Is 2:4). Spears will have to become pruning hooks. The myriad cultural dead ends of history will be finally forgotten and truly dead. I suppose the same will be true of cultural mediocrity, the half-baked and half-hearted efforts to make something of the world that never reached a point where they could be described as the "glory" of any cultural tradition.

And it seems certain that every cultural artifact will have to undergo a radical transformation of some sort—just as gold, translucent when beaten, will become capable of transparency. The best parallel, it seems, may be what Scripture instructs us to expect for our own bodies. We too, after all, will have to undergo a humbling and a judgment, and the body with which we will be raised, Paul assures us, will bear as little, and as much, resemblance to our current body as the oak tree bears to the acorn. Surely the same kind of judgment, purification and resurrection will happen for every cultural good that is brought into the city.

But just as we hope and expect to be bodily present, in bodies we cannot now imagine yet that we believe will be recognizably our own—just as the disciples met Jesus in a resurrected body that had unimaginable capabilities yet was recognizably his own—it seems clear from Isaiah 60 and from Revelation 21 that we will find the new creation furnished with culture. Cultural goods too will be transformed and redeemed, yet they will be recognizably what they were in the old creation—or perhaps more accurately, they will be what they always could have been. The new Jerusalem will be truly a city: a place suffused with culture, a place where culture has reached its full flourishing. It will be the place where God's instruction to the first human beings is fulfilled, where all the latent potentialities of the world will be discovered and released by creative, cultivating people.

And finally, in the midst of this metropolis there will also be the Garden where the whole story began:

> Then the angel showed me the river of the water of life, bright as crystal, flowing from the throne of God and of the Lamb through the middle of the street of the city. On either side of the river is the tree of life with its twelve kinds of fruit, producing its fruit each month; and the leaves of the tree are for the healing of the nations. Nothing accursed will be found there any more. But the throne of God and of the Lamb will be in it, and his servants will worship him; they will see his face, and his name will be on their foreheads. And there will be no more night; they need no light of lamp or sun, for the Lord God will be their light, and they will reign forever and ever. (Rev 22:1-5)

It is not just culture that is rescued, redeemed and transformed—nature also flourishes as it was always intended to, now that God has rendered judgment on "those who destroy the earth" (Rev 11:18). The tree of life is no longer prohibited or perilous. The city does not pave over the garden— the garden is at the city's heart, lush and green with life.

FURNISHING THE NEW JERUSALEM

Culture, then, is the furniture of heaven. (And indeed, Revelation makes it clear, in the words of Belinda Carlisle, that "heaven is a place on earth.") It is simply not true, according to Isaiah and John—and according to the whole sweep of the biblical story from beginning to end—that "souls" are the only eternal things or that human beings are all that last into eternity. To be sure, cultural goods without creators and cultivators would be inert and useless. But human beings, in God's original intention and in their redemptive destination, cannot be separated from the cultural goods they create and cultivate at their best.

So it's a fascinating exercise to ask about any cultural artifact: can we imagine this making it into the new Jerusalem? What cultural goods represent the "glory and honor" of the many cultural traditions we know? We already have biblical assurance that the ships of Tarshish will be there; perhaps they will share a harbor with an Americas' Cup yacht and a lovingly carved birch bark canoe. My own personal list of "the glory and honor of the nations" would surely include Bach's *B Minor Mass*, Miles Davis's *Kind of Blue* and Arvo Pärt's "Spiegel im Spiegel"; green-tea crème brûlée, fish tacos and bulgogi; *Moby-Dick* and the *Odyssey;* the iPod and the Mini Cooper. Of course I don't expect any of them to appear without being suitably purified and redeemed, any more than I expect my own resurrected body to be just another unimproved version of my present one. But I will be very surprised if they are not carried in by one or another of the representatives of human culture, for they are part of the glorious best that human beings have made of the twelve-tone scale, the flavors of the natural world, language, the microchip and the internal combustion engine. (For the cows' and fishes' sake, I suppose the transformed meals in the new Jerusalem will be vegetarian, but surely they will be a grand improvement on tofurkey.)

We should ask the same question about our own cultural creativity and cultivating. Are we creating and cultivating things that have a chance of furnishing the new Jerusalem? Will the cultural goods we devote our lives to—the food we cook and consume, the music we purchase and practice, the movies we watch and make, the enterprises we earn our paychecks from and invest our wealth in—be identified as the glory and honor of our cultural tradition? Or will they be remembered as mediocrities at best, dead ends at worst? This is not the same as asking whether we are making "Christian" culture. "Christian" cultural artifacts will surely go through the same winnowing and judgment as "non-Christian" artifacts. Nor is this entirely a matter of who is responsible for the cultural artifacts and where their faith is placed, especially since every cultural good is a collective effort. Clearly some of the cultural goods found in the new Jerusalem will have been created and cultivated by people who may well not accept the Lamb's invitation to substitute his righteousness for their sin. Yet the best of their work may survive. Can that be said of the goods that we are devoting our lives to?

This is, it seems to me, a standard for cultural responsibility that is both more demanding and more liberating than the ways Christians often gauge our work's significance. We tend to have altogether too short a time frame for the worth of our work. We ask if this book will be noticed, this store will have a profitable quarter, this contract will be accepted. Some of these are useful intermediate steps for assessing whether our cultural work is of lasting value, but our short-term evaluations can be misleading if our work is not also held up to the long horizon of God's redemptive purpose. On the other hand, knowing that the new Jerusalem will be furnished with the best of every culture frees us from having to give a "religious" or evangelistic explanation for everything we do. We are free to simply make the best we can of the world, in concert with our forebears and our neighbors. If the ships of Tarshish and the camels of Midian can find a place in the new Jerusalem, our work, no matter how "secular," can too.

THE UNEXPECTED KINGS

It may be a surprise, for many Christian readers, to discover the "kings of the earth" in the city at the end of the story (see Rev 21:24). But more surprises are surely waiting. The very concept of a king, like all other human cultural goods, will have to be properly purified. The pages of Revelation are populated with unexpectedly significant characters. The white-robed army of martyrs, whose lives were summarily snuffed out by human empire, play a central part in the end, and the "King of kings and Lord of lords" who rules over the whole city is a Lamb who was slain. In the new Jerusalem, as Jesus promised, the first are last and the last are first.

So we probably should expect some surprises when the "kings of the earth" are revealed bringing the glory of the nations into the city. Their names may or may not be recognizable from the history books. Tonight a mother is singing her child a lullaby. A nurse in a clinic without electricity is holding the hand of a man dying from AIDS. A hungry boy is sharing a scrap of food with his sister. They are not kings—now. But the gospel turns our assumptions about what is lasting, what is significant, what is "elite," upside down. The ships of Tarshish will have to be humbled before they can fit, as through the eye of a needle, into the new creation, but other cultural goods, which are now so small as to be invisible to our status- and power-obsessed world, will be exalted. God's new creation both levels the mountains *and* raises the valleys.

In Isaiah 57:15 God says, "I dwell in the high and holy place, / and also with those who are contrite and humble in spirit." Those little words "and also" are a key to Christian cultural discernment. Isaiah's and John's visions undoubtedly include "high" culture, that which is celebrated and cultivated by elites, the wealthy and the powerful—but any city ruled by a Lamb will include among its glories cultural goods that most of us overlooked, brought in by exemplary culture shapers whose names we never knew. There will be French fries as well as haute cuisine at the great and final Feast.

WORK AND PRAISE

John's vision of culture's place in the city has profound implications for our own vision of what eternity will be like. I've sometimes heard it said in church circles that human beings were created to worship God. More than once I've heard a worship leader say, "Worship is the only eternal thing we will do." (A flattering thought if you're a worship leader!) Without a doubt our original purpose and eventual destination is to love God with our whole heart, mind, soul and strength. But it is a great misreading of both Genesis and Revelation to suppose that the only way we will ultimately love God wholeheartedly will be through something like what happens in church on Sunday morning. To be sure, Revelation, with its tableaux of elders falling down before the throne of God and white-robed martyrs praising God, makes it clear that we will know an intensity and depth of praise in the new creation that we can only imagine now, even as right now we get to sing some of the same songs that will be sung eternally.

But the end of humanity as depicted in Revelation is more than a temple—an everlasting worship service. In fact, as we've seen, a temple is the one notable thing the new Jerusalem does not have (Rev 21:22). The new Jerusalem needs no temple because every aspect of life in that city is permeated with the light and love of God. In that sense worship as we know it—a sacred time set apart to realign our hearts with the knowledge and love of God—will be obsolete. What will take its place?

The most plausible answer, it seems to me, is that our eternal life in God's recreated world will be the fulfillment of what God originally asked us to do: cultivating and creating in full and lasting relationship with our Creator. This time, of course, we will not just be tending a garden; we will be sustaining the life of a city, a harmonious human society that has developed all the potentialities hidden in the original creation to their fullest. Culture—redeemed, transformed and permeated by the presence of God—will be the activity of eternity.

To be sure, life in that new city will be very different from the life we know now. Jesus told his contemporaries that in the resurrection there is no marriage (Mk 12:25). But John in Revelation makes it clear that in another sense the human cultural institution that is marriage will be echoed in the new Jerusalem, for the new Jerusalem itself will be one eternal wedding feast between Creator and redeemed creation. Likewise, work, in the sense we know it in human history, will not be the same in the new Jerusalem either. Yet if there is no work, there will surely be activity. Perhaps some of the "glory and honor of the nations," like a fine painting or sculpture, will be able to be simply enjoyed without new human effort. But much of the glory and honor of the nations, whether epic poetry or baroque fugues or fine cuisine, can be realized only when people "perform" it—when singers sing, chefs cook and dancers dance. From jazz we are familiar with the idea of improvisation—the creative reinterpretation of a fixed set of chord changes and a memorable theme. It seems likely to me that part of the activity of eternity will be endlessly creative improvisations upon the "glory and honor of the nations"—human beings using their creative capacities to their fullest to explore the depth and breadth of all that human beings made in their vocations as cocreators with God.

So culture will ultimately fulfill Genesis 1's mandate—humanity will ultimately comprehend and have our proper dominion over all of creation. The glory of the nations will include our best realizations of the potentiality of God's world—the best use of minerals, of sound, of color, of thermodynamics. And it will all be summed up as praise, because the ultimate meaning of the world is love. And true love calls forth praise of the beloved.

In the end this is what we will make of the world:

> You are worthy, our Lord and God,
>   to receive glory and honor and power,
> for you created all things,
>   and by your will they existed and were created. (Rev 4:11)

Wouldn't it be strangely empty to sing that song in a new world where all those things had lost their being and were now only a memory? To the contrary, they will be present in all their fullness, and our cultivation of them will prompt endless delight in the One who brought them into being. The hymn-writer Isaac Watts put it perfectly in his setting of Psalm 23: "Oh, may thy house be mine abode, and all my work be praise." In the new city our work will be praise.

11

THE GLORIOUS IMPOSSIBLE

Now that we have finished this all-too-short tour of the way culture is woven into the story of Scripture, perhaps it's time to step back and sum up what we've found.

To put it most boldly: culture is God's original plan for humanity—and it is God's original gift to humanity, both duty and grace. Culture is the scene of humanity's rebellion against their Creator, the scene of judgment—and it is also the setting of God's mercy. At Babel the nations try to insulate and isolate themselves from God through a city, where culture reaches critical mass—but beginning with Abraham God forms a nation that will demonstrate the goodness and faithfulness of dependence on God. Jesus himself, a descendant of Abraham, is both a cultivator of culture, dwelling in and affirming much that is good in it, and a creator of culture, offering dramatically new cultural goods that reshape the ho-rizons of the possible and impossible for Jews and Gentiles alike. He is crushed by culture, experiencing the full weight of its brokenness on the cross—yet his resurrection begins a slow but inexorable redemption of culture, offering a down payment on the hope that culture's story will not have a dead end but rather a new beginning. In the ultimate vision of that new beginning, the City is central, ushering all the best fruits of human love and labor into eternal, concerted praise.

In sum, the only story that can truly be named the "good news" is absolutely, completely saturated with culture.

And yet the gospel cannot be contained within culture. The gospel is not simply another cultural product that stands alongside other cultural products, comfortably reinforcing some version or another of the horizons of the possible. Indeed, if every culture defines the horizons of the possible and the impossible for its members, then the gospel always sits uncomfortably on that very horizon, hovering between possibility and impossibility. There has never been a culture where the gospel, in all its world-upending glory, simply and comfortably exists within the realm of the possible. The choice of an insignificant nation to represent the world's Creator, the arrival of that Creator in the form of a young man who was briefly active in a remote part of the world and then summarily executed, the alleged return from the dead of that man in glorified yet still-human form, the expectation that history itself has a surprise ending—all of this violates our deepest human assumptions and experiences.

In a lovely Christmas book for children, Madeleine L'Engle called the incarnation "the glorious impossible"—an unthinkable idea that nevertheless shines with possibility and hope. It's a good description of the gospel as a whole. And it is precisely the impossibility of the gospel that makes it so culturally potent and so perennially relevant. The gospel constantly challenges every human culture with the possibility that we live within misplaced horizons.

This is true even for the era of Christendom—the centuries when Constantinople or Rome imposed belief on vast parts of Europe or Asia. As Christianized as these cultures were, they could no more fully comprehend the gospel than a pagan culture could hearing it for the first time. This does not mean that there was not widespread assent to orthodox Christian faith at the height of Christendom—just that the cultural expressions of that faith often did as much to make the full gospel story seem implausible as plausible. Right in the midst of Christendom were firmly entrenched cultural practices—consider the Crusades and the relentless persecution of the Jews—that exhibited Christendom's failure to culturally embrace the gospel's key themes of peace and God's particular concern for his chosen people.

So wise Christian culture makers will abandon the hope for Christendom—a culture in which the gospel is at the center rather than at the margins of possibility. To be sure, there will be times and places where certain features of Christianity are relatively attractive and plausible. In the last century much of sub-Saharan Africa has become such a place. The age of rulers dramatically embracing Christian faith did not end with Constantine: I recently saw the video record of the baptism of the president of a major African nation. He had deliberated for years about whether to be baptized, since his culture rightly understands the world-shaking significance of a national leader allowing himself to be symbolically buried in water, then raised again from spiritual death. In his nation as in many others, the gospel has a freshness and a force that reminds us post-Christian Westerners of its raw and radical power.

But in Africa too the gospel will hover uncomfortably on the edge of possibility, no matter how many presidents and prime ministers are baptized. The 1994 genocide in Rwanda, one of the most Christianized nations in Africa, buried any easy hope for an African Christendom. The gospel, precisely because it so powerfully confronts all the human ways we try to supplant God, from the tower of Babel to the cross, is always mysterious and even dangerous to cultures that want to maintain their uneasy bargains with sin—whether those bargains take the form of tribalism or individualism, collectivism or consumerism. No human society—not even Israel, as the prophets lamented and insisted—can fully "enculturate" the gospel. Christendom is always purchased at the price of a reduced gospel that all too often reduces the cross to a piece of jewelry.

But just as the gospel never is comfortably contained in the realm of the culturally possible, it also never disappears from the horizon altogether. God's grace and mercy, his endless inventive capacity to respond to human waywardness, ensure that every culture can be reclaimed.

My friend Gary Haugen was in Rwanda weeks after the killing ended in 1994, directing the United Nations' effort to document and eventually prosecute the *génocidaires*. He waded through churches filled with bones and interviewed children who had survived by feigning death in piles of their slaughtered relatives.

When Gary returned to the United States, he could have returned to his relatively secure job in the Civil Rights division of the Department of Justice and continued an honorable career, serving as a cultivator of culture—tending and passing on the great legacy of American law. But haunted by the memory of those who had cried out to God for protection from their killers and received no answer in this life, he embarked on an audacious career of cultural creativity. The organization he founded, International Justice Mission (IJM), now advocates on behalf of victims of oppression in eleven countries around the world where the cultural goods of law and enforcement are generally unavailable to the poor. And while IJM's advocacy efforts are a drop in the ocean of worldwide injustice, their ripples may yet become a wave, as increasing numbers of Christians see securing justice for the oppressed as a basic component of their cultural stewardship.

Meanwhile in Rwanda, a new generation of leaders are rebuilding cultural structures that could make Rwanda a model of ethnic coexistence and peacemaking. Many of these leaders are animated by the same gospel that failed to stay the hand of murderers. They have caught a glimpse of possibility right in the midst of one of the most categorical and demonic denials of human possibility in our recent history. To be sure, their efforts are accompanied by all the fits and starts that cultural creativity entails. But the glorious impossible shimmers at the edge of their vision just as it does at the edge of ours, inviting us to create something new in faith and see what might become of our small efforts. It whispers a confirmation of what people in every culture have imagined and hoped for all along.

CHRIST AND CULTURE

Here, at the end of this section on the biblical story of culture, seems like the right place to digress to the most influential theological work on culture in the twentieth century, H. Richard Niebuhr's *Christ and Culture*. If you have been waiting impatiently for a reference to Niebuhr and his famous "types" or "motifs" of Christian responses to culture, the wait is over; if not, you may well want to skim or skip the next few pages, as it is hard to engage Niebuhr's important book without a certain amount of technical vocabulary. Indeed, I have waited this long to address Niebuhr directly because I believe it is important that our thoughts and imaginations be formed by a vivid and concrete picture of culture, and by the narrative of Scripture itself, before we engage with his theoretical approach to the subject.

Niebuhr's typology has framed nearly every conversation about culture among theologically minded Christians since he delivered the Alumni Foundation Lectures at Austin Presbyterian Theological Seminary in 1949. At one end of Niebuhr's scale are those who see Christ *against* culture and see the Christian duty as withdrawal from the world; at the other end are those who see culture as so fully agreeing with Christ that they can make him a Christ *of* culture. A more moderate version of the first is to see Christ and culture *in paradox*—to acknowledge the corruption of culture but still to believe that Christian life can and must be lived faithfully in it. A more moderate version of the second is to believe that while culture is good in and of itself, it cannot lead us all the way to a Christ who is *above* culture. Niebuhr's fifth type, Christ *transforming* culture, takes culture's fallenness seriously but hopes for "conversion" within it:

> Those who offer [the fifth type of answer] understand . . . that human nature is fallen or perverted, and that this perversion not only appears in culture but is transmitted by it. Hence the opposition between Christ and all human institutions and customs is to be recognized. Yet the antithesis does not lead either to Christian separation from the world as with [the Christ *against* culture type], or to mere endurance in the expectation of a transhistorical salvation, as with [the Christ and culture *in paradox* type]. Christ is seen as the converter of man in his culture and society, not apart from these, for there is no nature without culture and no turning of men from self and idols to God save in society.

Niebuhr may have been ahead of his time, or he may just have been exceptionally good at putting his time's insights into words. The understanding that "there is no nature without culture"—that we cannot separate the two, for human beings at least—is at the heart of all recent thinking about culture, especially in Peter Berger and Thomas Luckmann's book *The Social Construction of Reality*. This insight lies at the heart of the biblical

understanding of human beings as well. By associating this insight with
the "Christ transforming culture" approach, Niebuhr may well be stack-
ing the deck—suggesting that the other approaches to Christ and culture
were based on an impossible separation between culture and human nature. The "Christ against culture" motif comes across especially poorly in
this light. How indeed could Christ do anything for "man" except in the
context of culture? In that sense, how could Christ be "against" culture?

While Niebuhr does not conclude *Christ and Culture* with a ringing
endorsement of any of the five motifs, there is no doubt that most readers
have left their encounter with Niebuhr most inclined toward the language
of transformation. Initially the call for "transforming culture" was embraced by Niebuhr's fellow mainline Protestants, but it has become the
rallying cry for more conservative Christians as well. As I write, a Google
search for the phrase "transforming culture" produces 42,600 results—
probably more by the time this book is published. H. Richard Niebuhr is
indirectly responsible for many of them. And to the extent that Niebuhr's
book helped several generations of Christians, of all persuasions, reflect
on their own embeddedness in and responsibility for the culture around
them, it made a tremendous contribution to cultural creativity.

But we can note several ways in which Niebuhr was very much a product of his time—ways that his book might have been more helpful and
ways that it can easily mislead us today. Start with the title. In quintessentially modern fashion, Niebuhr framed his book in terms of two highly
abstract words: *Christ and Culture*. What kind of book would he have
written—what kind of cultural influence would his book have had—if he
had been assigned the title *Jesus and the Cultures? Christ* is a Greek translation of a Hebrew word; *Jesus* is the name of a Hebrew man who radically
redefined the meaning of that Hebrew word by applying it to his ministry of healing, confrontation, reconciliation and suffering. *Culture* is a
broad and abstract word, but the historical Jesus of Nazareth, and his first-
century followers and biographers, lived very consciously not in "culture"
but in the midst of many "cultures."

Niebuhr was well aware that his "Christ" was a flesh-and-blood first-
century Hebrew man, and that his "culture" was an abstraction away
from concrete cultures and cultural goods. But these nuances are hard

to perceive in monolithic phrases like "Christ above culture" and "Christ and culture in paradox." Niebuhr's motifs have worn grooves in Christian thinking, steering us toward the assumption that there must be one right answer: that "Christ" would always be "against" or "in paradox with" or "transforming" culture wherever and however it was expressed. In the language of chapter five, Niebuhr was describing a set of *postures* toward culture as a whole. But any culture as a whole is composed of myriad cultural goods, which might require many different *gestures*. If he had been quicker to decompose culture into its particular artifacts and goods, Niebuhr could have helped Christians be more attentive to the way that Jesus could call tax collectors to repentance while honoring tax collectors' feasts with his presence, subvert public justice for a woman caught in adultery while naming her adultery a sin, radically reinterpret the demands of the divine, culture-making law while also insisting that the law would never pass away.

There is another subtle temptation in the way Niebuhr framed his contribution to the conversation about Christianity and culture—the temptation to replace "Christ" with "Christians." As Niebuhr's typology made its way into the collective vocabulary of several succeeding generations, Christians often moved from "Christ transforming culture" to "Christians transforming culture." It is dangerous to abstract away from Jesus the Messiah as we meet him in the New Testament, turning him into a cosmic Christ who embodies a posture toward culture as a whole, but at least this is justified by the conviction of the biblical writers that Jesus did somehow participate in the life of cosmic Trinity through whom and for whom all things were created. But to move from speculation about what posture Christ, the eternal Son, might take toward culture as a whole to the posture that Christians should take is to assume that we could ever establish the transhistorical vantage point that the Trinity has on our little cultural efforts. And this danger was nowhere more clear than in Niebuhr's most popular category, Christ transforming culture, which quickly shaded over into the hope of "Christians transforming culture."

Indeed, while Niebuhr begins his examination of the "Christ transforming culture" motif with Augustine of Hippo, he ends with the Christian socialist F. D. Maurice, a figure who is all but forgotten today but who exemplified to Niebuhr a fully realized commitment to cultural transformation. Socialism was the natural outcome of a modern confidence in our ability to aspire to transform entire societies, and in the human potential to play Christ's redemptive role in society: "The conversionist, with his view of history as the present encounter with God in Christ, does not live so much in expectation of a final ending of the world of creation and culture as in awareness of the power of the Lord to transform all things by lifting them up to himself." But this shading toward the expectation of gradual transformation, and the emphasis on immanent human history, led and still leads to a confusion between what God in Christ may be doing in the grand sweep of human culture on the one hand and what Christ's followers can hope for in their cultural activities on the other hand.

There is a reason that modern and postmodern Christians have gravitated toward the language of "transformation." Culture is not something that Christ could simply lift us out of, rise serenely above or be utterly against. It is too closely bound up with the original purposes of the creation of humanity in God's creative image. And *transformation* also seems to be the best way to describe Revelation's final vision of cultural goods brought into the new Jerusalem, redeemed and included in an eternal city. Whatever God is up to with his wayward and willful creation, the restoration and reclamation of culture will be an indispensable part of the story. But the only consistently Christian conviction is that transformation arrives within history, and will arrive at the end of history, as a radical gift. As we will see in part three, the temptation to take matters into our own hands, to take over God's role as the transformer of culture, leads to folly.

If there is one theme woven through the whole biblical witness on culture, it is this idea that culture, in all its best forms, is God's gift. From the leather skins of Genesis 4 to the supper in the upper room, culture finds its true potential when God blesses it with his presence and offers it in transformed form as a gift back to humanity. And from the fig leaves to the tower of Babel to the cross, culture is at its worst when human beings take on the role of cultural strategists, attempting to provide for themselves apart from God. This does not mean that human beings do not participate in essential ways in the transformation of culture—but it does mean that when transformation happens for the better, the one who gets the credit is the Creator. But *credit* will be too weak a word for the culmination of the whole wonderful and terrible cultural story. The gospel is the *glorious* impossible—for as God continues, completes and consummates his creative activity in the midst of culture, the only adequate word for that new creation will be *glory*.

And this is perhaps the one other limitation of Niebuhr's subtly this-worldly interpretation of transformation, tempered by his realism about the frailty and fragility of human efforts. Any careful reader of Niebuhr understands by the end of *Christ and Culture* just how precarious our cultural activity is, just how subject to distortion and disappointment. But perhaps *Christ and Culture* does not do justice to culture at its best, which is to say culture in the hands of Christ: the sheer delight and joy that comes when Jesus takes the most basic stuff of the world, breaks it, blesses it and offers it back to us, made whole and made new. We may taste that kind of joy at weddings; we may taste it at funerals. I have tasted it in a village in India, in the form of a freshly cracked coconut offered by a ten-year-old girl who months before had been a slave; I've tasted it in the form of a four-course dinner, served by generous and gracious hosts, overlooking the Pacific Ocean in Southern California. Sometimes the taste is fleeting and only makes us more hungry; sometimes it is overwhelming and spoils us for anything less lovely. Only when culture gives us that kind of joy will it be fully transformed—and when it is transformed that way, in fulfillment of the whole sweep of the story from beginning to end, it will indeed be Christ who deserves the glory, honor and praise.

PART THREE

CALLING

WHY WE CAN'T
CHANGE THE WORLD

A few years ago my friend Nate Barksdale encouraged me to try a simple experiment. We asked HOLLIS, the search engine of the Harvard University library system, for all books whose titles included the phrases "change the world," "changing the world" or "changed the world." Out of the 216 results returned in the winter of 2004 (only a fraction of the 1,670 results that Amazon.com offered at that time), 75 had been published in the four years since 2000—more than one-third. A few examples: *The Riddle of the Compass: The Invention That Changed the World, Mauve: How One Man Invented a Color That Changed the World, 100 Bible Verses That Changed the World.*

Another 101—nearly half of the entire total—were published in the 1990s. *(Five Equations that Changed the World, Five Speeches That Changed the World, Thirteen Creative Men Who Changed the World, Twelve Lesbians Who Changed the World.* And, injecting a note of realism, *Patent Nonsense: A Catalogue of Inventions That Failed to Change the World.)*

Eighteen such books were published in the 1980s, four in the 1970s, eight in the 1960s and four in the 1950s. A total of six were published in the first half of the twentieth century.

Of the 1.5 million titles in the Harvard collections published before 1900, how many included a reference to changing the world?

Zero.

You don't want to know how many results the Internet search engine Google returned for the same query—*change the world, changed the world* or *changing the world*—in mid-2007.

Okay, you do: 8,770,000.

(I feel compelled to note a pet peeve here: you get very different results from Google's search engine when searching for phrases *with* and *without* quotes. Simply searching for "change the world" without quotes in Google produces a prodigious 870 million results—because *change* and *world* are exceedingly common words, and Google includes any page that includes them both. Likewise, searching for "Andy Crouch" without quotes produces 1.8 million results—searching for the name with quotes produces, well, far fewer. So the next time a journalist breathlessly informs you that they got 9.5 million results for some seemingly obscure phrase, try the search with quote marks yourself. The world may not be changing quite as quickly as they want you to think.)

We moderns certainly can't be accused of lacking self-confidence. The explosion of books about "changing the world" fits our self-image—we are world changers. There is indisputable literal truth to the phrase. Powered by the twentieth century's explosion of technology, humanity has multiplied our effect on the natural world with measurable global results, from the deepest ocean to the thinnest outer atmosphere. Six billion human beings, whose total mass is less than one millionth of a billionth of one percent of the mass of earth, all of whose works, even today, are invisible from space (except at night, when our cities radiate light skyward), are changing their own and only world in extraordinary, not entirely predictable and possibly irreversible ways.

And we are world changers because we are culture makers. As we have seen already, *making something of the world* is of the very essence of what we are meant to be and do. For Christians this is not just an empirical observation about humanity, but an opportunity and an obligation rooted in our relationship with the world's Creator.

So perhaps it's not surprising that Christians have enthusiastically embraced the language of "changing the world." A major college ministry defines its mission as producing "world changers." A recent Christian conference for pastors handed out copies of a book—a secular guide to environmental responsibility—called *Worldchanging*.

But the more carefully you listen to the people who study the mechanisms of culture—sociologists and anthropologists, along with their poor cousins, the journalists—the more you may begin to doubt that we can change the world at all. A major theme of contemporary sociology, influenced deeply by scholars like Peter Berger, is not how we can change the world—it is how thoroughly the world (including the world of culture) changes, shapes and even determines us. When I was first presenting some of the ideas that form the core of this book, a sociologist asked me a perceptive question. "I'm concerned that when you talk about being 'culture makers,'" she said, "you're granting individuals a great deal of agency." Translated from the technical language of her field, she was asking whether we are as free to create culture as we imagine—or whether indeed we are free to shape culture at all. All of her training had equipped her to be exquisitely sensitive to the ways that culture constrains and determines our choices, and to be suspicious of any suggestion that we are cultural free agents.

Indeed, the great irony with the North American Christian community's obsession with becoming world changers, as outsiders like Alan Wolfe and insiders like Ron Sider have documented, is that so far and on the whole we are much more changed than changing. The rise of interest in cultural transformation has been accompanied by a rise in cultural transformation of a different sort—the transformation of the church into the culture's image.

So we are confronted with a paradox. Culture—making something of the world, moving the horizons of possibility and impossibility—is what human beings do and are meant to do. Transformed culture is at the heart of God's mission in the world, and it is the call of God's redeemed people. But changing the world is the one thing we cannot do. As it turns out, fully embracing this paradoxical reality is at the very heart of what it means to be a Christian culture maker.

DEFINING "WORLD CHANGING"

What would it mean to "change the world," after all? As with many grand slogans, it's well worth probing the particulars. When we say "change the world," what we generally mean is "change culture"—change the horizons of possibility and impossibility that serve as the "world" in its full biblical sense. Perhaps sometimes we use that phrase for damming the Yangtze River, irrigating the American Southwest or digging the Suez Canal— culturally driven changes in the natural world on a large scale. But most of the time we recognize that for human beings, "the world" is just as much cultural as natural. And as we have seen, the only way cultures truly change is through the introduction of new cultural goods. A compass, an equation or the color mauve—world changing always comes down to something concrete and specific. Even the "twelve lesbians who changed the world" did so by offering some specific cultural good to their world.

So world changing begins with a cultural good—but to rise to the level of "changing the world" that good would have to be taken up by an in- credibly wide public. If something were to literally "change the world," it would have to be adopted by and shape the horizons of possibility for every one of the world's six-plus billion people and their descendants. Which leads us to the deflating observation that not a single human cul- tural artifact has changed the world at that scale—neither the compass nor indeed any other application of magnetism, the Gettysburg Address nor any other work in the English language, Einstein's theory of gen- eral relativity nor any other set of mathematical formulas. Even the color mauve hasn't changed the world in that sense.

Yet because culture is so all-encompassing for human beings, such a thoroughly world-making reality, there is another sense in which *for any given human being in a particular cultural environment*, all it takes to change their world—to change the horizons of possibility and impossibility for them—is to change the culture right around them. In my personal expe- rience of the world, it matters surprisingly little that China is damming the Yangtze River in the largest public works project in human history, but it matters a great deal that there are bridges over the Delaware River. And this is what we usually implicitly mean when we talk loosely about changing the world: we are referring to cultural goods that have changed *our* world—that have shaped the horizons for a smaller but not inconsiderable subset of humanity that happens to include us. "Change the world" becomes shorthand for "change the culture at a particular time and place." And once we get to that scale, we can recount endless examples of cultural goods that, for a certain group of people at a certain time, have surely changed their world.

Yet here we run into a subtle and serious problem. It is one thing to look back and see how the interstate highway system, Marx and Engel's *Communist Manifesto* or even (possibly) the color mauve "changed the world." That is essentially what historians do—narrate cultural change through the stories of particular goods and the people who made them. But is it possible to look *around*, much less look *forward*, and predict which cultural goods will have a world-changing effect? Chances are that at the time the color mauve was rising in popularity, someone else was energetically promoting a different color palette—perhaps involving fuchsia or periwinkle or burnt orange. Had we been there at the time, could we have reliably predicted which color was going to move the cultural horizons?

As a matter of fact, thanks to the pervasive commercialization of culture, we have a very good sense of whether such predictions are possible, because they are precisely the kind of predictions that financial investors must make all the time. Investing is basically a way of placing bets on which cultural goods will grow in world-changing importance, as measured (however imperfectly) by their financial return to their producers. Suppose we want to invest profitably in a hot arena of cultural change: the wireless communications industry, say. We compile a list of all the companies that operate in that space, fill in an extensive spreadsheet with their growth rates, profit margins and stock prices, and set out to make an investment decision. Our investment will essentially be a prediction of which cultural goods will be most successful. How well will we do?

Surprisingly, the answer is that most people, most of the time, will get more predictions wrong than right. An extensive body of literature has shown that most actively managed mutual funds—bundles of bets on cultural trends that are managed by highly compensated, highly trained analysts—perform worse than they would have if their managers had simply blindly invested the money in proportionate amounts in every company on the market. Individual investors, who do not have access to anything like the same amount of information, training and analysis as industry professionals, do worse still. One of the most successful investors of the twentieth century was Peter Lynch, who put his instincts at the service of investors in Fidelity's Magellan Fund, which returned 29 percent per year for thirteen years. Yet many individual investors in Lynch's fund lost money because of their inability to resist tinkering with their investments, moving their money in and out of the fund with impeccably bad timing.

A profusion of common phrases sheds light from various angles on the humbling truth of how little we know about what will happen next. "Past performance is no guarantee of future results"—this disclaimer, or something like it, is required by the federal government to protect investors from their easy assumptions. Unfortunately, no matter how frequently the warning is repeated, investors seem to ignore it. Our inability to accurately anticipate the direction of cultural change is one of the most commonly affirmed realities of human existence—and one of the most commonly ignored.

SURVIVOR BIAS

A more subtle and insidious way of being misled by past performance is to fall victim to "survivor bias." If we are not careful, our list of potentially world-changing wireless companies will exclude a very important group: the companies that no longer exist at all because they failed and went out of business. But ignoring these failed companies and focusing only on the survivors will give us a exaggerated sense of the promise of our investments.

It is amazing how much cultural analysis of all sorts is tainted by survivor bias—how often we forget to mention that at the same time as mauve was taking the world by storm, periwinkle and burnt orange were smoldering on the ash heap of history. (University of Texas at Austin fans, to be sure, will beg to disagree.) Most of us, unless we are very careful historians, form our impression of the past by the books that are still in print and the music that is still performed, forgetting that while some cultural goods (Victor Hugo's *Les Misérables*, say) were bestsellers then and are bestsellers now, many others that were the talk of the town then are now completely forgotten, and some that we now consider classics were barely noticed at the time (such as the works of J. S. Bach, which largely languished until they were championed by Mendelssohn eighty years after Bach's death).

"History is written by the winners" alludes to another kind of survivor bias: the survivors get to write the stories of how culture changed. But until the rise of forms of history that seek to recover the experiences of the poor, the enslaved, women and children, it would also be true to say that history was written *about* the cultural winners—not just the literal victors on the battlefield or in the marketplace, but about the people and cultural goods that were sufficiently prominent and influential to get noticed, even as losers. As long as Americans remember the Civil War, they will remember not just General William Tecumseh Sherman but also General Robert E. Lee, even though Lee's army lost—but they are much less likely to remember the lieutenants on either side who had been thought to have great promise for generalship, but never quite made it up the ranks.

History and historians make our lives easier by preselecting the most salient, world-changing cultural goods by sheer force of time and attrition. We learn about and remember the inventions, equations and colors that changed the world. But we can easily forget that at the time, which invention, equation and color would prevail was an entirely open question. And then we can easily deceive ourselves into thinking that changing the world is a great deal easier than it actually is.

Take the movie business—please. There is no doubt that Hollywood is one of the most powerful culture-shaping forces on the planet, competing only with Coca-Cola and Christianity for the sheer reach of its cultural goods into every nook and cranny. (Though like Coke and the church, it still falls far short of "changing the world" in the strongest sense described previously.) Yet perhaps the most famous aphorism in Hollywood comes from the screenwriter William Goldman, describing how this huge cultural industry produces its blockbuster, world-changing hits: "Nobody knows anything." After mobilizing countless focus groups, deploying marketing budgets in the tens or hundreds of millions of dollars, gauging audience interest and the "bankability" of stars and story lines, no one in Hollywood can reliably claim that they know whether a movie will recoup its investment.

Consider the movie *My Big Fat Greek Wedding*, produced for a total of $5 million. To the astonishment of everyone involved, the film grossed $241 million in the United States, one of the great breakout hits of Hollywood history. In retrospect we can see that not only did the film package an appealing—not to say textbook—Hollywood storyline with a winning young actress, it was produced by Tom Hanks, one of Hollywood's leading men, and his wife Rita Wilson, a Hollywood power couple if ever there was one. With Hanks and Wilson behind it, the film had opportunities few other "indie" films could ever hope to have. Surely its success was assured the moment that Hanks and Wilson signed on?

Well, no, since Hanks's other production credits (if that is the right word) include 2006's *The Ant Bully*, produced for $50 million, which grossed $28 million domestically; 2004's *Connie and Carla* (starring *My Big Fat Greek Wedding*'s winning young actress, Nia Vardalos) produced for $27 million, which grossed $8 million domestically; and slightly more successfully *The Polar Express*, produced for $165 million, which did manage to gross $162 million at the domestic box office and probably turned a profit on strong overseas results. Even when Hanks and Wilson tried to capitalize on the success of *Wedding* by creating a TV series called *My Big Fat Greek Life*, it ran for all of seven episodes before being summarily canceled.

"Nobody knows anything." And this is true in an industry that has ruthlessly clear measurements of cultural success and massive financial incentives to motivate its key players to succeed in their cultural production. If it is true of Hollywood, why would we expect other, more murky arenas of cultural activity, from politics to poetry, to be any easier to understand? The truth is that culture, precisely because it is world-sized, is simply too complex for anyone to control or predict. And this truth is cruelest to those who have momentary cultural success—the "survivors" toward whom the system is biased. There are, at any given cultural moment and in any given cultural field, a handful of people who have demonstrated great aptitude in anticipating cultural change: fabulously wealthy hedge fund managers, prescient journalists and fashion mavens, as well as politicians with good poll numbers and pastors with star power. But of course there are—just as in any group there is someone who is the tallest. That doesn't mean that he has been especially diligent in doing his stretching exercises—it just means that someone has to stand out. But unlike height, which does not change much after we reach adulthood, culture is constantly changing in small and large ways. Past performance is no guarantee of future results, and when peering forward into the future, it is always worth repeating under your breath: nobody knows anything. Or, for variety, you can murmur the words that have been variously attributed to Mark Twain, Niels Bohr and Yogi Berra: "It is difficult to make predictions, especially about the future."

A SCUFFED CIRCLE OF DIRT

Surely most readers will be strenuously objecting at this point. Haven't journalists like Malcolm Gladwell, in his fascinating book *The Tipping Point: How Little Things Can Make a Big Difference*, shown exactly how culture is changed—in Gladwell's account, by the intersection of well-connected people ("mavens," "connectors," "salespersons") who mobilize networks to transmit "memes" the way a virus spreads in an epidemic? Is the cultural influence of Madonna or Bono, or on a smaller scale someone like Gladwell himself, just as randomly distributed as height or hair color? Doesn't their evident talent have something to do with their ability to change culture? How about their cultural prominence—can't we predict that the next cause Bono takes on will be more likely to succeed because he is involved? To put it in crass commercial terms, would you rather finance the next U2 album or a debut album by the garage band down the street?

The first key to answering these questions is to invoke a favorite distinction of philosophers: the difference between *necessary* and *sufficient* conditions. If you hope to make Hush Puppies a profitable, fashionable brand of shoes (one of the examples used in Gladwell's book), the factors that Gladwell describes are indeed *necessary*. Your shoes will need to be on the feet of some well-connected young urban influentials; fashion mavens will need to tell their friends to buy a pair. Your shoemakers and your marketing department, your distribution system and your accounting system will need to be robust and, as they say, "scalable"—in other words, your organization will need talent. And if you are an established brand in the marketplace, you are more likely to be able to successfully introduce a new line of shoes that will capture the hearts and wallets of consumers. All these are *necessary* conditions for cultural success.

But they are not *sufficient*. You can fulfill every one of the necessary conditions—indeed, you must, since that is what *necessary* means—and still fail completely to sell enough shoes, let alone "change the shoe world." For at the same time as you are busily fulfilling all the necessary conditions of cultural influence, your competitors are doing the same. And even if you have the best-selling shoe one year, that becomes *past performance*—and you know the rest. In 2007, Amazon.com introduced a feature that asked its customers to rate how fashionable a given pair of shoes was compared to others with a similar style. A perfectly decent-looking pair of Hush Puppies men's clogs was rated fifteenth out of twenty-six, well behind offerings from two manufacturers, Simple and Skechers, that were just becoming known to the general public when Gladwell published his book in 2002.

So what are the all-important sufficient conditions for cultural influence? The sobering truth is that *at a large enough scale, there are no sufficient conditions for cultural change.* There is no way to ensure cultural success—to ensure that a given cultural good will shape horizons in the way its creator may hope.

This leads to a second key insight. Our ability to change culture—or, if you like, "change the world"—is a matter of *scale*. On a small enough scale, nearly everyone has the power to change the world. A few years ago my father hung a swing from a tree limb twenty feet high in our back yard for our children, Timothy and Amy, to use. That swing has become one of the icons of their childhood, and they have spent countless hours lazily swinging back and forth, scuffing their feet on the lawn at the bottom of each oscillation. Not surprisingly, there is no lawn left under the swing, just a dusty, compacted dirt circle marking the gradually lengthening reach of their feet. The swing is culture, and so is the circle of dirt—a change in the world. At this scale, every human being, except the youngest, oldest and most infirm, "changes the world" daily.

At the relatively small scale of my family's life together, there are many ways in which I profoundly shape our shared world—setting bedtimes and waking times, deciding where we will vacation, choosing what is for dinner, buying (or, in our case, not buying) a television, choosing and using the nicknames for one another that only the four of us know. Within the walls of our house, all four of us have real power to shape the very real culture we, and we alone, share.

But as we move into larger scales of culture we quickly leave behind our ability to change very much about the cultural world we find ourselves in. Even before I leave my property, with my modicum of ability to control the natural and cultural world there, I am dependent on the cultivation and creativity of countless other people who supply electricity, water and security (not to mention high-speed Internet service), and influence the safety or danger of the very air I breathe by their decisions about how to operate power plants and factories down the street and on the other side of the planet. Should I want to travel to the city, I consult a train timetable that someone else has set or drive on roads that someone else has planned and maintained. My ability to make small changes in my local world is dwarfed by my dependence on the changes other people make at larger scales of culture.

Ah, you may say, but there are people who have the power to make those changes! Someone planned the road, set the timetable and keeps the electricity on. So someone has the power to "change the world." That is true—but their power is sharply circumscribed. Ask any civil engineer, urban transit planner or utility executive how much power they have to "change the world" where they are, and you'll quickly discover that there are many changes they believe should be but cannot be made, even in their own domain of cultural expertise and authority. And when they leave their office—the scale of cultural activity where they have some real power—they are subject to all the same dependencies that I am.

So can we change the world? Yes and no. On a small enough scale, yes, of course we can. But the world is sufficiently complex, not to mention sufficiently broken, that the small scale of our own cultural capacity is never sufficient. And this remains true no matter how much power we accumulate—true for the CEO of the telephone company just as much as it is true for the lineman, true for the general of the army as well as for the private.

At whatever scale we have the capacity to bring change, we discover, for myriad reasons, that power to bring the change we truly seek lies beyond our grasp. How else can we explain the failure of the world's most allegedly powerful nation, led by the person who holds what has been called "the most powerful job in the world," to bring cultural transformation in a relatively small country in the Middle East, despite the deployment of awesome resources of power?

This should not inspire confidence. The record of human efforts to change the world is mixed, to say the least—no matter how many books chronicle the attempt. And the larger the scale of change we seek, the more mixed the record becomes. At the largest scale, the changes in the world we most deeply would wish for, the record is bleak indeed, and our best efforts sometimes seem not much more impressive than children scuffing a dirt circle in the lawn.

THE POWER OF CULTURAL GOODS

To further complicate our hopes of changing the world, it is worth remembering that world-changing power resides much more in cultural goods themselves than in the people who created those goods. For the very nature of cultural goods is to go beyond the reach of their creators. They leave the circle of our influence and are taken up by a wide public, and very often the consequences of their adoption could never have been foreseen. Indeed, many of the most culturally influential goods succeed precisely because they have effects on the horizons of the possible and impossible that their creators only dimly imagined. The telephone, the iPod, the interstate highway and the atomic bomb—all have had tremendously consequential impact on human history, yet none has remained, or could have remained, fully within the control of their creators.

Indeed, over time, the *unintended* consequences of a given cultural good almost always swamp the *intended* consequences in magnitude, as people continue the culture-making process, making new culture in response to the changed horizons. The interstate highways were surely never designed to gut America's inner cities or accelerate the growth of fast-food restaurants, but those were two of their most powerful effects. The telephone was not designed to increase geographic mobility by making it possible to move far from home and yet still feel connected to one's family and friends, but that may be its most important contribution, for better and for worse, to American life. Such unintended consequences compound over time, increasing in importance and unpredictability the further out we go from the original creation.

The law of unintended consequences applies in spades to high technology like the Internet, a cultural good whose principal quality is its indeterminacy. The Internet is designed to be used for almost anything you want to use it for and to circumvent most restrictions on its use. It may be the most flexible and unpredictable cultural good since the invention of electricity—meaning also that its consequences are the hardest to anticipate. One of its first massive unintended consequences, still being played out as this book is written, has been the decimation of the twentieth-century music industry and the empowering of both individual musicians and individual music consumers, at the expense of established record labels and artists. When the peer-to-peer music-sharing (or, depending on your point of view, music-stealing) service Napster was at its height of popularity in 2000, the heavy metal rock band Metallica became the improbable spokespersons for the old regime, arguing vociferously against file-sharing. Drummer and cofounder Lars Ulrich memorably testified before Congress, making a simple plea: "I want to continue to control what I create." Ulrich had not yet learned the first lesson of culture making. If there is one thing culture creators cannot do, it is to control their creations.

None of this should really be a surprise to Christians. After all, our central story begins with a Creator who set into motion a cultural process that had myriad consequences that were never within his original intent. Because all culture is shared and public, all culture is also a risk, dependent on the cultivation and creativity of present and future generations. Adam and Eve certainly did "change the world," but not in the way their Creator had surely hoped.

CHANGING THE WORLD AS TEMPTATION

And this leads to our final caution about setting out to change the world: the unspoken assumption in nearly every Christian use of that phrase is that our cultural activity will change the world *for the better*. But why do we assume this? Changing the world sounds grand, until you consider how poorly we do even at changing our own little lives. On a daily basis we break our promises, indulge our addictions and rehearse old fantasies and grudges that even we know we'd be better off without. We have changed less about ourselves than we would like to admit. Who are we to charge off to change the world?

Indeed, I sometimes wonder if breathless rhetoric about changing the world is actually about changing the subject—from our own fitfully suppressed awareness that we did not ask to be brought into this world, have only vaguely succeeded in figuring it out, and will end our days in radical dependence on something or someone other than ourselves. If our excitement about changing the world leads us into the grand illusion that we stand somehow outside the world, knowing what's best for it, tools and goodwill and gusto at the ready, we have not yet come to terms with the reality that the world has changed us far more than we will ever change it. Beware of world changers—they have not yet learned the true meaning of sin.

That is the humbling reality at the private level. And at the other end of the scale, Christians have learned from the Gospel of John and the letters of Paul that "the world" is a name for a realm of systemic active rebellion against God's purposes. We are wrestling not against flesh and blood—even our own fleshly inclinations, though that would be challenge enough—but against spiritual powers in high places (Eph 6:12). And any honest reading of history suggests that one of the most successful strategies of that cosmic rebellion is to twist well-intentioned endeavors in precisely the wrong direction, using human greed, fear and pride for extra leverage.

All the same, we *are* made to change the world. We are made to do so at small scales and (occasionally, and probably not as often as we think, hope or expect) at large scales. We are culture makers. But when we thoughtlessly grasp for the heedless rhetoric of "changing the world," we expose ourselves to temptation. We find ourselves in a situation similar to Adam and Eve's in the Garden. "You will be like God, knowing good and evil," the serpent insisted. Made in God's image, Adam and Eve were, in fact, already "like God." And yet the serpent invited them to use their God-given power to extend their grasp just a bit further. The serpent's invitation succeeded partly because it was so close to truth. It just called them a step beyond truth, into a fantasy that ended up destroying the very capacities they sought to extend.

Is there a way to change the world without falling into one of the many traps laid for would-be world changers? If so, it will require us to learn the one thing the language of "changing the world" usually lacks: humility, defined not so much as bashfulness about our own abilities as awed and quiet confidence in God's ability. Is the Maker of the world still at work "changing the world"? If so, what are the patterns of his activity, and what would it mean to join him in what he is doing in every sphere and scale of human culture? How can we join his culture making and live out our own calling to make something of the world, without slowly and subtly giving in to the temptation to take his place?

You may have read this chapter with a fair amount of impatience because you are a person with real cultural power who wants to use that power for good. Or you may have read with a mixture of relief and depression because you think *I can never be a culture maker—I'm too insignificant*—especially after reading a chapter on why we can't change the world! But this kind of caution, it seems to me, is the only way to begin finding our cultural calling with any hope of true success. And strangely enough, as we'll see, whether you feel powerful or powerless, you are exactly the sort of person that God has a track record of deciding to use.

13

THE TRACES OF GOD

The Christian faith is a historical faith. We believe that the world's Maker has made himself known in history—not just in visions, inward dispositions or psychological experiences. And *history* is just another word for the story of how cultures have changed through time. The Jewish and Christian claim, as unlikely or even scandalous as it often seems, is that God has been involved in culture making from the very beginning.

But how, exactly, is God involved? All efforts to pin down the details of where and when we can say that God is working in history are fraught with the danger of self-deception, if not outright blasphemy. The commandment not to take the Lord's name in vain seems especially to apply to human attempts to recruit God for one cultural movement or another. The warning that "history is written by the winners" should caution us that any attempt to discern God's activity in particular historical events runs the risk of self-justification, claiming after the fact that God was on our side all along. This has not stopped leaders through the ages from claiming God's blessing on their culture-making endeavors. A notable exception was Abraham Lincoln, whose Second Inaugural Address contained profound reflections on the divine purpose in the agonizing cultural conflict of the Civil War. "Both [sides] read the same Bible and pray to the same God, and each invokes His aid against the other. . . . The prayers of both could not be answered. That of neither has been answered fully. The Almighty has His own purposes."

We could do worse than follow Lincoln's unwillingness to assign God a side even in a conflict as apparently just, in hindsight, as the Civil War. There is no disagreement—from this distance in history—that slavery was every bit the evil Lincoln believed it was. But the prosecution of the Union side was a fallen human cultural project like all others, Sherman's brutal march through the South being just one of many moments where the horizons were surely misplaced. Most of all it was subject to all the same laws of unintended consequences as any cultural good over time. The bloodiest war in American history kept the Union together but failed to ensure real justice for the descendants of Negro slaves. Human cultures at their best and their worst are often determinedly conservative, and the South found ways to guard institutions of racism long after the Civil War ended; yet the North, for its part, institutionalized racism in ways that even today are more subtle and slippery, and just as enduring. It is certainly true that the prayers of neither side—even their noblest prayers—have ever been answered fully.

And yet. We who are no longer in the thick of conflict as Lincoln was (he delivered his Second Inaugural Address one month before his assassination) should feel uneasy not somehow recognizing the hand of God in the outcome of the Civil War and all the long struggle for racial justice that has followed. Don't we have a sense that Lincoln's very reticence to claim God's blessing, coupled with his "firmness in the right as God gives us to see the right," was the sort of faithfulness that God seeks and rewards? The concluding words of his address echoed with God's own self-disclosure in Scripture: "let us strive on to finish the work we are in, to bind up the nation's wounds, to care for him who shall have borne the battle and for his widow and his orphan, to do all which may achieve and cherish a just and lasting peace among ourselves and with all nations." If we cannot recognize God at work in these seminal words of American history, we may doubt that we will ever find him in the pages of history anywhere.

Is there a way to talk about God's purpose for culture that does not fall into the idolatry of our particular cause and moment? If there is, it will require us to go back to the places, times and texts where the Christian tradition declares unambiguously that God has been revealed. And in that tradition two events stand out, not only for their central place in the biblical narrative but for their indisputable culture-making power: the exodus and the resurrection.

The exodus and the resurrection are the center of their respective Testaments of the Bible. All of the Hebrew Bible radiates outward, as it were, from the liberation of God's people, the moment when God reveals his name, his character and his purposes fully to his people: "I am the LORD [in Hebrew, the divine name or Tetragrammaton, YHWH] your God, who brought you out of the land of Egypt, out of the house of slavery; you shall have no other gods before me." God's unpronounceable name alone would not be enough to make him known—he is known because he brought a particular nation out of oppression by another particular nation, at a particular time. Indeed, Israel's religious obligation to have no other gods besides YHWH is rooted not merely in the kind of abstract principle of monotheism that might be articulated by a philosopher of religion, but an act: "I brought you out of the land of Egypt."

The exodus does not just have religious significance. It stakes a claim to human history. To be sure, more than a few moderns question whether the events recounted in the Bible happened the way they were recorded. Undoubtedly the biblical texts, like all texts, streamline or condense certain features of the historical events. Yet those who would deny the basic historicity of the exodus, like those who deny the historicity of the resurrection, are left with a daunting historical problem: how to convincingly explain the coming into being of such a distinctive people, with such deeply rooted and enduring religious, ethical and cultural practices, *without* any cataclysmic event like the deliverance from Egypt. One need only compare the exodus account to the crazy quilt of national origin stories in Greek or Roman mythology. We have to admit that a pantheon filled with a wild variety of gods of various sorts and conditions, playing favorites and capriciously intervening in history in an endless cosmic competition, seems much better suited to the haphazard process of cultural consolidation in the ferment of the Mediterranean Basin than the idea of a single Creator God who has chosen a particular people and sticks with them with the ferocity of covenant love. Even in spite of their admitted temptations to assimilation and syncretism, even through cycles of marginalization and exile, the Jewish people maintained a tenacious and culture-shaping faith in that one God, YHWH. They did so despite living, generation after generation, in cultural contexts where monotheism in general and worship of YHWH in particular was all but impossible. In the face of such an extraordinary religious and cultural achievement, something like the exodus comes much closer to being the simplest and most plausible explanation.

Likewise, we have already seen that the historical resurrection of Jesus is quite possibly the only adequate explanation of the myriad cultural effects that still follow, like the aftershocks of an earthquake, two thousand years after Jesus' death. Simply explaining the resurrection as an inward experience or perhaps shared hallucination of a few of Jesus' disciples, let alone a story invented by those disciples to somehow affirm that Jesus' spirit "lived on" in their community, seems to fall far short of accounting for the cultural power of the movement that within a few generations was altering the direction of the Roman Empire. Neither exodus nor resurrection was a "religious" event as we often understand that word. They were historical, cultural events that compete with any other event in history for culture-making preeminence. And yet the resurrection, like the exodus, is indeed a profoundly religious event, in that it reveals the true nature of God, vindicating Jesus' claim to be God's own and only Son. Without the resurrection, Jesus would be yet another intriguing and perhaps exemplary human being, and we would search his life and teachings for clues to truth in the same way we probe the sayings of Gautama Buddha or the dialogues of Socrates. But if the resurrection is true, then Jesus' life, death and victory over death give us unprecedented confidence that his way of life (and death) discloses something reliably true about the reality of God.

THE POWERLESS AND THE POWERFUL

So if the exodus and the resurrection are the two moments in human culture when God has made himself most definitively known, what do they tell us about God? And since they are historical interventions in culture, what do they tell us, in particular, about his purposes in culture?

One inescapable feature of both events is that they show *God at work in the lives of the powerless*. As we will see in chapter fourteen, creating cultural goods by definition requires cultural power. The Hebrews enslaved under Egyptian rule and Jesus of Nazareth on a Roman cross are the last people we would expect to be able to be "culture makers." At the low point of Hebrew enslavement, when the entire community has been targeted for genocide through the murder of a generation of infant sons; at noon on Good Friday, when the hands that once shaped wood and broke bread have been nailed to a cross—at these moments all hope of creating culture, even simply of cultivating and sustaining culture, seems completely lost. The exodus and the resurrection are utterly unlikely events in the lives of a people and a person who have run out of other options, who have been crushed by those with cultural power—Pharaoh's Egypt and Caesar's Rome—and who lack the means to save themselves.

These historical events echo a recurring theme in the revelation of God in both the Old and New Testaments: his concern for "the poor, the widow, and the orphan," the three groups in ancient societies (and many modern ones) who together form a kind of triptych of powerlessness. Unlike the gods of surrounding cultures, who concern themselves largely with "godlike" heroes (often the gods' own progeny) and founders and rulers of nations, the God of Israel is concerned with those who seem least culturally important, who have the least to recommend themselves as potential culture makers. Indeed, the people of Israel, small and insignificant compared to the empires that surround them, and the person of Jesus, hailing from the remote town of Nazareth, are themselves signs of God's strange preoccupation with the powerless—as God reminds his people, "you yourselves were once strangers in Egypt." Yet in the exodus and resurrection, God's preoccupation with the powerless is translated into astonishing and visible deliverance from the worst that the culturally powerful can do.

These two defining cultural events also reveal a surprising additional theme on closer inspection. Not only do the exodus and resurrection signal God's concern for the powerless, they display his ongoing engagement with the *powerful*. When the time comes for exodus, the people of Israel are not simply spirited away from Egypt in the dark of night. Instead, God enters into a lengthy dialogue with Pharaoh, who along with his magicians and counselors is given every opportunity to let God's people go. (Whatever we make of God's statement that he has hardened Pharaoh's heart, Pharaoh is clearly presented as responsible for his choice to keep the Israelites enslaved.) The exodus does not circumvent Pharaoh's cultural and political power—it directly engages it, ultimately at great cost to Pharaoh and his people.

But there is another culturally powerful player in the story besides Pharaoh: the Hebrew named Moses, who was raised in Pharaoh's court. Moses is not simply another member of the oppressed minority. Like his distant ancestor Joseph, he has lived at the very center of Egyptian cultural power and has presumably become fluent in the language and relationships that surround Egypt's ruling class. Like many members of ethnic minorities since, Moses has had the opportunity to "pass" as a member of the majority. Until his frustration boils over in his murder of an Egyptian slave driver, we are led to believe that Moses has had access in every way to the inner workings of the elite culture of Egypt. When he returns from exile in Midian to deliver YHWH's call to Pharaoh, then, he is speaking a language and walking into a palace that he has known from childhood. Moses' cultural fluency is a key human ingredient in the story of God's confrontation with Pharaoh's cultural power.

So the exodus is not just the story of a powerless people escaping a powerful ruler. It is also the story of a culturally powerful person whose power, while not sufficient by itself to bring about liberation, is a central means by which God confronts injustice and offers those in power the opportunity to become partners with his purposes.

When we turn to the story of Jesus we see a similar pattern. Jesus is not simply a revolutionary who is bent simply and solely on the overthrow of the current powers, whether those in the temple or those in the Roman procurator's palace. Rather, he offers opportunities to both sets of cultural elites to respond to his message and change course. In the extraordinary dialogue John records with Pilate on the eve of his crucifixion, Jesus parries the procurator's assertion, "I have power to release you, and power to crucify you," by insisting, "You would have no power over me unless it had been given you from above" (Jn 19:10-11). Jesus spends a week in the temple in dialogue with the priests and scribes, challenging them but also opening himself to their questions and critique. He does not lob parables, let alone missiles, over the walls without coming near to the centers of power; instead he offers the urban powerful the same opportunities as the rural powerless to ask questions and draw near to the kingdom of God.

And once again, in the midst of a largely negative story of rejection and condemnation at the hands of the powerful, we find more than one powerful person who seeks Jesus out and becomes, in one way or another, a partner in his purposes. Nicodemus, a member of the Sanhedrin, approaches Jesus with his most searching questions (Jn 3), defends him before his fellow Pharisees (Jn 7) and eventually assists in his burial (Jn 19). (From the fact that we hear so much about Nicodemus in the Gospel of John, the early tradition that Nicodemus eventually became one of Jesus' followers seems plausible.) A Roman centurion sees his valued servant miraculously healed (Lk 7). In the Gospel according to Mark, even the centurion who oversees Jesus' crucifixion becomes the clearest witness of Jesus' true identity in the end: "Truly this man was God's Son" (Mk 15:39). After the resurrection a student of Gamaliel, the most influential rabbi of Jesus' day, turns dramatically from his role as the most prominent persecutor of the early church to become its most energetic evangelist and theologian—the apostle Paul.

Above all, the crucifixion and resurrection of Jesus are the culmination of the most extraordinary possible convergence of power and powerlessness. If the Roman centurion is right, Jesus on the cross becomes simultaneously the most powerful and the most powerless person who has ever lived. The Son of God becomes not just a Judean subject to Roman rule but a human being subject to the power of death. The one through whom all things were created, to whom the very world owes its existence, humbles himself to the point of nonexistence. In Jesus Christ power and powerlessness meet completely in one inestimably consequential human life. For Jesus, in life, death and victory over death, is not simply powerless—"Jesus meek and mild." His way of life; his command over unclean spirits, illness and hunger; and his parables and actions all display his extraordinary power, even before his resurrection from the dead confirms his ultimate authority over heaven and earth. And yet this power is contained and even disguised in a Nazarene whose very accent betrays his culturally marginal status in an insignificant client state far from the streets of Rome.

In the paradox of Jesus Christ—Yeshua from Nazareth, anointed One of history—the paradox of God's cultural agenda is summed up most perfectly and completely. God is *for* the poor—the oppressed, the widow and the orphan—and he is *for* humanity in our collective poverty, our ultimate powerlessness in the face of sin and death. But he makes known his redemptive purposes for us *through* both the powerless *and* the powerful, using both to accomplish his purposes. When God acts in culture, he uses both the powerful and the powerless alongside one another rather than using one against the other. To mobilize the powerless against the powerful would be revolution; to mobilize the powerful against the powerless would simply confirm "the way of the world." But to bring them into partnership is the true sign of God's paradoxical and graceful intervention into the human story.

I believe this pattern—God working with the poor and the rich, the powerless and the powerful—serves as a kind of template for seeking out what God might be doing now in our human cultures. When elites use their privilege to create cultural goods that primarily serve other elites, that is nothing but the way of the world, the standard operating procedure of culture. Furthermore, even when the culturally powerful deign to share their blessings with the powerless, but in ways that leave the powerless dependent and needy, this too is simply another marginally kinder version of the way of the world. Likewise, when the powerless cultivate and create culture that simply reinforces their oppression without bringing any real change in the horizons of possibility and impossibility, or when those in desperate circumstances rise up against the powerful, simply creating new structures of power in their place, we rightly recognize what is happening as business as usual.

So it is no surprise, for example, to discover that two-thirds of American philanthropy actually goes to institutions (whether museums, orchestras or churches) that primarily serve the rich—essentially, the wealthy underwriting their own cultural experiences with the benefit of a tax deduction—or that the futility of American urban life has given rise to misogynistic, nihilistic forms of music that simply underwrite broken horizons of masculinity and femininity with the alleged credibility of "the street." It is also no surprise that most money is made on Wall Street providing financial services to people who already have extraordinary amounts of money, that most advertising targets a thin (literally and figuratively) slice of prosperous young people, and that much of the rich world's research into new medicines target the disorders that disproportionately affect the rich world. Nor is it a surprise that in the name of economic and political empowerment, dictators like Pol Pot and Robert Mugabe have expropriated allegedly ill-gotten wealth from cultural elites—yet in the end only further impoverished and imprisoned their own people.

Now, thanks to common grace, much that happens according to "the way of the world" still can be affirmed, cultivated and even created by Christians. Not all horizons are misplaced, and it is by no means wrong to provide excellent financial services to the wealthy, to create technological devices that solve problems only the prosperous have, or to serve with all the excellence you can in a government that is compromised by corruption—any more than it is wrong to perpetuate God's original act of cultural mercy by sewing garments, even leather ones. Much of our lives as Christians, by choice and circumstance, will be spent doing the same good cultural things our neighbors do, working alongside them to cultivate and create.

And yet I think Christians who are seeking their cultural calling need to look for the distinctive template of God's work in culture, the work announced by Jesus in his own "inaugural address" recorded in Luke 4:

> The Spirit of the Lord is upon me,
>   because he has anointed me to bring good news to the poor.
> He has sent me to proclaim release to the captives
>   and recovery of sight to the blind,
>   to let the oppressed go free,
> to proclaim the year of the Lord's favor. (vv. 18-19)

Jesus is reading from the scroll of the prophet Isaiah, and it is Isaiah, prophesying with his gaze on both the present and future horizons of

Israel's destiny, who most eloquently sums up God's cultural purposes in history, the horizons of possibility God intends to use human beings to create:

> Every valley shall be lifted up,
>   and every mountain and hill be made low;
> the uneven ground shall become level,
>   and the rough places a plain.
> Then the glory of the LORD shall be revealed,
>   and all people shall see it together,
>   for the mouth of the LORD has spoken. (Is 40:4-5)

The valleys—the places of poverty and powerlessness—will be raised up. The mountains and hills, sites of power and privilege (not to mention present-day gated communities and million-dollar real estate!), will be humbled. This is a cultural vision that includes both the powerless and the powerful. It does not glorify poverty but predicts that the poor will eventually have cultural power of their own and more than enough resources (in God's time the hungry will eat rich food and the thirsty will drink fine wine [Is 55]); it does not bow to privilege but can envision, as we saw in chapter ten, that the cultural achievements of the powerful will find their own place in God's redemptive design.

Perhaps Isaiah's most eloquent and surprising statement of God's willingness to partner with both the powerful and the powerless is found in Isaiah 57:15:

> I dwell in the high and holy place,
>   and also with those who are contrite and humble in spirit,
> to revive the spirit of the humble,
>   and to revive the heart of the contrite.

There is good news here for the poor—God dwells with them, and has plans for them. But this is not unequivocally bad news for those who dwell in high and powerful places—provided they discover their need for God and allow him to make their own rough places plain, as humbling as that will be.

So what is God doing in history, according to his own revelation in the pages of Scripture and in Israel's history, culminating with Jesus Christ?

He is at work lowering the high places and raising the low places—so that *all flesh*, low and high, will see his glory together, the glory of the one who brings the possible out of the impossible, the one who raises the dead.

A JUST AND LASTING PEACE

In our own time we have seen this very kind of dramatic cultural change: major shifts in the horizons of possibility in places that seemed fiercely resistant to the kind of raising and lowering of which Isaiah speaks. Few would have predicted in the 1980s that the white minority of South Africa would peacefully give up their hammerlock on cultural power, enforced through the allegedly Christian practice of apartheid. Yet President P. W. Botha, a defiant defender of white rule, was followed in 1989 by F. W. de Klerk, who, astonishingly, released the long-jailed African National Congress leader Nelson Mandela and proceeded to negotiate a peaceful transition to democracy. De Klerk, who fully represented the power of the white South African elite, sought reconciliation with Mandela, the representative of a subjugated people. Perhaps most amazing of all was the cultural credibility and overall success of the Truth and Reconciliation Commission, which in a wide range of cases made "a just and lasting peace," in Abraham Lincoln's words, possible against all odds, allowing perpetrators and victims to honestly come to terms even with heinous crimes without invoking a destructive cycle of vengeance. This process was at every step undergirded by the prayers of disciplined and determined Christians of every race—yet it engaged a pluralistic culture that included many people, like Mandela himself, who did not share the Christian faith.

While there have been other examples before (the Civil Rights movement in the United States) and since (the dismantling of the Soviet Union and the "color revolutions" in many former Soviet republics), the end of apartheid in South Africa strikes me as the most extraordinary sign of God's work in culture in my lifetime. During my college years in the late 1980s, when I was avoiding Shell gas stations because Royal Dutch Shell did business in South Africa, and when some of my friends were being arrested calling for divestment of our college's funds from the apartheid regime, I think all of us would have been astonished to be told that within a few years, not only would the white minority hand over power peacefully, but that such a deeply Christian process of "truth and reconciliation" would take place in an entire society. "That which exists is possible," said the economist Kenneth Boulding. The end of apartheid, prayed for—and died for—by followers of Jesus over several generations, is a sign that God is at work wherever the powerful are willing to humble themselves and the poor are willing to receive the good news as good for themselves *and* the culturally powerful.

Like every epochal cultural change, the transition of South Africa to majority rule has not been perfect or seamless, and there is plenty to critique in the ANC's stewardship of power. But this should not eclipse the sign that God has not exited the business of cultural change. When this kind of change is possible, who can be fully satisfied simply tending the existing horizons? We were made for more, and God is already there in a thousand places where the horizons are misplaced, seeking partners for his new horizons among the powerful and the powerless alike.

The end of apartheid, of course, was cultural change on a massive scale. But it is clear from Scripture that God is equally interested in smaller-scale cultural change—and many of the most momentous changes start small. The household codes of the New Testament often provoke modern discomfort because they do not seem to pay enough attention to "equality" between masters and servants or husbands and wives. But considered as divine interventions in a cultural context where the horizons of possibility did not even include real friendship between a husband and wife (something many Greeks and Romans considered unthinkable), where masters had unlimited power over their slaves, and where children prompted not a shred of our post-Victorian sentimentality, the instructions for how Christians are to conduct their relationships turn out to envision massive restructuring of the existing horizons. When Paul asks husbands to love their wives as Christ loved the church (Eph 5:25), he is inviting them into a level of intimacy and servanthood that was all but unknown.

One of Paul's most audacious exercises in horizon moving is the cultural artifact called the letter to Philemon, in which the apostle uses every persuasive move he can pack into a short letter to change the way the master Philemon sees the runaway slave Onesimus—changing the relationship from one of mastery to brotherhood. Crucially, in intervening in this broken relationship between a powerful man and a powerless one, Paul invites *both* to take risks in moving the horizons (since Onesimus is returning voluntarily, with Paul's encouragement, to his master) and envisions changes in the way *both* carry out their culturally prescribed roles. He also specifically includes the wider community of which both Philemon and Onesimus are a part, going out of his way to greet Philemon's friends Apphia and Archippus and "the church in your house" (Philem 2). This will not be a merely private transaction, no matter how happy the outcome might be, but one that will set in motion a change in how a whole community perceives one of the central cultural institutions of Roman society.

FINDING OUR CALLING

Each of these final chapters will end with some diagnostic questions we can ask to discern where we might find our calling in the midst of culture. For Christians, calling does not fundamentally begin with questions about ourselves but about God. Like the Pevensie children in C. S. Lewis's Narnia chronicles, we will very likely find ourselves suddenly snatched from a known and comfortable world to another one, where extraordinary things are expected of us that seem far beyond our own talents and capabilities. But as the Pevensies learn, what matters at those times is not so much what they bring to Narnia's moment of cultural crisis as that "Aslan is on the move." If we believe that God is still on the move in human cultures, then our most basic questions have to be, *What is God doing in culture? What is his vision for the horizons of the possible and the impossible? Who are the poor who are having good news preached to them? Who are the powerful who are called to spend their power alongside the relatively powerless? Where is the impossible becoming possible?*

These questions cannot be applied too narrowly, merely to questions of "social justice"—although they surely apply there. Our creativity will be called for and we will find a divine wind at our back whenever we discover a place where the current horizons deprive people of their full humanity. For example, people who have the means to travel by airplane are not, in any literal sense of the word, the "poor." But I can testify that the horizons of the possible in most airports are desperately limited, producing in the most frequent flyers (a category which, alas, includes me) the most acute symptoms of anxiety, depression and stress. Furthermore, much of this dis-ease is not allayed by a first-class seat or a membership in an exclusive airline club—the refuges of those with enough money or clout to buy a bit of quiet and privacy.

Cultural creativity of a deeper sort is required. The designers of the central concourse at Charlotte Douglas International Airport exercised some of this creativity several years ago when they placed several dozen white wooden rocking chairs under the hardy (or perhaps plastic) trees that line the atrium across from the food court—creating a space where mothers rock their babies, college students read novels, and senior citizens watch travelers walk by. It is vastly more welcoming and humanizing than most luxury airport clubs I have visited (including the perfectly pleasant US Airways Club just a few steps away). Nearby, the wine producers of North Carolina opened up a wine bar that serves local wines by the glass at reasonable prices. In about one hundred square feet they created a surprisingly refreshing and welcoming oasis where the usual tense anonymity of airline travel is often broken by smiles and relaxed conversation. These cultural stewards recognized the way that air travel can disempower and thus dehumanize even cultural elites, and provided a way back to more generous and gracious horizons—in the case of the wooden rocking chairs, at no extra charge. Is the Charlotte airport a perfect cultural environment? By no means—and yet it is a place where good news whispers just a bit more audibly.

This is the kind of culture making that is needed in every place. It is needed in exurban neighborhoods, where lasting friendship and a sense of significance beyond consumption are as rare as Hummers are plentiful. It is needed in urban-core neighborhoods—whose deficit of significance and surplus of Hummers is not so different from the exurbs after all. It is needed in places where the lure of the new and cool keeps up an insistent and steady beat, and in places where conformity and complacency tempt people to settle for easy comforts. Culture making is needed in every company, every school and every church. In every place there are impossibilities that leave even the powerful feeling constrained and drained, and that rob the powerless of the ability to imagine something different and better.

At root, every human cultural enterprise is haunted by the ultimate impossibility, death, which threatens to slam shut the door of human hope. But God is at work precisely in these places where the impossible seems absolute. Our calling is to join him in what he is already doing—to make visible what, in exodus and resurrection, he has already done.

14

POWER

You can make a strong case that the two most influential women of the twentieth century were a British princess and an Albanian nun. Certainly they were the most widely known. Wherever she went, Diana, Princess of Wales, held the attention of courtiers, commoners and cameras. She had the seeming good fortune to fall in love with the Prince of Wales and marry him in the magnificence of St. Paul's Cathedral—a wedding and a marriage that shaped the hearts and imaginations of a whole generation. Even after she became estranged from Prince Charles, she retained the public's sympathy, and no one could fail to feel a catch in their heart on the Sunday morning when we woke up to discover that this beautiful, winsome young woman had died in a moment of horrible folly in a Paris underpass.

Within a week of Diana's death, the other most recognizable woman in the world died too—not in a luxury car but in a convent in Calcutta. Mother Teresa had moved from her native Albania to the slums of India to serve the dying—not even to cure them but simply to witness and love the presence of her Savior in their "distressing disguise."

Our global celebrity culture is relentlessly intrusive and informal, so that the world readily called the Princess of Wales "Diana." Strangely, though, you rarely heard anyone speak of the nun from Calcutta as "Teresa." To those who served in her home for the dying and to her fellow nuns, in fact, she was simply "Mother." If titles are a sign of power and deference, somehow Mother Teresa compelled a reverence and respect that even the Princess of Wales could not. Yet her title spoke intrinsically of relationship, not just her role in a monastic hierarchy.

Ever since their deaths, I have felt that the princess and the nun offer us a kind of parable of power, and a picture of two paths to cultural influence. The fundamentalists' grandchildren, still commoners and populists at heart, have access to power that their grandparents could not have imagined—or would only have imagined with a shudder. I wrote part of this chapter on a train to two days of meetings with fellow Christian believers at the Union League Club and the Yale Club in New York City—places where, for all our society's aspirations to (or pretensions of) democratic equality, the power of privilege still broods with almost palpable weight. Before I left I was perusing the website of an African evangelist that featured rotating pictures of the evangelist visiting with British royalty, standing in front of his private plane, and, alarmingly, shaking hands with the little-loved former dictator of his home country. Then I read a lengthy story in the *New York Times* profiling a young actress who proclaims faith in Christ, while also wearing thigh-high leather boots and exuding, in the paper's words, "sex appeal." Our most photogenic fellow believers may not yet occupy quite such a privileged place as the late Princess of Wales, but it may only be a matter of time.

The moralistic turn to take at this point is to urge us all to become more like Mother—to take up the vocation of service to and among the poor, foregoing the accumulation of possessions and privilege. And there is no doubt that when Jesus met at least one young man of privilege, he invited him to do exactly that. There's a difference, as the black preacher said, between having a title and having a testimony. "Diana had the title," I can hear him say, "but Mother had the testimony."

Furthermore, there is an unsettling asymmetry between the Princess and the Mother. I dare say that precisely no readers of this book ever could, in any possible scenario, take Princess Diana's place—either her royal station, her worldwide celebrity or her magnetic grip on every nearby camera. Leaving aside the fact that most of us are not subjects of the British Crown, you and I are simply not cut out for the job. Princess Diana's singular life was just that, singular. There will be, in our lifetime, an absolutely tiny number of women (or men) who will charm the cameras and manipulate the celebrity press so effectively that they reach her level of fame. For the rest of us to chase that kind of popularity and visibility would be both foolish and futile. Of course, the sad conclusion of Diana's short life is that even for them to chase that kind of popularity and visibility would be both foolish and futile.

And yet there is nothing—absolutely nothing—stopping us from taking Mother Teresa's place. None of the intrinsic barriers to taking up the life of a celebrity princess apply to those who might want to take up the life of a servant to the poor. As I write there are hundreds of people volunteering at the Missionaries of Charity's home for the dying in Calcutta. Some have been there for a day or two; others have stayed for years or decades. They obviously will not necessarily achieve Mother's worldwide recognition, but they are living, in every material respect, the life she lived. At the end Mother Teresa was a wizened old woman whose face bore a crease for every year of her life. With all the plastic surgery money could buy, you or I will never look like Princess Diana in her prime—but for absolutely no cost except a life of love, we could all look like Mother Teresa.

For nearly all of us, becoming a celebrity is completely, categorically impossible. For all of us, becoming a saint is completely, categorically possible.

So why are so many trying to become a celebrity and so few trying to become a saint?

POWER DEFINED

Strangely enough, I think the reason we are so attracted to the life of the princess and so little attracted to the life of the saint is that we understand just enough about power to be dangerous.

Cultural power can be defined very simply as *the ability to successfully propose a new cultural good*. This definition builds on several of our previous observations about culture. Culture changes when new cultural goods—concrete, tangible artifacts, whether books or tools or buildings—are introduced into the world. But not all artifacts automatically become truly horizon-shaping cultural goods—not, at least, at the scale which their creators intended. If I write this book and eight people read it but then never speak a word about it to their friends or family, it will not have moved the horizons in any measurable way for a broad public. It will be like Christo's *Gates* five years before its exhibition—brilliant or flawed as the case may be, but culturally inert.

An important corollary of this definition of power that *no one* has the power to *impose* a cultural good. The public nature of culture means that in principle, any cultural good can be refused. Even the instruments of state authority, police forces and armies, that have the power to enforce certain kinds of cultural horizons depend on the acquiescence of the individuals who drive the tanks and aim the guns. Illegitimate, violent exercises of raw power—such as terrorism—clearly can destroy individual lives, but they still depend for their "success" on whatever kind of response the public who survive choose to make. Cultural goods cannot be imposed—they can only be *proposed*. How the public responds is never fully in anyone's grasp—and that is as true for parents serving chili as for presidents declaring war.

Consequently, venturing the proposal of a new cultural good is a risky thing. My publishers and I have gone out on a limb to offer this book for sale, putting money and time at risk in a bet that, objectively speaking, fails or fizzles most of the time. We can do our best to estimate the chances of success and allocate resources accordingly, but as we saw in chapter twelve, such exercises are haphazard even in the hands of experienced professionals. The truth is that as I write these words, I simply have no idea whether this cultural good, with the ideas, vocabulary and vision it contains, will move the horizons for any significant public.

And yet we can handicap, as it were, the odds of success, because power is a reality—some would say the only reality—in culture. The bare fact is that some people are much more likely to succeed in proposing a new cultural good than others. Sometimes this power comes from a title. When the CEO of a company speaks in a meeting after a presentation by a junior-level staff member, we know that the CEO's words and ideas will carry more weight. (Note how we resort to a metaphor which is not literally true at all—"carry more weight"—to express the intangible but universally acknowledged reality of power.) In some cultural contexts certain words, tones of voice or even entire realms of grammar are reserved for those who carry certain kinds of power. In our relatively fluid society, though, power is often distributed more informally. Most of us have experienced being in a context where our jokes were funny, our ideas provoked interest and excitement, and we felt light and quick on our feet, able to realize our vision with little sense of friction—and then being in another context where the same jokes and ideas fell completely flat and we found ourselves tongue-tied and embarrassed. The difference was, in a word, power.

Power, in this sense, is deeply and absolutely dependent on the nature of the particular public we find ourselves among. A brilliant academic researcher whose peers defer to her at academic conferences may find herself adrift and ignored in an investment firm's board room. A hard-charging executive in that firm can travel fifteen minutes from his downtown office and find a street corner where his clothing and manner of speech provoke only indifference or outright hostility—just as a young man on that street corner, whose word is his bond and who has the "respect" of the street, will be ignored or even ejected should he try to walk into the executive's office building. Each of these people has the ability to successfully propose new cultural goods—for a given public, in a given context. Elsewhere they are at the mercy of those with power—which is why those who do have power in some cultural context become deeply averse to spending time in places where their power is of no use. Indeed, much of the energy and resources of the powerful is spent securing their access to a seamless experience of powerfulness—finding a home, a workplace, a vacation spot, a set of friends where their power will be validated and not negated. To leave the circle of one's power is a deeply, existentially unsettling experience.

SEX, MONEY AND POWER

The Christian tradition has often recognized the three basic arenas of human temptation as sex, money and power, corresponding roughly to the apostle John's list: "the desire of the flesh, the desire of the eyes, the pride in riches" (1 Jn 2:16). The three are, as both sinners and saints have observed, somewhat interchangeable, and much of human existence is oriented toward the pursuit of one, two or all three at once. But of the three, power is by far the most slippery and dangerous, for two simple reasons: no one ever knows how much power they have, and no one ever has enough.

No one ever knows how much power they have. You know, certainly, when you are having sex. You can count your money. But there is no way to reliably measure power, especially at the moments when we most want and need it. I can be reasonably sure that tomorrow morning my children will obey me when I call them to breakfast—in that sense, I know something about my power within the cultural sphere of my family. But my attention and anxieties are elsewhere, focused on a phone call I am hoping someone will return, a proposal I hope my colleagues will embrace, or a book I am about to finish and launch into the world. In none of these areas am I at all sure how much ability I have to ensure that my proposed cultural goods will be adopted. All true cultural creativity happens at the edges of the horizons of the possible, so by definition our most culturally creative endeavors have a high risk of failure. No matter how much I try to gauge the chances of success beforehand, there is simply no way to tell except to try.

And no one ever has enough power. Our culture's standards for what counts as "enough" wealth and sex are amazingly elastic, yet at some point any reasonable person would be satisfied with some (large) amount of both. Microsoft founder Bill Gates has enough money—in fact, he has so much money that the great challenge facing him, and many other people of great wealth, is how to spend it purposefully and effectively. But even Bill Gates does not wake up every morning and feel that he has all the power he needs to create what he would hope to create. The world is too broken, too intractable. The only people who are serenely confident that they have sufficient power have closed their eyes to their own mortality and have eradicated from their hearts the last vestige of compassion. When any of us reflect in even the most cursory way on the insults to dignity that our fellow human beings are suffering right now in places of violence, poverty and famine all over the world, we become aware that we are woefully incapable of bringing the kind of change we would want to see. We could never create enough cultural goods to alter their horizons of possibility.

Indeed, while wealth and power are somewhat interchangeable—wealth can buy you influence in many cultural domains, and power can give you access to wealth—it is striking that as a means of influencing culture, even great wealth is often deucedly difficult to use well, and after a point, using it well becomes more difficult the more we have. The great challenges of our time—the proliferation of weapons, from land mines to rifles to nuclear bombs; the corruption of junior and senior officials in countless nations; the will to fight and treat diseases that primarily afflict the poor, to name a few—are only minimally responsive to inputs of more money. After a certain point, as the practitioners of international aid have found to their chagrin, more money can actually make the situation worse. While billions or trillions of dollars may genuinely be needed to address these challenges, the money is actually the easy part. What is most needed is the creation of new cultural goods, new structures of possibility and impossibility built on new forms of culture that do not yet exist. To create those new goods and see them successfully adopted by the public at large will require cultural power. And no one in the world has enough to do so with full confidence that they will succeed.

All this means that for all the attention paid to the temptations of lust (the insatiable desire for sex) and greed (the insatiable desire for money), the quest for power is the most insidious temptation of all. Since we never know for sure how much we have, and in fact never have enough, we are constantly tempted to try to acquire a bit more to hold in reserve or to use at a moment of crisis. As with all temptations the temptation to amass power is most acute when it is coupled to the best of intentions. In the grip of the temptation to accumulate power, we begin to fall prey to the fallacy of strategy, imagining that we can plot our way into cultural success by manipulating the right levers of relationship, access and fame.

Furthermore, unlike money, which can be measured and stored for the future, power is a fluid capacity that must be maintained, since it is always in danger of slipping away if we lose the attention or respect of the public. At the end of all our angling for power, we will be just as unsure of our ultimate ability to "change the world" as we were at the beginning, but now we will be enmeshed in a web of obligations that constrain us and can easily leave us with less power than we had before.

An instructive example of the temptations of power is found in the rise of the Christian Coalition under Ralph E. Reed Jr., the young and energetic leader who brought Pat Robertson's political organization to national prominence in the 1990s. The Christian Coalition sought to mobilize Christians to influence local and national politics on a range of issues. "80 percent of Americans believe there is a problem of declining morality within our nation," said the Coalition's 1995 document "Contract with the American Family," designed to influence the agenda of a Congress where Newt Gingrich and a new generation of Republicans had just taken control in midterm elections. The Christian Coalition was widely credited for at least part of the Republican triumph in Congress—enough for *Time* magazine to put Reed on its cover in 1995 with the headline "The Right Hand of God"—thanks to shrewd alliances. Christian conservatives, by themselves, were not enough of a constituency to form a majority bloc in the Republican Party, so Reed and his partners had reached out to the Party's probusiness, antitax wing, a group that would have placed the "problem of declining morality" far down on their list of concerns. This alliance surely accounts for one of the planks in the Contract's ten-point platform that seemed distantly related to the issue of moral decline: "Family-Friendly Tax Relief."

The logic of the Christian Coalition's strategy under Reed was simple. Their Christian constituency did not have enough power to move American culture decisively in their direction on the issues that mattered most to them—notwithstanding the "80 percent" of Americans who might agree with a very general statement about moral decline. So it would have to form alliances with others who did conceivably have enough power. The leaders of the Coalition would leverage their ability to mobilize Christian voters to achieve results far greater than those voters alone could expect to have.

In principle there was nothing wrong with such a strategy. The creation of large-scale cultural goods requires large-scale cultural partnerships. The pursuit of a common good requires working in common with people who will not agree with us on every point. Some of the scorn that more left-leaning Christians have heaped on the Christian Coalition's alliance with probusiness Republicans is misplaced, since any Christian, regardless of political philosophy, who wants to be part of creating something new in culture will find him- or herself in various kinds of partnership with otherwise unlikely allies.

But power's temptation is insidious. Because we can never have enough, and because we never know how much we have, we are constantly tempted to let the end start dictating the means. We begin to accumulate power for its own sake, which requires separating our quest for power from the goals that originally motivated it. We begin to measure our significance by our access to powerful people and institutions, not by how faithful we remain to the cultural goods we were seeking to cultivate and create.

In Reed's case, the quest for access and power not only led him beyond the Christian Coalition to a much more conventional life of lobbying, political consulting and "public relations," but to a relationship with another Republican lobbyist named Jack Abramoff. The former president of the Christian Coalition found himself collaborating with Abramoff on advocating for, of all things, the interests of Native American gambling, writing to Abramoff in November 1998: "Hey, now that I'm done with the electoral politics, I need to start humping in corporate accounts! I'm counting on you to help me with some contacts." In less than four years, Ralph Reed had gone from decrying America's moral decline to "humping in corporate accounts."

THE GOODNESS OF POWER

The temptation to power does not just afflict those who work in politics, any more than the temptation to greed only afflicts those who work in banks. Power, the ability to successfully propose cultural goods, suffuses every culture, every sphere and every scale. It was (and is) a reality in the halls of the Missionaries of Charity's Home for the Dying in Calcutta, where choices have to be made daily about how to shape the culture of care and prayer, just as much as it was (and is) a reality in the halls of Buckingham Palace. Even the smallest cultural change, at the smallest scale of culture, requires power, and cultural change at larger scales requires major cultural power.

The church is often a particularly difficult place to discuss power. We prefer to pass quickly over the fact that even within our Christian community, there are some who can more readily propose new cultural goods than others. When we leave the church building, some of us take up positions during the week that give us tremendous scope for cultural creativity, while others take up positions that largely are constrained by the power of others. This is a reality every bit as pressing as the fact that we have widely varying amounts of money in our bank accounts and that we are each beset by particular callings and temptations in our sexual relationships. Our churches are not generally likely to win any awards for dealing honestly with any of these three perennial arenas of both blessing and temptation, but while it is likely that you have heard at least one sermon on how to think in a Christian way about sex and the requirements of church budgets make money an annual topic, chances are you have never heard a sermon on how to be stewards of cultural power. Given this silence it is not completely surprising that there were plenty of Christians who blithely followed the Christian Coalition into its dubious alliances, and few who were in a position to question Ralph Reed's stewardship of his power.

There is also a durable Christian tradition, rooted in the Anabaptist protest against established religion, that is deeply suspicious of Christians who wield power, especially state power, which is supported by the threat of force. The Christian argument over the legitimacy of war is beyond our scope here, though it is an argument well worth having. But while a just war could possibly *restrain* the worst that human beings can do, even the most adamant proponents of just war will agree that war is utterly unable to create. The best war can do (and pacifists make a bold case that it cannot even do this) is prevent cultural destruction. When wars end, whether Christians supported them or not, the work of creating new cultural goods remains—and to do that requires cultural power. How are we to understand this potent and potentially distorting force?

The only place to begin is with the *goodness* of power and with the recognition of power as a *gift*. When God invites Adam to name the animals in Genesis 2, he is doing nothing other than giving Adam cultural power: inviting him to successfully propose new cultural goods, the names that each animal will bear. But this power is not something that Adam successfully wrestles out of God's grasp by a series of clever strategies. It is simply what God chooses to give to Adam in order that Adam can fulfill his destiny to be a culture creator in God's image.

If the creation of cultural goods is the very essence of our original calling as human beings, and if that original calling is as good as God said it was, than the power to create those cultural goods must also be essentially good, no matter how distorted by sin. But like all goods, this is one we cannot grasp. The very model of grasping for cultural power is the citizens of Babel: "Come, let us make bricks. . . . Come, let us build ourselves a city, and a tower, . . . and let us make a name for ourselves" (Gen 11:3-4). The threefold repetition of "let us," and the escalating scale of their cultural ambitions, from bricks to a tower to "a name for ourselves," is an all-too-accurate summary of the human quest to secure enough power to become finally free from dependence on God, finally able to thrive without God's gifts.

There is another way to approach power. Rather than seeking to build our way up to the pinnacle of power, we can make the move that God invites us to make: to see ourselves, in relationship to the world's Creator, as in possession of more power than we could ever dream. Exodus and resurrection, the most dramatic divine interventions in history, both declare that there is a grace-filled power loose in the world that far outstrips our greatest human ambitions and can quiet our deepest human fears. We enter into the work of cultural creativity not as people who desperately need to strategize our way into cultural relevance, but as participants in a story of new creation that comes just when our power seems to have been extinguished. Culture making becomes not just the product of clever cultural strategy or the natural byproduct of inherited privilege, but the astonished and grateful response of people who have been rescued from the worst that culture and nature can do.

THE DISCIPLINES OF POWER: SERVICE

These are, perhaps, lovely sentiments. But how, in practice, can we approach the inevitable opportunities of cultural power and the frustrations of powerlessness with any hope of treating power as a gift rather than a strategic achievement? We face similar questions with the two other good gifts that tempt and challenge Christians, sex and money. In each case the answer is to embrace a certain kind of discipline: to make deliberate choices that both rob the temptation of its hold on us and unleash the gift in all its intended glory. In the case of sex, these disciplines go by the names of chastity and fidelity, the twin choices to limit our sexual activity in the name of greater fruitfulness. In the case of money, the core disciplines are simplicity and generosity, regularly giving beyond our comfort level in order to rob money of its claim to secure our lives apart from God, and to release its blessing in the lives of the materially poor.

So what are the corresponding disciplines for dealing with the gift and temptation of power? In his important book *The Challenge of the Disciplined Life*, Richard Foster chooses the word *service*. Indeed, the language and imagery of servanthood is central to Jesus' own extensive teaching on power, seen most vividly when he washes the feet of the disciples in the upper room the night before his death. When Jesus explains his mission and ministry in the Gospel of Mark, he uses the language of servanthood:

> You know that among the Gentiles those whom they recognize as their rulers lord it over them, and their great ones are tyrants over them. But it is not so among you; but whoever wishes to become great among you must be your servant, and whoever wishes to be first among you must be slave of all. For the Son of Man came not to be served but to serve, and to give his life a ransom for many. (Mk 10:42-45)

When we take up the role of servants, we do precisely what the powerful prefer not to do: put ourselves in a position where our power is of little use. Rather than asserting the privilege the powerful have to control their environment and avoid humbling experiences, we seek Christ in the places where we will not be noticed, will not seem useful and will not receive praise. Servants are anonymous and often all but invisible, and the more powerful we become, the more we should seek out opportunities for anonymity and invisibility. Just as the only real antidote to the temptations of money is lavish generosity, so the only real antidote to the temptations of power is choosing to spend our power in the opposite of the way the world encourages us to spend it: not on getting closer to the sources of additional power or on securing our own round-the-clock sense of comfort and control, but spend it on getting closer to the relatively powerless.

One of the basic disciplines I have put in place in my own life is travel outside the developed world, about once a year if our family budgets of time and money allow. In some respects, of course, international travel is an expression of tremendous cultural power and wealth. But I have found that my annual trips outside the developed world are among the most challenging and humbling things I have ever done. Placing myself in a context where I am dependent on the hospitality of strangers, as well as Christian brothers and sisters, is for me a singularly unnerving experience. I am used to considering myself a fairly culturally savvy and resourceful person, but in the cultural context of my hosts I am generally of very little use, especially since I usually travel in a private capacity, not representing any great store of Western money or influence. All I can offer is my willingness to listen, learn and pray to brothers and sisters who are much farther along the road of discipleship, and observe with awe their cultural creativity in the face of crushing odds.

On one such trip my friend Bill and I were walking along a dusty street in Nairobi bustling with people on their way to and from the slum where one quarter of the population make their home. "When I'm in places like this," he said, "I like to look at people's butts." He laughed at my confused expression. "Because I figure that when we're all in the new Jerusalem around the throne of the Lamb, I'll have barely made it into the room—I'll be in the cheap seats, while these folks will be up front. So this will pretty much be the view I'll have in eternity. I might as well get used to it now."

Bill's perspective helps to correct a potential danger in the language of service. In our cultural context, *service* often implies condescension, not in the earlier sense of that word that meant the powerful treating all they met with dignity and respect, but in the sense of maintaining our sense of superiority even while we offer charity to those "less fortunate." It also quickly conjures up images of volunteers in a soup kitchen ladling out resources for "the poor." But it does not readily carry with it the idea that the very people we might serve are in fact people with their own untapped cultural capacities—people whom we might end up needing as much as they need us. And so *service* does not always carry with it the astonishing biblical insight that when God works in history, he does so through partnership between powerful and powerless alike.

For the basic thing we are invited to do with our cultural power is to *spend it alongside those less powerful than ourselves.* The more customary phrase would be *spend it on behalf of the powerless*, but that is not the way power works in God's economy. The way to spend cultural power is to open up for others the opportunity to create new cultural goods, adding our resources to theirs to increase their chance of moving the horizons of possibility for some community. And while there are a few categories of people—the very young, the very old and the very ill—who might be truly said to be powerless (and who do especially require our service), the stories of exodus and resurrection convince us that God's power is available even to those who do not seem to have any power of their own.

We do not approach the relatively powerless as recipients of our charity but as sources of a power that we who are relatively powerful may not even know. When we put our power at their service, we unlock their creative capacity without in any way diminishing our own—and in this way, spending power is very different from spending money. When we transfer money to another person, their net worth increases while ours decreases, but the power to create cultural goods rarely has this zero-sum quality. Indeed, as we'll see in chapter fifteen, the only way we can truly create cultural goods is in partnership with others, in a process where power does not so much flow from one participant to another as accrue to the overall creative capacity of a community of people, who become more and more able to contribute new and good things to the world.

THE DISCIPLINES OF POWER: STEWARDSHIP

So there is another discipline we need to embrace alongside service, one that recognizes the capacities of even the seemingly least culturally powerful. And here another biblical word may be useful: *stewardship*. Stewards, by definition, are custodians of cultural power—responsible, as many of Jesus' parables make clear, not just for their masters' wealth but for representing the masters' interests when they are away. Stewards possess an outsized proportion of influence, gained not simply by their own striving or success but by virtue of their relationship with their employers. And so—for all of its unfortunate connotations with end-of-the-year "stewardship" campaigns—*stewardship* is a very good word indeed for we who are custodians of God's resurrection power in the midst of the world.

What does it mean to embrace stewardship as a spiritual discipline? It is different from service, which requires setting aside our power entirely for a time. Stewardship means to consciously take up our cultural power, investing it intentionally among the seemingly powerless, putting our power at their disposal to enable them to cultivate and create. This is different from charity, which is simply the transfer of assets from rich to poor. It is closer to investment. Investors expect a return—indeed, they expect their own resources to grow alongside the success of the enterprises they invest in. Investors begin from a position of wealth, but they also are aware of the capacities and gifts of those in whom they invest, capacities they themselves do not have. Stewards are simply those who invest with resources they know are not their own, in places where there will only be a return on investment if God is indeed at loose and at work in the world.

Needless to say, this does not require a trip to a Nairobi slum. I know graduate students who have chosen to invest extra portions of time in tutoring the lagging students in their classes, even though academia encourages them to consider a teaching fellowship as simply a means to support the process of research and relationship building that leads to a tenure-track position. Some of my former students at Harvard had joined consulting firms and spent most of their days advising profitable businesses how to become more profitable, but they also volunteered in a nonprofit nearby, helping to streamline its operations while also learning from an ex-con who knew how to get a group of alcoholics to talk.

Not long ago I had the privilege of meeting Catherine Rohr, a former Wall Street investment banker who realized that the same skills that she had learned in business school could be used to prepare prisoners to reenter society as entrepreneurs rather than unemployed recipients of charity. Her Prison Entrepreneurship Program brings executives and business school professors into prisons to train inmates in the skills needed to launch new enterprises of cultivation and creativity upon their release. Catherine realized that even prisoners, seemingly deprived of any cultural power, in fact could become a tremendous resource to their communities if the culturally powerful came alongside them—and that those prisoners will start businesses their mentors could not have dreamed of or successfully led, precisely in the places that most need growing businesses and new jobs. She is a steward of her power, helping both the seemingly powerless and the seemingly powerful to be better stewards themselves.

In Manila, there is a garbage dump called "Smokey Mountain," a perpetually smoldering heap of trash nearly one hundred feet high. There, as in many garbage dumps all over the world, there is a community of people who eke out an existence, essentially, as recyclers, taking the trash of the city and extracting economic value from small pieces of string, tinfoil and cardboard. When I feel frustrated with the limits of my cultural power, as I do more often than I would like to admit, I like to think about the inhabitants of Smokey Mountain. By the world's standards—certainly by the standards of the privileged and powerful journalists, artists, activists, executives and church leaders I get to spend much of my time among—their options are painfully limited. There is no reason to think that they have any less innate capacity for cultivation and creativity than any other group of human beings made in God's image, but they were born in a place where, instead of cultural goods being proposed and going on to reshape the world, the detritus of culture is brought to decompose and die. Their existence is a rebuke, to say the least, to my self-pity.

But I also know just enough about this community in Manila to know that they neither need nor want my pity. In 1980 a Catholic priest named Father Ben relocated to Smokey Mountain from the seminary where he was a promising young scholar. He brought the residents there the good news about Jesus. And he began to instill in them the confidence that God had not forgotten them—indeed, that God was ready to breathe life into their efforts at making a better life for their families. The community of garbage-dump workers persuaded the city to provide them with water and electric services. They have built modest but dignified concrete homes at the edge of the dump, replacing shacks of cardboard and tin. They even built a community center where children play games and older people gather to pass the time.

So the residents of the Manila garbage dump are not, for me, primarily a moral object lesson in my relative affluence, a ready-to-mind guilt trip that I could use to browbeat myself into being more charitable. Rather, they are a reminder of the inexhaustible human capacity to cultivate and create, and the transformative power of partnerships that accompany God in his world-upending plan to level the mountains and raise the valleys. They are a reminder that in exactly the places where the image of God seems to be in most danger of being extinguished, human beings can find the resources to create something that moves the horizons—even the horizons of a garbage dump.

Like the disciplines of fidelity and chastity, simplicity and generosity, acts of service and stewardship are not just quaint or pious exercises to make us better people. They are down payments on our faith that the reality of power, that most slippery of all human realities, is not as it appears. The lesson of both exodus and resurrection is that the powerless are never as powerless as they seem. Perhaps that is the truest sense of the "good news to the poor" that Jesus came to proclaim: the poor are not as poor as they, and we, think they are. The creative God of history has made his resurrection power available to them. He has made his power available to us if we will become poor in spirit—no longer simply accumulating power but freely sharing it.

THE LURE OF POWER

A few years ago I was at a Christian conference with many friends and colleagues from the world of university ministry. Among them was my own campus minister from undergraduate years, Bob, who had contributed greatly to my Christian formation as a college student. We happily arranged ahead of time to share a dinner in the packed hotel ballroom to catch up on the many years of life that had passed since we last talked. When the time came, we chose two spots at a table full of other conference-goers.

Within a few minutes I discovered that the person seated on my left was a man named Duane, whom I had been wanting to meet for some time, the new executive director of a private foundation that had supported my work under his predecessor. Not only was this a strategic relationship, but as we chatted I discovered we had a great deal in common, including shared stints in the world of Harvard University and many mutual friends. Duane and I ended up having an animated conversation for most of the rest of the dinner. Bob, meanwhile, knew the person to his right well enough that they were able to carry on a cordial conversation, but by the end of dinner I had spoken only a few words to Bob, meanwhile giving silent thanks that I had had the good fortune to sit down next to Duane.

I didn't reflect on this incident at all until a few weeks later, when I was having lunch with a friend who works in Washington, D.C. He was describing the frustration of the D.C. social scene, where everyone has mastered the art of seeming to be interested in their current conversation, even while they scan the room for someone more important to talk to. We were trading stories of particularly galling or adroit "handoffs"—when I realized that was exactly what I had done to Bob. In an instant and subconscious calculation I had spotted Duane's potential to be a powerful ally in a way that Bob could not be.

I am not prepared to say that the Christian thing to do is steadfastly to ignore all opportunities to build relationships with those who seem more powerful than we are. To the contrary, if God's basic work is to build partnerships between the powerful and the powerless, to cut ourselves off from people with cultural power is to deprive both them and ourselves of an opportunity to see God at work. Duane and I have gone on to have several more conversations where, thankfully, neither of us were looking over the other's shoulder for better opportunities that might be coming along. My instinct that he could be a challenging and valuable friend certainly was not misplaced. But I recognize in my quick handoff of Bob precisely the kind of heart that I need spiritual disciplines to change.

And the sad end of "the people's princess" is a reminder of the grave dangers of our attraction to power. The daughter of Earl Spencer had tremendous resources of cultural power at her disposal—resources which she did put to work in the later years of her short life, especially in addressing the global scourge of land mines—but she was also, as Tina Brown's biography makes excruciatingly clear, utterly absorbed in a never-ending effort to guard her power by stage-managing her relationship with the celebrity-hungry press. The most recognizable woman in the world expended vast resources of personal time and energy trying to control her own celebrity and image. Even if the pursuing paparazzi did not play the decisive role in her death in a brutal car crash in a Paris underpass, no image better captures the tragedy of a life spent chasing power: an ever-accelerating luxury car careening out of control. It was an ending that had nothing of the quality so many admired in Diana—grace.

It could have been otherwise. Diana and Mother Teresa only met a few times, the last time at a Missionaries of Charity home in New York City just two months before their deaths in the same week in the late summer of 1997. They might have met more often. Mother might have been a better friend than most that Diana found. And together they might have been partners in creating something new in the world.

FINDING OUR CALLING

What questions for our calling emerge from these reflections on power? The first question for each of us must be to honestly assess the extent of our current cultural power. *Where have we successfully proposed a new cultural good?* Where are the cultural contexts where our cultivation and creativity bears fruit? The most important discipline here is to resist strategy—to avoid plotting our way into greater cultural influence. We will have the greatest cultural effect where we already have cultural influence, where we have already cultivated a community that recognizes our ability to contribute something new. Honestly and gratefully assessing where we already have cultural power is also an essential antidote to the futile process of desperately trying to amass more.

We also can ask, *With whom am I sharing my power?* How am I making it possible for others to cultivate and create culture? How can I become a steward, investing my cultural power in the dreams and plans of those with less cultural power than myself?

And most fundamentally, we can ask whether our own transformation is keeping pace with the cultural power we have been given. Are we engaging in acts of service that take us into places of anonymity and invisibility? Do we sense stillness and confidence at the bottom of our own heart, or are we all too close to being passengers in a luxury car going far over the speed limit? Do we dream of climbing a slippery pole to achieve enough cultural power to accomplish our goals, or do we seek transformation in the hands of the One who is already at work in history before and after us?

It shouldn't be entirely surprising that these questions, asked with sufficient intensity and answered with sufficient honesty, will bring us to the core question of faith, because culture making is, in the end, a call to faith. In whose power do we trust? The best way to find out is to observe what we do with our power—and what we do with our powerlessness.

15

COMMUNITY

For many years I lived in the 8th Congressional District of Massachusetts, home of one of the most powerful and popular politicians of the twentieth century, Thomas P. "Tip" O'Neill Jr.

O'Neill wielded nearly unprecedented power as Speaker of the House during the Reagan administration, but he was an Irish Catholic boy from North Cambridge, Massachusetts, to the end of his days. His parish was not the urbane and cosmopolitan St. Paul's in Harvard Square—it was St. John the Evangelist, a broad-shouldered building fronting unceremoniously on Massachusetts Avenue in North Cambridge. When O'Neill died, after serving in the House of Representatives for thirty-four years, St. John the Evangelist was thronged with well-wishers from all over the world.

There's a famous Saul Steinberg *New Yorker* cover showing America as viewed, supposedly, from Manhattan's Upper East Side. Ninth Avenue is lovingly detailed, with pedestrians, cars and architectural features all perfectly visible. Beyond, and a bit smaller, is 10th Avenue. Then comes the Hudson River, then a strip of land vaguely labeled "Jersey." There are a few inches of green space with Chicago, Kansas City and Nebraska perfunctorily noted, with the Pacific Ocean beyond (just a bit larger than the Hudson River in the foreground). Three indistinct hills on the other side of the Pacific are labeled "China," "Japan" and "Russia."

And that's about it.

You could draw a similar picture to describe the world as seen from Harvard Square, where I lived and worked for ten years. In that drawing, North Cambridge would be hardly a blip on the way to Lexington, the gracious, green, crushingly expensive suburb where many Harvard faculty live. New York's Central Park, Washington, D.C.'s, Dupont Circle or for that matter San Francisco's Union Square would probably all figure more prominently than the stretch of Massachusetts Avenue where Tip O'Neill was baptized, worshiped and was buried.

Tip O'Neill's longest-lasting legacy—beside the Central Artery Project in Boston, the massive public works project that he pushed through Congress as a parting gift to the citizens and construction industry of Boston—is his axiom, "All politics is local." Even while leading a national political party, negotiating from the opposition with the president of the United States, and appearing on national news programs, he remembered the interests of his neighbors in North Cambridge. He didn't want to succumb to the distortions of the map as seen from Capitol Hill or Harvard Square, the "Beltway Fever" that is said to afflict the long-term denizens of places where power concentrates.

O'Neill's aphorism surprised and provoked because it's not literally true. Some politics is truly local, affecting roughly as many people as are directly involved and no more—the politics of a small business, a neighborhood block association or the elders' board of a small church. When the House of Representatives raised the minimum wage or cut taxes, it was affecting an entire nation. Yet O'Neill was signaling not just his awareness that he was an elected representative from a particular place and group of people—he was also naming the concrete personal experiences, networks and places that lie at the roots of every political actor and action, and acknowledging that even politics on the largest scale only matters because it affects concrete, particular places and people. To be an effective political leader, for O'Neill, was never to give in to the schematic way of thinking of the world where some places are dispensable and unimportant. O'Neill was effective, even revered, as a national political leader precisely because he was baptized and buried at St. John the Evangelist.

THE 3, THE 12 AND THE 120

Is there any sense to the idea that "all culture is local"? Mandarin Chinese, Coca-Cola, the common law system of jurisprudence and the twelve-tone musical scale form the horizons of possibility for millions or billions of people. They are as far from "local" as you can get, and they are cultural goods of tremendous importance, for better or worse.

Yet there is one crucial way that all culture is local: all *culture making* is local. Every cultural good, whether a new word, law, recipe, song or gadget, begins with a small group of people—and not just a relatively small group but an *absolutely* small group. No matter how many it goes on to affect, culture always starts small.

And this means that no matter how complex and extensive the cultural system you may consider, the only way it will be changed is by an absolutely small group of people who innovate and create a new cultural good.

The optimal size of this small group? I suggest three. Sometimes it is four or five, and even two can occasionally pull it off. But three is the perfect number.

Three people can fit in a Mini Cooper (barely) with room for luggage. Three people can talk on a conference call, convene around a table in a meeting room, or chat online without anyone getting bored or distracted or feeling superfluous. Three people can sit in a single booth at a restaurant and hatch plans.

Now, for any cultural good to reach its full potential, the efforts of more than three people will be required. There will need to be concentric circles of people around the initial three who join in refining and shaping the three's initial proposal. But the surprising pattern that emerges when you start studying the propagation of cultural goods is that these concentric circles are never very large. They may not be absolutely small—the size of a group that could fit in a compact car—but they are always relatively small: relative, that is, to the size of the culture that they affect.

And the optimal size for these concentric circles, I suggest, is 12 and

120. These circles are still small enough that they can include people who know one another's faces and names, who are intimately acquainted with one another's talents and limitations, who know how much to trust and how much to verify.

Not all culture is local. This book, as a cultural good, is not local—you, the reader, are probably not my geographic neighbor and have never met me in person. But the *making* of this book was local, in the sense that it was based on personal relationships and intimate collaboration: the product of the 3, the 12 and the 120. In the circle of 3 were a publisher, an editor and an author; in the circle of 12 were an editorial director, a marketing director, publicists, designers and a few trusted reviewers and readers. In the circle of 120 were the endorsers whose comments you read on the cover; editors and producers at magazines, newspapers and broadcast media; and some key friends who helped shape the content, strengthen the concepts and spread the word.

This is why most books include acknowledgments. Read the acknowledgments carefully—sometimes you have to read between the lines—and you'll invariably find a few key people thanked especially profusely (the 3), another group of people given particular mention (the 12), and a host of others whose names couldn't be omitted without the author dishonestly taking more credit for the final product than he really deserved (the 120). Of course, the numbers won't always line up quite precisely, but the proportions will always be roughly 3 : 12 : 120—and the inner concentric circle, the small group without whom the book simply would never have been written, will never be much more than 3.

Once you start looking for the pattern of 3 : 12 : 120, you see it everywhere. Movie credits: an executive producer, a producer and a director (3); the other producers and key crew members (12); the crew (120 or more— because a major motion picture is one of the most complex cultural goods our society creates, up there with jet airplanes and computer operating systems). Companies of almost any size: the so-called C-level executives (CEO, COO, CIO, CFO)—3 to 5 leaders; the board—12 or so; the key staff, which in small businesses is the whole team and in larger businesses may be the leaders of various business units. The founders of Google, two former Stanford graduate students, Sergey Brin and Larry Page, added a third executive, Eric Schmidt, when the company began to grow. The executive branch of the government of the United States comes down to a surprisingly small group of people: the president, the chief of staff and one or two of the president's most trusted advisers; the Cabinet (admittedly, at this writing it numbers twenty—a bit more than twelve); and the people who can reasonably expect personal access to the Oval Office in any given week (not much more than 120—the entire list of appointed White House staff, including assistants and deputy assistants, is only forty-nine).

When the Poincaré Conjecture, one of the trickiest and most obscure problems in mathematics, was finally proved early in the twenty-first century, the key contributors were Grigory Perlman, Richard Hamilton and William Thurston—the 3. The number of people in the entire world who were qualified to confirm that the proof actually was complete and correct was not much more than 12. And the number who could explain the proof's significance to fellow mathematicians probably numbered a few hundred at best—even though the proof of the Poincaré Conjecture has effects on fields populated by hundreds of thousands of specialists that shape the horizons for billions of human beings.

This distinction between absolutely and relatively small groups is important. At the small end of the 3 : 12 : 120 pattern is an *absolutely* small group. At the large end is a relatively small group—small, that is, relative to the cultural domain for which the cultural good is intended. So the 120 is a more flexible number than the 3. The Ford Motor Corporation, one of the giants of modern American industry, had about three hundred "senior-level officers" in 2006—still a relatively small group compared to the scale of its worldwide operations. Yet its executive leadership—CEO and CFO, plus three executive vice presidents—numbered only five, an *absolutely* small number.

On the other hand, a business like a catering firm that serves a small town may have its owner and one or two key employees (the 3), its most trusted suppliers and workers (the 12), and perhaps just a few dozen people, whether customers or friends, who often refer new business to the firm (its version of the 120). The 120 for a small business may actually be fewer than 120 people, but it is still a *relatively* small number of people compared to the thousands of people a catering firm may serve over the course of a year at weddings and banquets.

Perhaps the most dramatic example of the power of the 3, the 12 and the 120 in recent years have been social networks like MySpace, Facebook, LinkedIn and no doubt several more by the time this book reaches your hands. MySpace was the first to become wildly popular, acquired by Rupert Murdoch's News Corporation in 2006 and boasting 200 million worldwide users by 2007. Murdoch is the sort of person we think of when we think of the phrase *culture maker*—a person of tremendous wealth and power. Yet he did not—and could not—build MySpace, which grew organically out of interlocking networks.

Paradoxically, given its millions of users, MySpace is a vivid example of the small scale of culture-making networks. MySpace stretches Americans' already-thin definition of the word *friend* to its breaking point: the founder, "Tom," is registered as a "friend" of every single MySpace member, thanks to the magic of software, and MySpace users are notorious for promiscuously "friending" people they barely know. A MySpace user's list of "friends" is likely to be the widest possible measure of their social network, ranging from their best friends and family to people they wouldn't recognize if they passed each other in the grocery store.

Yet the average number of "friends," even by this absurdly broad definition, is surprisingly low: sixty-eight.

You might expect that in an era of mobility and technology, a site like MySpace would be a "global village," leading to an explosion in the number of relationships available to any given person. But in fact MySpace—and every other space, online or off—turns out to be a globe *of* villages, collections of small networks of people. Anthropologists speculate, in fact, that we are hardwired for small groups—that human beings are simply designed to operate in a village, even if that village exists in the midst of a vast metropolis or on computer servers that host a million other villages simultaneously.

There is much variation, of course—Gladwell's "connectors" are the handful of people who sustain relationships with an above-average number of other people. Some of us seem wired for networking, while others stick with a very small group their whole lives. While the average number of friends on MySpace is sixty-eight, many members have only three or four friends, many others have hundreds, and a few have thousands or more, even without the benefit of the automatic "friending" Tom enjoys. But even for these few MySpace celebrities, you can be sure that their actual social network (the people whom they know by face and name) and their culture-making network (the people with whom they could create something new) is measured in the low three digits at the very most. The producer and rap star Kanye West, perhaps the most prolific producer in hip-hop in the 1990s and 2000s, had 24,956 "friends" on MySpace in 2006—but he had produced albums for only fifty-nine artists over roughly ten years.

Rupert Murdoch had the cultural power to buy MySpace and to try to extract some economic benefit from it (a very uncertain prospect at the time this book went to press). Yet while Murdoch's own circles of 3, 12 and 120 include persons of great wealth, creativity and power, no one in those circles could have *created* MySpace. That piece of culture making was beyond his grasp. But it was within the grasp of Tom Anderson, Christopher DeWolfe and a few others—a circle of 3 who mobilized their circles of 12 and 120 to invite, eventually, millions of users to create culture for themselves.

The essential insight of 3 : 12 : 120 is that every cultural innovation, no matter how far-reaching its consequences, is based on personal relationships and personal commitment. Culture making is hard. It simply doesn't happen without the deep investment of absolutely and relatively small groups of people. In culture making, size matters—in reverse. Only a small group can sustain the attention, energy and perseverance to create something that genuinely moves the horizons of possibility—because to create that good requires an ability to suspend, at least for a time, the very horizons within which everyone else is operating. Such "suspension of impossibility" is tiring and taxing. The only thing strong enough to sustain it is a community of people. To create a new cultural good, a small group is essential.

And yet the almost uncanny thing about culture making is that *a small group is enough*. To be sure, the distribution of a cultural good may require hundreds of thousands or even millions of people. Malcolm Gladwell's book *The Tipping Point* popularized this process, pointing out the role of people who sustain unusually large networks or wield unusually large influence over the choices of their friends. But as we saw in chapter twelve, the mavens and connectors are merely necessary, not sufficient, conditions for cultural change. At the end of the day there is a profound mystery to which cultural goods are taken up into the wider culture—whether that is the global media culture or the pattern of life on a city block—and which fail to reshape the horizons of possibility. But even the most influential cultural good—the iPod, the interstate highway system or the omelet— began with groups of 3, 12 and 120 who invested their scarce time and talents in its creation, often with nothing except their own confidence or hubris, or an unaccountable sense of grace, to assure them of success.

Are all cultural goods the products of the kind of consumer-marketing wizardry and technological drive that led to the iPod? Are all cultural goods even intentional creations at all? Of course not. The origin of the omelet is lost to history, but it may well have developed, slowly and organically, in some set of country kitchens in medieval France, and it certainly developed without meetings, marketing budgets or master plans. We can be sure that it did not become a widely adopted cultural good without mavens and connectors—people who spread the word, perhaps without even trying, about a wonderful new way to cook eggs. Yet somewhere in the omelet's early history are a few cooks, very possibly servants or peasants, gathered in a kitchen; a dozen or so "early adopters," and perhaps a blacksmith or two cajoled into crafting an ideally shaped pan; and the 120 lucky first customers, perhaps spread over many years. They may not have been intending to reshape the horizons of egg-based cuisine, but they did. The omelet, like the iPod, began with the three.

THE GOOD NEWS OF THE THREE

Scripture, of course, is also the story of 3, 12 and 120. God's first decisive cultural intervention, narrated in Genesis 12, is the choosing of a people, beginning with an absolutely small group of people: a nomad named Abram, his wife Sarai and their household. The biblical shorthand description of that first stage of cultural intervention names the iconic figures of the first three generations: Abraham, Isaac and Jacob—three men linked by blood, risk and shared stories of astonishing personal encounters with the God their ancestors had much more dimly known. Then the circle widens to Jacob's twelve sons and their families—the 120. From this very small beginning—as God pointedly says, "the smallest of all the nations"—emerges a distinctive cultural tradition extended through time and space.

So when Jesus sets out to redeem the cultural project called Israel, he uses the same pattern. The Synoptic Gospels stress the pivotal role of the three disciples closest to Jesus—Peter, James and John—whom Jesus invites most deeply into the disclosure of his extraordinary mission to be sacrifice, model and source of a new way of living in the world. Jesus chooses twelve men to be close to him at the key moments of his teaching and demonstration of the kingdom. While Christian imagination has focused on the Twelve, it is clear that many women were just as close to Jesus as the twelve male disciples (at the crucifixion and resurrection, the women were much closer indeed), and the band of disciples was even larger still. At one point Jesus sends out seventy disciples in pairs to proclaim the kingdom he is inaugurating (Lk 10), and just after the resurrection, in the days leading up to Pentecost, there are 120 believers gathered in Jerusalem (Acts 1:15). Three, 12, 70, 120—through these concentric circles of men and women the kingdom's distinctive cultural goods, like parables, deeds of miraculous power, and new ways of organizing everything from time ("the sabbath was made for humankind, and not humankind for the sabbath") to meals (where "sinners" sit with the "righteous" in one welcoming banquet) begin to reshape the cultural horizons of Judea. God's own culture making, for all its universal scope through millennia and across continents, flows through absolutely and relatively small groups of people—perhaps because the original creative initiative that is the prerequisite for any human creativity came from an eternal society of three divine persons, united in their loving purpose.

The pattern of 3 : 12 : 120 is marvelously good news. Faced with the immense scale and scope of culture, we often retreat into postures ranging from condemnation to consumption. We feel overwhelmed, justly concerned about many features of our culture that we will never be able to change. The temptation to withdraw or accommodate, to get away or just go along, is strong.

Yet nearly every human being—certainly everyone who is able to read this book—has a "3." Your "3" is an absolutely small group of people whom you know and trust, with whom you share passion and conviction and commitment, with complementary gifts, talents and needs. You may even be part of more than one such small group, though probably not more than a few.

And your "3" has a "12"—a handful of others whose passions, interests, gifts and commitments are closely linked with yours, people who would be quick to help if you gave them the chance. It may be harder to see or believe that the "12" have a "120," and the actual number may be slightly smaller or larger, but they are there, waiting for something worthwhile and compelling in which to invest their time and energy.

The crucial, central fact is that all of us have a "3"—and none of us have a large number of "3s." When it comes to culture making, we are on relatively level ground in this respect: we all will make something of the world with an absolutely small number of people, many or most of whom are already intimately involved in our lives.

At first this may not seem to be true. The president of the United States can phone anyone in the country, perhaps the world, and reasonably expect them to take his call. Hollywood moguls and celebrities and chief executives have bulging Rolodexes and access to resources that most of us do not have. Aren't they the real culture makers, with the rest of us simply pawns in their game of power?

Yet on a daily basis, in how many people can the president put his trust? Who helps him decide which phone numbers to dial? It's an absolutely small number—somewhere between three and twelve. Whom does a producer talk to before deciding whether or not to greenlight a movie? They are on speed-dial on his cell phone, and there aren't more than ten or so, no matter how extensive the research and preparation that go into the decision.

On the other hand, there are many forms of culture that even the president cannot touch, and this too is limited by his or her access to personal relationships. The president could make a big splash at the elementary school in our neighborhood by scheduling a visit there, perhaps to announce some dramatic new legislation—for a day. But our neighbor Beth, who has invested several years in relationships with other parents, administrators and teachers, can create culture in our school district in ways that the president of the United States cannot. Her "3," "12" and "120" include creative partners who are essential to making the culture of our school district what it is, and the relationships and trust they share are inaccessible even to the president of the United States.

FINDING OUR CALLING

Absolutely no one makes culture alone. There may be periods of solitude where we work alone to shape our contribution to our own cultural sphere and scale. But for our work alone to bear any fruit at all, we will need to join with a 3. So one of the most important questions for our calling is, *Who are your 3?* Who are the few people you trust enough to risk creating something together? What is the cultural sphere and scale where you could imagine successfully proposing a cultural good? Who might be members of your 12? Who might be drawn into the circle of the 120 who will eventually lend their effort and energy to moving the horizons of possibility with you?

This question applies to friends who want to change the horizons of their neighborhood just as much as it applies to friends who want to change the horizons of their nation. The nature of the 3, 12 and 120 people we can imagine joining for cultural creativity is an indication of the sphere and scale at which we are currently called to create. I have friends who can convene some of our society's most celebrated and well-known creators of culture. I have other friends who work in a single urban neighborhood that is largely cut off from those wider social networks. My own ability to create culture is located at a scale somewhere in between those two extremes—indeed, my own calling includes bringing those friends together, bridging the spheres and scales that rarely intersect. But while some of us have more apparent power or status—measured by the scale and sphere where we can gather a creative community—the truth is that none of us has full access to the networks the others have. All of us are needed. None of us are dispensable. Each of us, with the 3, 12 and 120 we can gather around us, can create something that no one else in the world can create.

Our circles of 3, 12 and 120 are not static. My circles of creativity at age thirty-nine are different from my circles at twenty-nine or nineteen. The spheres and scales that I have been called into have changed as well—and not always in an ever-widening direction. When I was twenty-nine I was just beginning the most important cultural calling of my life, shaping the culture of a family that today includes just four people, which, if we are blessed, will widen over the generations, just as my family of origin began with four but now cannot even fit around the large dining table in my parents' home. Scaling down can be as important as scaling up—I never expect to have better partners in shaping culture than Catherine, Timothy and Amy. Small things can become greater over time—those who are faithful with little are sometimes, just as Jesus said, given the chance to be faithful with much—but small communities can always create things that are out of reach of wider, thinner networks.

The quest for the three, the recognition that all culture making is local, the willingness to start and end small, all seem to me to be the only approaches to culture making that do justice to the improbable story of God. Christian culture making grows through networks, but it is not a matter of networking. It is a matter of community—a relatively small group of people whose common life is ordered by love. Love is a fragile thing that does not scale well. It seems small beside the towers of Babel and Babylon. It is like a mustard seed, tiny and seemingly vulnerable. But it is the unseen truth of the universe, the key to the whole story.

Mercifully, very few of us will be given the gift and the cross of fame—access to and responsibility for circles of 3, 12 and 120 that touch the largest scales of culture. Those who are given that vocation will only survive it to the extent that they are surrounded by a robust community of fearless friends. And it is such communities, not just their famous representatives, that can actually transform culture. Communities are the way God intervenes to offer, within every culture, a different and better horizon. To be Christian is to stake our lives on this belief: the only cultural goods that ultimately matter are the ones that love creates.

16

GRACE

As a campus minister at Harvard University, I got to know hundreds of students who had made it through the gates of one of our culture's most influential institutions. I've found that when you ask students at most colleges or universities why they are attending their particular school, you get a story. They talk about being charmed by the location, impressed by a professor or welcomed by an admissions officer. They talk about their school being close to home or far from home, about financial aid or financial need, about escaping their religious upbringing or pursuing it, about the high-school grades they had or didn't have, all of which may have shaped their final choice.

At Harvard it was a bit different. Almost every time I asked a wide-eyed first-year student why they attended Harvard, I heard the same reply, often delivered with a note of awe: "Because I got in." Harvard's West Coast competitor, Stanford, can only count on about half of the students it admits actually accepting the invitation—but 80 percent of students admitted to Harvard end up joining the freshman class. Being accepted by Harvard, it seems, is all the story you need.

Over time, I found that I could roughly divide the students into three groups. There were the "strivers"—kids who had been prepared day and night since elementary school, or nursery school, to make it to Harvard (or, as acceptable fallback options, Princeton or Yale). They walked quickly and carried bulging backpacks. They sat in the front of the lecture hall, staying afterward to ask questions. They were up late and up early.

Then there were the "legacies," as they were inelegantly known—children of alumni, plus the heirs of other kinds of privilege, whether celebrity, power or wealth. The strivers' dominant trait was anxiety—they were sure the admissions office had somehow made a mistake. The legacies' dominant trait was, well, dominance. They carried themselves with a serene sense of entitlement, at home in Harvard's world, since it had been their home all along.

After a few years, though, I realized there was a third group, smaller than the first two. They arrived at Harvard seeming nothing but delighted and surprised at the letter that had landed in their mailbox on a spring day. I met students who hadn't even thought to apply to Harvard until their high-school guidance counselor suggested it, including a few who were the first in their extended family to ever go away to college. They could have their moments of anxiety, or they could be perfectly self-assured. But what you remembered about them was the lightness in their manner, a sense of fun and even play that accompanied them into the dining room, the classroom and the lab. Not the play of the entitled who were at Harvard more for the social capital than the schoolwork; just the enjoyment of the very good life of studying, learning and growing that can be found at any college at its best. Harvard psychiatrist Robert Coles wrote a series of books called Children of Crisis, with one volume called *Children of Privilege*. I came to think of these students as children of grace.

Of all the students I met who received the coveted summa cum laude for their senior thesis (still an accomplishment even with grade inflation), nearly every one was in this third group—neither a striver nor a legacy but a quietly brilliant child of grace.

Of the many students I met who grew in their faith and trust in God during four years at one of America's allegedly most secular institutions, relatively few were strivers, and not that many were legacies. The strivers tended to be too busy for faith; the legacies had a hard time seeing the need for it. The children of grace tended to grow deeply and quickly, discovering and wanting more and more of God.

I have kept up with many of these students over the years, as well as some legacies and strivers who found their way to grace during college or afterward. Some of them are thriving and creating culture in forgotten corners of the world; some of them are thriving and creating culture in corner offices. Like all of us, they have their bad days—but more than most of us, they still seem delighted and surprised by the whole experience.

The funny thing is that every Harvard undergraduate could be a child of grace. Harvard admits about 10 percent of the high-school students who apply in a given year. In the remaining 90 percent are strivers every bit as driven and talented as the strivers in the 10 percent; in that 90 percent are plenty of children of alumni (the days of automatic admission being long gone), the famous and the wealthy. There is no one in any class at Harvard who could not have been replaced by someone else equally gifted or connected. A great deal of luck weaves its way through the process from application to acceptance. For that matter, no one even gets the chance to apply to Harvard without an extraordinary number of lucky breaks. My colleagues in campus ministry at other universities would talk about the stress of divorce and "blended families" on their students, but I rarely met a student whose family of origin was not intact. Students at Harvard are disproportionately oldest or only children, recipients of plenty of undivided attention. Just to buy a ticket in the lottery that is the Ivy League admissions process, you have to win a series of lotteries you did not even know existed. Every student I met, anxious, confident or otherwise, had been the recipient of a gift. Only a few of them knew it.

Spend any amount of time in the black church and you'll soon hear someone pray: "I thank you, Lord, that I woke up this morning in my right mind, and with the use and activity of my limbs." The first few times I heard that it seemed a little, well, rudimentary. And yet that prayer sustained a people who were continually reminded of their powerlessness by small and large humiliations, reorienting them to the gifts that no oppression could take away. It affirmed the power to think and move in the world—it was a dignity-sustaining prayer, a repudiation of powerlessness and despair. The black church had very little ascribed cultural power, but they woke up in their right mind, with the use and activity of their limbs, and led a transformative movement in American culture. As a people, historically speaking, they were children of crisis, but every time they prayed that prayer they were children of grace.

I have become convinced that little good comes from straining to "change the culture." To do so is indeed, as the sociologists would say, to grant human beings too much agency. We will end our efforts to change the world exhausted and spent, less sure of ourselves and less sure of God—or, worse, we will end *more* sure of ourselves and less sure of God. I am also convinced that culture is sufficiently broken that none of us can simply afford to marinate in privilege, enjoying the fruits of power at a time when Christians have reentered the cultural mainstream and many of us have access to the best that a prosperous society can offer. Nor can we simply leverage our privilege and power, in the ways that come naturally to elites, and expect to contribute anything distinctive to the world.

The way to genuine cultural creativity starts with the recognition that we woke up this morning in our right mind, with the use and activity of our limbs—and that every other creative capacity we have has likewise arrived as a gift we did not earn and to which we were not entitled. And once we are awake and thankful, our most important cultural contribution will very likely come from doing whatever keeps us precisely in the center of delight and surprise.

MULTIPLICATION

In the search for grace, one of Jesus' parables has become especially helpful to me in pointing the way.

> Listen! A sower went out to sow. And as he sowed, some seed fell on the path, and the birds came and ate it up. Other seed fell on rocky ground, where it did not have much soil, and it sprang up quickly, since it had no depth of soil. And when the sun rose, it was scorched; and since it had no root, it withered away. Other seed fell among thorns, and the thorns grew up and choked it, and it yielded no grain. Other seed fell into good soil and brought forth grain, growing up and increasing and yielding thirty and sixty and a hundredfold. (Mk 4:3-8)

As with so many of Jesus' parables, this one is initially confusing. This is an unusual sower. Not many experienced farmers would waste their time and seed on ground thick with weeds or rocks, let alone on the packed dirt of a footpath. To borrow the title of another parable, this is a prodigal sower, whose method of farming seems, at least initially, to be economically and agriculturally foolish. On the other hand, he is fortunate enough to find some prodigal soil as well—soil that yields an extraordinarily fruitful harvest of grain.

When Jesus' disciples approach him in private to ask the meaning of this strange tale of prodigal sower and seed, he makes it clear that this is not a parable about agriculture. It is, in fact, a parable about parables—an explanation of the whole parable-telling strategy. "The sower sows the word," Jesus says, and the word falls not onto various kinds of ground but into various kinds of *hearts*. The parables, compact and opaque on their own, are like seeds. The sower of parables has to be prodigal in scattering them—preaching to huge crowds on mountainsides and seashores—for a simple reason. Any experienced farmer can inspect the ground, note where the path, rocks and weeds are, and direct his attention to the best soil. But there is no way to similarly inspect the human heart. The sower of the word cannot predict ahead of time who will ignore the word altogether, who will initially delight in it but quickly lose interest or who will hear the word but become distracted by "the cares of the world, and the lure of wealth, and the desire for other things" (Mk 4:19). But he knows that somewhere in the crowd are hearts that are like good soil—prodigal hearts—that will pursue the parable-teller and, like the disciples, ask more questions, questions that will bear lavish fruit.

The parable of the prodigal sower is first of all about Jesus' own ministry strategy. But it also applies very closely to the work of culture making. Parables, after all, are cultural goods—new ways of making something of the world. The teller of parables faces the same risks every culture maker does: the risk of seeing the cultural goods we propose flatly rejected, seeing initial enthusiasm and success wither into nothing, or perhaps worst, seeing our cultural goods survive but not thrive, bearing none of the fruit we had hoped for or even being turned against their original purpose. A farmer can inspect and prepare the soil, but no one has enough power to assure that much of his or her culture making will not fall onto bad soil.

What we can do, however, is pay careful attention to the fruit of our cultural work. Do we see a divine multiplication at work after we have done our best? Does a riotous abundance of grain spring up from a tiny, compact seed? This is grace: unearned, unexpected abundance that can leave us dizzy with joy. It is a return on investment that exceeds anything we could explain by our own effectiveness or efforts.

If God is at work in every sphere and scale of human culture, then such supernaturally abundant results are potentially present whenever we take the risk of creating a new cultural good. Hard experience tells us that we, like the prodigal sower, can never be sure beforehand what we will find. However, the parable and Jesus' interpretation offer us guidance in how to pursue our calling. Having reaped such a tremendous harvest, the next time the sower goes out he will surely spread extra seed on the good soil. Having scattered his parables widely, the parable teller waits to see who responds—and then tells them that they have discovered "the secret of the kingdom." They are the good soil, and so the prodigal sower invests deeply in them. He offers more to them. They become, indeed, his partners in shaping a new culture.

When I honestly examine my own life and work, I can discern results very similar to the sower's. Some of what I have tried to do has simply failed, early and decisively, like the awkward interviews with ad agencies and investment banks in college that led nowhere. Other attempts at culture making have seemed initially to succeed, only to quickly fade—my enthusiasm for basketball as a tall seventh grader that foundered on my own athletic limits once other boys caught up to my height, or my acceptance into an exclusive club that never became a truly welcoming set of friendships and eventually felt more like a burden than an opportunity.

But my most subtle and difficult challenges in culture making have been like the seed that falls among thorns, which does indeed produce a leafy green plant, but never produces fruit because of the thorns entwined around its roots. As a preteen I found that I had an aptitude for computer programming, beginning on the mainframe computers at the university where my father taught and moving on to the personal computers that became available during my teenage years. I still love to tinker with technology—

the computer language Ruby is one of my recent interests, a mind-bending and mind-expanding exercise that requires keen concentration and provides glimpses of pure mathematical beauty. But while computers are a diverting hobby, my attempts to actually make something of the world of computers—to produce a public cultural good in the world of information technology—have never borne notable fruit. This is not to say that I can't accomplish *something* when I sit down at a computer. But what I accomplish is directly related to the sweat of my brow, the long hours of coding and testing. The end result can be a satisfying little application that serves my needs, but it never has the abundance of divine multiplication. I have worked hard, and I have what I worked for—but I have never written a computer program and got up from the computer feeling awed and grateful for unimagined, fruitful results.

Indeed, one of my perennial temptations is to channel my cultural efforts into avenues where the fruit, if any, is simply wrung painstakingly from the effort I put in. I may finish these efforts with a sense of pride, but I do not finish with a sense of gratitude. Early in my adult life, on the days when my job was frustrating and disappointing, and in an era when skills in technology were being handsomely rewarded, I would cherish the idea of leaving ministry behind to simply put in the hours as a systems analyst, cashing a generous paycheck far from campus ministry's risks and failures. It took me several years to face the futility of that fantasy and recognize that such a career move, for me, would lead to a choked life of "the cares of the world, the lure of wealth, and the desire for other things." I had to admit that over and over, even in the midst of long hours and hard work, I had come to some moment of harvest—a conversation with a student, a night of song and prayer, an opportunity to teach—where the results, in terms of change and growth and joy vastly out of proportion to any contribution I had made, left all involved nearly speechless with gratitude. And the more I let go of my fantasies of securing my own life and avoiding the pain of the particular work I was called to do, the more frequent were these moments where my students, my partners and I glimpsed something I can only call glory.

But some of my colleagues in ministry had the opposite experience. We labored under a subtle but real dichotomy between sacred and secular, granting full legitimacy only to callings to "ministry" under the pretext of subverting Harvard's lure of wealth, fame and power. So we recruited more than one young associate with the rhetoric of renouncing their ambitions (as we called it, "leaving their nets"), only to see them struggle doggedly to produce the kind of abundance we had promised. More than one eventually left us and took up "secular" jobs—where they found a sense of freedom and joy that they had never experienced in our demanding company of workers for the gospel.

Is it possible to participate in culture, to create culture, outside of the church and experience every bit as much divine multiplication as those who work inside the church? For centuries many Christians would have answered no. A few had "vocations"—a word that still today, in Catholic contexts, refers to a specifically religious life—and the rest did not. To have a vocation was to withdraw to the edges of culture (although monasteries and churches were once more culturally central and culturally creative than they often are today).

But there are two serious problems with this approach to vocation. First, even a full-time sacred agenda turns out to be no guarantee of either holiness or fruitfulness. Segmenting off a "sacred" set of cultural activities sets us up for disillusionment when the sacred specialists turn out to be no more creative and no less corruptible than their secular counterparts. Second, it becomes impossible to do justice to the biblical story, in which the whole world was created good, the first human beings were given a cultural task, not just instructed to be dutiful worshipers (unlike in other creation myths of the time), and the Son of God himself spent most of his life as a carpenter.

The religious or secular nature of our cultural creativity is simply the wrong question. The right question is whether, when we undertake the work we believe to be our vocation, we experience the joy and humility that come only when God multiplies our work so that it bears thirty, sixty and a hundredfold beyond what we could expect from our feeble inputs. *Vocation*—calling—becomes another word for a continual process of discernment, examining the fruits of our work to see whether they are producing that kind of fruit, and doing all we can to scatter the next round of seed in the most fruitful places.

GRACE AND THE DISCIPLINES

I believe the single best question for discerning our calling—the specific cultural sphere and scale where we and our communities of 3, 12 and 120 are called to cultivate and create—is *Where do you experience grace—divine multiplication that far exceeds your efforts?* But three immediate qualifications must be made.

The first is that grace is no exemption from the disciplines: the careful, painstaking cultivation of the part of culture where we are called to be creators. God provides the growth that makes our cultural vocations truly fruitful, but that does not mean, to paraphrase the apostle Paul, that we can skip the hard work of planting and watering. Grace is not a shortcut around our effort; it is the divine blessing on efforts that are undertaken in dependence and trust on God. Grace is certainly not another word for entitlement, simply living off the dividends of the cultural capital of our parents, community or nation, enjoying the good life rather than seriously trying to make something of a broken and recalcitrant world.

Indeed, the disciplines that undergird any effort at culture making are an essential path to grace. Disciplines are private and invisible, preparing our hearts to handle the pressures of our work becoming public and visible. Disciplines are small and by themselves inconsequential (like the scales that professional musicians play every day), attracting no notice and deserving no prize, humbling us in advance of the occasions when our work will be recognized and applauded. Disciplines are difficult, revealing all too clearly our laziness and foolishness, preparing us for the times when fruit seems to burst from our smallest efforts. No matter how accomplished we become, disciplines always bring us up against the limits of our ability, offering us an opportunity to reclaim our dependence on Another to complete our inadequate work.

All this is true of the spiritual disciplines that every Christian must pursue, the practices of prayer, solitude and fasting that are at the core of any serious attempt to learn dependence on God. But the disciplines specific to our vocation are equally opportunities for cultivating that kind of dependence. As a musician I can allow the daily practicing of scales and vocalizations to become opportunities for prayer. As a writer I can take the daily difficulty of sitting down before a blank page as an opportunity to acknowledge my complete dependence on God, not just for the fruit but for the seed as well. As a producer I can see the dogged pursuit of potential funding sources and the tedium of hours in the editing suite as practice in patience and trust. Of course, it is equally possible for any of these to become means of striving self-justification. Perhaps on most days we will face the empty page with fear, or we procrastinate so we don't have to face it at all; we will breeze through perfunctory and substandard imitations of the rudiments of our instrument; we will avoid the hard phone call and postpone the tedious work of cultivation. Even then the disciplines can school us in just how wayward our hearts tend to be, humbling us further by exposing the fear and pride that make us so easily distracted and of so little lasting use. There may be no greater value to the disciplines than to regularly bring us to these moments of disillusionment with ourselves. Grace is for the poor in spirit, and the disciplines bring us, no matter our ascribed power or actual wealth, to keen awareness of our fundamental poverty.

GRACE AND FAILURE

One of my favorite professional baseball players for several years has been Philadelphia Phillies shortstop Jimmy Rollins, who was named the National League's Most Valuable Player in 2007. From the moment he runs onto the field for pregame warm-ups, Rollins is on the balls of his feet, bringing a boundless kinetic energy and joy to his fielding and his hitting. Behind his consistently stellar performances, I know, are hours in the gym and thousands of practice swings at the plate, the disciplines that have kept his talent honed for seven years and that led to a thirty-eight-game hitting streak in 2005 and 2006, the longest in Phillies history and the longest in the major leagues for twenty years. Few players play with a more tangible sense of grace than J-Roll.

Over his career in major league baseball, as of this writing, Rollins's on-base percentage is .331.

Which means that two out of every three times he steps up to the plate, he fails.

Baseball is a tough game (by comparison, basketball's leading scorer in the 2006-2007 season, Kobe Bryant, had a .344 percentage for his three-point attempts, and overall saw half his shots go into the basket). But it's certainly no harder than creating culture.

Most of the time most of us propose a new cultural good, we will fail. Sometimes our failure will be temporary—sometimes it will be perennial. The prophet Jeremiah spent his entire life attempting to change the course of Judah's international relations, warning several kings in a row that they were courting disaster by leaning on foreign alliances and neglecting God. He watched as the Babylonian army swept into Jerusalem and carted away its entire ruling class, a brutal and effective form of cultural decimation. At the end of the book of Jeremiah we see the last of the kings Jeremiah had tried to counsel, Jehoiachin, winning the feeble victory of release from a Babylonian prison, but still eating every day at another king's table while his fellow Israelites sing:

> By the rivers of Babylon—
>> there we sat down and there we wept
>> when we remembered Zion.
> On the willows there
>> we hung up our harps.
> For there our captors
>> asked us for songs,
> and our tormentors asked for mirth, saying,
>> "Sing us one of the songs of Zion!"
> How could we sing the LORD's song
>> in a foreign land? (Ps 137:1-4)

In 1998 two friends and I (three, once again) took over the leadership of a magazine called *re:generation quarterly* that was on the brink of failure. We sensed the call of grace in the opportunity to keep *re:generation* alive, a chance to deepen our friendships and offer a different kind of Christian magazine to the world, intelligent and design-savvy, orthodox and creative. Over five years we poured our time and plenty of money (both others' and our own) into the work. Magazines are an even worse business than baseball—70 percent of new magazines fail after the *first issue*. By that absurdly low standard, *re:generation*'s five years under our stewardship were a success—but in 2003, our new owner closed the doors, for very good financial and strategic reasons. What remains of all the late nights and long plane flights are some dusty back issues—a momentary burst of cultural productivity that left the horizons of the possible awfully close to where they were when we started.

That's not all to the story, fortunately—what also remains are some of the best friendships I ever hope to have, still-creative communities of former readers who found one another through the magazine, and the careers of some writers whom we were among the first to publish when they were young and unknown. Five years later I still hear stories of new culture that is being created because *re:generation* existed. But the fact remains that *re:generation*, for all the creativity it sparked and friendships it formed, failed. I spent nearly a year after its demise doing little beside mourning what we had lost—not quite in the cistern where Jeremiah found himself at his lowest ebb, but lethargic and lonely all the same. Then I roused myself from my low-grade depression and began to write this book—a book I probably would never have written had I not changed course from campus ministry to another kind of cultural creativity.

Grace is not an exemption from failure. It is, however, what makes it possible to sustain hope in the midst of failure. Even though our magazine had certainly not produced dollar returns on investment of thirty, sixty or one hundredfold, none of us close to the project could fail to see that it was bearing other kinds of fruit. Even when the challenges of running a small nonprofit kept me up late at night, it never felt like anything but a gift. We had taken on the challenge of *re:generation* with a commitment not to be strivers, committed to enjoy God and one another along the way. Grace surrounded the beginning and the ending in remarkable ways, including one last donor who made it possible for us to end with our debts paid and our readers as well served as we could. On the wall of my office is a plaque with handwritten notes from my partners in the magazine— the "12" (though actually at the end we numbered nine) who risked and worked to see what we could create together. All of them, in one way or another, say thank you, because all of us, even in failure, received a gift.

GRACE AND THE CROSS

In 2006 the Catholic Church made public the letters of Mother Teresa as part of the process of her candidacy for canonization as a saint. The letters reveal a lover of Jesus who suffered for almost her whole adult life from a searing sense of the absence of God. "If I ever become a Saint—I will surely be one of darkness," she wrote to her spiritual director. Even while Mother Teresa's ministry was bearing fruit of thirty, sixty and a hundredfold, she herself experienced, decade after decade, abandonment right alongside that abundance.

And this is the final and greatest difficulty with grace: the very divine multiplication that gives us joy and delight in the midst of our cultural calling also leads us directly to the places where the world is most in pain. Finding grace is not a matter of taking an aptitude test, discovering our gifts, and happily restricting our activities only to those things we find pleasant. Rather, over and over in the lives of God's people we see a pattern: abundance alongside suffering, growing fruit but also dying seeds, grace and the cross. Grace itself leads us to the world's broken places.

So Mother Teresa wrote to the members of her order:

> My dear children, without suffering, our work would just be social work, very good and helpful, but it would not be the work of Jesus Christ, not part of the redemption—Jesus wanted to help us by sharing our life, our loneliness, our agony and death.
>
> All that He has taken upon Himself, and has carried it in the darkest night. Only by being one with us He has redeemed us.
>
> We are allowed to do the same: All the desolation of Poor people, not only their Material poverty, but their spiritual destitution must be redeemed and we must have our share in it, pray thus when you find it hard—"I wish to live in this world which is far from God, which has turned so much from the light of Jesus, to help them—to take upon me something of their suffering."

Or as N. T. Wright puts it in reflections on calling at the end of his marvelous book *The Challenge of Jesus:*

> If we are to be kingdom-announcers, modeling the new way of being human, we are also to be cross bearers. This is a strange and dark theme that is also our birthright as followers of Jesus. Shaping our world is never for a Christian a matter of going out arrogantly thinking we can just get on with the job, reorganizing the world according to some model we have in mind. It is a matter of sharing and bearing the pain and puzzlement of the world

so that the crucified love of God in Christ may be brought to bear healingly upon the world at exactly that point. . . . Because, as he himself said, following him involves taking up the cross, we should expect, as the New Testament tells us repeatedly, that to build on his foundation will be to find the cross etched into the pattern of our life and work over and over again.

Or as the writer to the Hebrews puts it, Jesus himself, "for the sake of the joy that was set before him endured the cross" (Heb 12:2). Jesus' cultural creativity led him to a cross; the cross led him, and us, to joy. Any Christ-shaped calling is cross-shaped.

This does not mean that we masochistically baptize every experience of suffering or adversity, seeking out the least rewarding and most painful possible vocation in order to demonstrate how thoroughly disinterested our culture making is. There is a regrettable tradition stretching back at least to the philosopher Immanuel Kant that insists that the only things worth doing, morally speaking, are things we do not enjoy. So we are led to believe that only following Christ as a missionary "to Africa" could possibly qualify as "bearing the cross" (as if Africa still needed missionaries and as if it were not a continent with some of the world's most joyful believers). This is quite wrong. Our calling is not to the maximum amount of suffering—in taking on the world's fundamental alienation from God, Jesus has already been there and set us free from that. But our callings do mean that we will find ourselves at the places of pain, offering new creation in the midst of brokenness and forsakenness. We cannot expect to be in those places without being touched and even broken by their pain. We can expect that even there abundance will be germinating under the ground, ready to bring fruit for which we can only say thank you.

So where are we called to create culture? At the intersection of grace and cross. Where do we find our work and play bearing awe-inspiring fruit—and at the same time find ourselves able to identify with Christ on the cross? That intersection is where we are called to dig into the dirt, cultivate and create.

We are marvelously different enough from one another that the simple quest for each one's intersection of grace and cross will take us to every nook and cranny of culture. For my friend Elizabeth the intersection of grace and cross is found in raising three children who sometimes tax her to the very limit, creating a family culture of forgiveness, play and prayer. For my friend Megan the intersection is indeed in Africa, far from her upbringing among privilege, connecting the worlds of American wealth with African orphans, and also connecting African hope with American emptiness. For Karl the intersection is found as an executive in a technology firm that creates new horizons of the possible, while also wrestling with the ways corporate life can constrain one's hopes, dreams and fears. For my wife, Catherine, the intersection is found in teaching not just supremely gifted students but also students whose cultural backgrounds still bear the marks of an oppressive past, who began at a starting line far behind the children of privilege. For me, the intersection is found in finding ways to tell stories no one would otherwise hear from the margins of our world and contemporary Christianity, and in daily sitting down to the hardest job I have ever tried to do, risking words for things far too deep for words.

Frederick Buechner writes that your calling is found "where your deep gladness and the world's deep hunger meet." In all those places, at the intersection of grace and cross, these friends of mine, who are just names to you but who are the greatest treasures in the world to me, cultivate and create. And of course this is just one snapshot of the many places to which each of us is called, since Elizabeth is also a writer, Megan is also an artist, Karl is also a lay leader in his church, Catherine is also a musician and mom, and I am also a dad. There is not space enough to tell all the ways we have become partners in one another's culture making, friends and comrades, suffering and rejoicing together—the amazingly resilient and creative communities of friendship and family that can grow and bear fruit over our short human lives.

So do you want to make culture? Find a community, a small group who can lovingly fuel your dreams and puncture your illusions. Find friends and form a family who are willing to see grace at work in one another's lives, who can discern together which gifts and which crosses each has been called to bear. Find people who have a holy respect for power and a holy willingness to spend their power alongside the powerless. Find some partners in the wild and wonderful world beyond church doors.

And then, together, make something of the world.

POSTSCRIPT

Artist in His Studio

In Boston's Museum of Fine Arts there is a painting by the Dutch master Rembrandt van Rijn called *Artist in His Studio*. Housed in a glass case in the middle of a room full of grand, dark canvases by Rembrandt and his contemporaries, this small work, painted in oil on a wooden panel, is easy to miss. But it has become one of the handful of paintings around the world I would make a trip just to see, because it is such an evocative portrait of a human being in the midst of culture making.

The artist has set up a canvas, facing away from us, at one end of his simply furnished studio. He himself stands far back from the easel at the far side of the room, so that from our perspective he is a small figure, dwarfed by the canvas in the foreground. It has an almost fearsome aspect, looming large and dark like a living, waiting thing. Yet as the light from a window or skylight out of our view reflects off its surface, it seems to have become its own source of light in the room, illuminating the corners of the space with a glow that suggests this canvas may still be entirely white, and thus entirely empty. But since it faces the artist, not us, we can only guess at what is already there or what is yet to be.

Artist in His Studio, painted when Rembrandt was only twenty-two, is usually counted among his many celebrated self-portraits. But it is an unusual one. While the artist's clothing—a green and gold robe that seems neither luxurious nor penurious—is carefully rendered, the artist's face is barely realized. His nose is a little curve of shadow, his eyes are two cartoonlike black buttons—no more. If this is a self-portrait, the artist has left the most telling aspect for us to fill in for ourselves. And this is all the more striking given that Rembrandt's greatest contribution to Western art may well be his faces—the astonishingly detailed visages that still leap out from museum walls to confront, comfort and disturb us. This face is nothing like those. The craggy lines and wrinkles are found, instead, on the wood of the easel in the foreground—and on the wood of the door which is, for now, partly blocked by the easel itself.

One consequence of the buttonlike eyes is that we are not sure whether the artist is looking at the painting or at us. If he is looking at us, who are we? Are we the artist's subject, so that the painter is looking at us to gauge our likeness? Are we the artist's patron, here to observe how well he is fulfilling our commission? Are we a dealer who will represent his work to potential buyers? Are we one of his fellow artists, peers or students, who visit his studio to be inspired and instructed? At first glance the painting seems to be all about the solitude of the creative task, but the more time we spend with it the more aware we become that we, the viewers, in whatever role we may play, are just as necessary to this painting's essence as the artist. The canvas exists to be eventually turned around so that others can see it. Even if the artist is alone in his studio, his studio is for others. It contains multitudes.

I have come to see *Artist in His Studio* not primarily as a portrait of a person but of a posture. The artist steps back from his work. His weight is on his back foot—he is contemplating, waiting, watching. But the brush is already in his hand. He will soon step forward to the canvas that looms before him with all its possibility and danger. He contemplates in order to act. He is still in order to move. He is alone in order to offer something to others. He is small and humble, recognizing that what he is creating is in some sense more lasting and of greater import than himself. But he is also dignified by this moment of waiting and watching. The painting depends on him, on his willingness to risk being a creator.

Indeed, it is possible to see most of the postures we can take toward culture in the moment Rembrandt captures. There is always the possibility that this canvas, like many other works by young and unformed hands, will need to be scrapped, condemned as a failure and discarded or painted over. That very possibility generates the artist's intense self-critique, the watchful waiting that evaluates the worth of what he has done so far and still has to do. There will inevitably be a certain amount of copying, borrowing the techniques of others who have gone before—their achievements in perspective, light and shadow, the conventional colors and subjects that form the common visual language of that artist's place and time. And at some point—perhaps the moment we are witnessing, if the canvas is not empty but rather complete—the artist and his community will consume, enjoying the finished work without needing to improve it. Surely Rembrandt is making an eloquent case for the essential dignity of the cultural task the artist cultivates: the importance of conserving and passing on the accumulated excellence of artistic history, its brushes and palettes and easels and canvases that wait for each generation to learn to use.

But none of these postures—condemning, critiquing, copying, consuming, even cultivating—would provide the unique sensation of energy that suffuses this compact little painting. That energy comes from creation—the creating the artist has already done and has yet to do. This painting captures human beings at their most characteristic moment, the moment when we are most ourselves.

The painting may also shed light on one of the most perplexing and profound questions I have been asked in the course of writing this book. If the cultivation and creation of culture is our basic human task and will carry over into the new Jerusalem, what exactly will that eternal creativity be like? Will Bach go on composing, Rembrandt go on painting, Dante go on writing tercets, and for that matter programmers go on programming, engineers go on engineering and plumbers go on plumbing? Culture and creativity for us are intimately bound up with time, yet surely the eternal life of the new heavens and new earth is not simply just more time. It will be, we suppose, a different kind of time, an eternal now rather than an eternal series of moments. But how can the inherently time-bound act of creating and cultivating culture be condensed into an eternal now? How will there ever be an end to history?

Of course we do not know. But there is something in Rembrandt's painting that suggests to me we *do* know in part, through a glass darkly, what creativity in the eternal now will be like. The same painting that is full of drama and even tension—the intense relationship between the artist and his work—is also composed with exquisite stillness. The artist, caught up in the moment of contemplation and creativity, does not move. He is as still and silent as his work—as still and silent as we are, watching. And yet his stillness, and ours, has nothing in it of laziness or lifelessness. It is a stillness that is completely alive.

Athletes, musicians, writers, gardeners and lovers all attest to the experience the psychologist Mihaly Csikszentmihalyi calls "flow"—the times when our work or play so absorbs and attunes our energies that we lose track of time. For a little while time seems to both expand and contract, becoming spacious rather than constricting, making room for our creativity and activity, and we lose the self-consciousness that wraps itself around most of our waking hours, even as we become most fully awake and alert to the possibilities of what lies in front of us.

In this world, this life, "flow" comes to an end. The canvas is dry, the fugue is complete, the band plays the tag one more time and then resolves on the final chord. And, too, the book is finished, the service is over, the lights go up in the darkened theater and we emerge blinking into the bright lights of the "real world." But what if the timeless, creative world we had glimpsed is really the real world—and it is precisely its reality that gave it such power to captivate us for a while? What if our ultimate destiny is that moment of enjoyment and engagement we glimpse in the artist's studio?

Perhaps the Bible's most profound meditation on time and eternity is Psalm 90, attributed to "Moses, the man of God." It may have earned that attribution because it rings with a kind of ancient loneliness:

> For a thousand years in your sight
> are like yesterday when it is past,
> or like a watch in the night.
> You sweep them away; they are like a dream,

> like grass that is renewed in the morning;
> in the morning it flourishes and is renewed;
>   in the evening it fades and withers. . . .
> All our days pass away under your wrath;
>   our years come to an end like a sigh. (Ps 90:4-6, 9)

And yet the same psalm ends with a prayer, repeated twice for effect:

> May the favor of the Lord our God rest on us;
>   establish the work of our hands for us—
>   yes, establish the work of our hands. (Ps 90:17 TNIV)

All our culture making must be bound up in this prayer—that what we make of the world will last after the world itself has been rolled up like a scroll. When we are fully able to bear the beauty of God resting upon us, when our work and worship are one, we will live in the eternal now of creators made in the Creator's image. And, once more, it will be very good.

ACKNOWLEDGMENTS

The 120: Dakota Pippins, Denise Rosetti, Francis Chen, Jimmy Quach, Christine Teng, Eddie Simmons and the students of the Harvard-Radcliffe Christian Fellowship, Harvard-Radcliffe Asian-American Christian Fellowship, and Boston College's InterVarsity Christian Fellowship first heard much of this material in October of 2004 and helped to make it much better. HRCF was an amazing home for ten years, with several circles of 3, 12 and 120 all its own—including Curtis Chang, whose friendship was a great gift at the end of this work and long before the beginning. Bill Haley and Joe Maxwell were my first partners in *re:generation*—fortunately, we've all managed to fail upward. Laura Andersen, Nate Barksdale, Brian Broadway, Annalaura Chuang, Michaela and Patton Dodd, Ever and Soren Johnson, Helen Lee, David McGaw, Karl and Elizabeth Wirth, Adrianna Wright, Danny and Sue Yee, and Val Zander were all fellow travelers for various parts of those five years. Kurt Keilhacker, Kelly Monroe Kullberg, and Ted and Ashley Callahan were (and are) unreasonably good friends. In The Vine, Jennifer Jukanovich created one of the most fruitful communities I ever hope to experience. Christina O'Hara and Will Truesdell prayed with me at a critical time. Far above Cayuga's waters, Elaine

Howard Ecklund asked careful questions with great enthusiasm and Karl Johnson extended one marvelous invitation after another to be part of the work of Chesterton House. David Neff, Mark Galli, Stan Guthrie and Madison Trammel have all rejected (or at least strongly objected to) something I've written over the years, for all the right reasons; John Wilson's high expectations have taken me places I would not have gone otherwise. Keith Blount, an unapologetic English atheist, created the marvelous cultural artifact called Scrivener, a program which justifies the existence of the Macintosh computer all by itself and which made completing this project an unexpected joy. Gabe and Rebekah Lyons, Jeff Shinabarger, and Danielle Kirkland have been great friends and allies. Shane Hipps, Erik Lokkesmoe, Eric Metaxas, Mike Metzger, Dick Staub, W. David O. Taylor, James Emery White and Gregory Wolfe have inspired and challenged me to improve my "posture." In one brief visit and hours of mind-expanding audio, Ken Myers has been a great encouragement, and it's worth acknowledging, once more, that it is his keen journalistic clarity that produced the phrase *what we make of the world*. The congregation of First Presbyterian Church, Berkeley, gave me just the final dose of intelligent enthusiasm I needed. Cam Anderson, Jon Boyd, Carrie Bare and many others on the IVCF GFM staff are invaluable partners in crime (in Carrie's case, I suspect, literally!). Jeff Barneson's tenacity and creativity in campus ministry is one of the great wonders of Cambridge and an unending source of encouragement. Nate Clarke's curiosity and commitment to excellence have led to some of the most gratifying culture making of my life. Gary Haugen, Larry Martin, Bethany Hoang and the senior fellows of the IJM Institute spur me toward Jesus and toward justice—and we'll try to keep just how much fun we have when we're together a closely guarded secret. Brian McLaren asked me to write a book about what I was for rather than what I was against—here you go, Brian! Alan Jacobs is my hero, an essayist non pareil, and has been kind enough to also be my friend.

Several anonymous reviewers provided invaluable critique and correction to this book in its early stages, and I am deeply grateful to them.

The 12 (but who's counting?): John Kingston, Fritz Kling, Mark Labberton, Fred Smith, Harold Smith and Lauren Winner have each opened doors and pulled me through them, often coming along for the adventure; Mark Tindall, Geof Morin and John Yates have been invaluable brothers in a new land. Al Hsu, Andy Le Peau, Jeff Crosby, Bob Fryling and the team at IVP have brought passion, intelligence and excellence (not to mention patience) to this project—it is better in countless ways because of their creative contributions. It is unusual to acknowledge an editor who didn't get the book, but Julianna Gustafson's enthusiasm and tenacity got me started and kept me going long after the contract with IVP had been signed—Julianna, I owe you one, or more! I owe the deepest debt to my parents, Wayne and Joyce Crouch, to my sister Melinda Ricker, and to Barbara and John Hirshfeld for the ways our families have shaped my horizons, making much possible that would otherwise have been impossible.

The 3, *sine quibus non*, are in this case just two. Michael Lindsay asks astute questions, gives gracious answers, always hopes and always perseveres, and his friendship and intellectual companionship have been one of the great gifts I have received in the process of writing this book.

Catherine Hirshfeld Crouch is my daily companion in cultivating and creating, and only with her help have any of the ideas in this book come off the page into our lives. I'm grateful to live with her at the intersection of grace and cross.

NOTES AND FURTHER READING

A book on a subject as sweeping as culture is dependent on a vast number of more focused works. In these notes, rather than exhaustively documenting every source, I have tried to credit the principal influences on my thinking, while also pointing toward the source of direct quotations and particularly improbable statistics and assertions. I encourage readers to pursue the works cited here—they are a treasure trove of creative reflection on faith and culture.

INTRODUCTION

page 10   "the second most complicated word in the English language": Terry Eagleton, *The Idea of Culture* (Malden, Mass.: Wiley-Blackwell, 2000), p. 1.

page 11   Abraham Kuyper's thought is most famously summarized in his *Lectures on Calvinism* (Grand Rapids: Eerdmans, 1943).

CHAPTER 1: THE HORIZONS OF THE POSSIBLE

page 19   "it is likely that art was the first of the human professions": Paul Johnson, *Art: A New History* (New York: HarperCollins, 2003), p. 9.

page 20   The *Enuma Elish* is well worth reading and can be found at <http://ccat.sas.upenn.edu/~humm/Resources/Ane/enumaA.html>.

page 20   "there is no violent conflict among gods and monsters here": for a less sunny reading, readers may want to consult Gregory A. Boyd, *God at War: The*

Bible and Spiritual Conflict (Downers Grove, Ill.: InterVarsity Press, 1997), esp. pp. 102ff. While Boyd recognizes that Genesis 1 presents a distinctively harmonious account of creation, he argues that other parts of the Hebrew Bible place more emphasis on divine conflict with the forces of chaos.

page 23 "Christian cultural critic Ken Myers": the producer of the marvelous *Mars Hill Audio* and the author of one of the best contemporary books on popular culture, *All God's Children and Blue Suede Shoes: Christians and Popular Culture* (Westchester, Ill.: Crossway, 1989). He defined culture as "what human beings make of creation, in both senses," in Albert Louis Zambone, "But What Do You Think, Ken Myers?" *re:generation quarterly* 6, no. 3 (2000).

page 25 "Every human society is an enterprise of world-building": Peter L. Berger, *The Sacred Canopy: Elements of a Sociological Theory of Religion* (1967; reprint, New York: Anchor, 1990), p. 3. Also see Peter L. Berger and Thomas Luckmann, *The Social Construction of Reality: A Treatise in the Sociology of Knowledge* (Garden City, N.Y.: Doubleday, 1966).

page 29 "*what does this cultural artifact make impossible*": While the wording is mine, the insight really belongs to the philosopher of technology Albert Borgmann. I cannot overstate my intellectual debt to Borgmann and his work. The best starting point is his foundational book *Technology and the Character of Contemporary Life: A Philosophical Inquiry* (Chicago: University of Chicago Press, 1984); another valuable work of his that makes more explicit contact with Christian concerns is *Power Failure: Christianity in the Culture of Technology* (Grand Rapids: Brazos Press, 2003). An important theological interpreter of Borgmann is Marva J. Dawn in her book *Unfettered Hope: A Call to Faithful Living in an Affluent Society* (Louisville, Ky.: Westminster John Knox, 2003). Working in the same vein, but more influenced by Marshall McLuhan, is Shane Hipps, *The Hidden Power of Electronic Culture: How Media Shapes Faith, the Gospel, and Church* (El Cajon, Calif.: Youth Specialties, 2006).

pages 30-32 Those who want more on the glories of omelets (and who would not?) should start with Robert Farrar Capon's extraordinary work of cookbook theology, *The Supper of the Lamb: A Culinary Reflection* (Garden City, N.Y.: Doubleday, 1969).

page 34 "Culture is not optional" happens to be the name of a wonderfully quirky and creative group of friends who publish thoughtful guides to various aspects of culture at <www.cultureisnotoptional.com>.

page 35 "81 minutes a day in our cars": this figure is from 2001, according to Nick Timiraos, "Aging Infrastructure: How Bad Is It?" *Wall Street Journal*, August 4, 2007, p. A5.

CHAPTER 2: CULTURAL WORLDS

page 37 "in the wrong place and the wrong time and in the wrong scale": James Bar-ron, "Dressing the Park in Orange, and Pleats," *New York Times,* February 13, 2005.

pages 37-40   New York City's official website for *The Gates* can be found at <www.nyc .gov/html/thegates>.

page 40   "real artists ship": the title of an essay by Andy Hertzfeld, one of the engineers for the original Macintosh, found at <www.folklore.org/StoryView .py?story=Real_Artists_Ship.txt>. Hertzfeld does not directly attribute these words to Jobs in this story, however.

page 44   "bourgeois bohemians": this phrase is the linchpin of David Brooks's book *Bobos in Paradise: The New Upper Class and How They Got There* (New York: Simon & Schuster, 2000), which also pays homage to the Gryphon Café.

CHAPTER 3: TEARDOWNS, TECHNOLOGY AND CHANGE

page 51   "a scientist named Charles Townes": "An Unexpectedly Bright Idea," *The Economist,* June 9, 2005.

page 56   "Stuff, Space Plan, Services, Skin, Structure, and Site": Stewart Brand, *How Buildings Learn* (New York: Viking Penguin, 1994), p. 13. Thanks to Frederica Mathewes-Green for first alerting me to Brand's work and its cultural relevance in her essay in Leonard I. Sweet, et al., *The Church in Emerging Culture: Five Perspectives* (El Cajon, Calif.: Youth Specialties, 2003).

page 56   "Adolescents are obsessed by fashion, elders bored by it": Stewart Brand, *The Clock of the Long Now: Time and Responsibility* (New York: Basic Books, 2000), p. 36.

page 58   "No city . . . can stop terrorists altogether": "London Under Attack," *The Economist,* July 7, 2005.

page 60   "technological 'solutions' to our deepest cultural 'problems'": in addition to Albert Borgmann, credited earlier, no one has made this point more trenchantly than Dorothy L. Sayers in her supremely important book *The Mind of the Maker* (1941; reprint, San Francisco: Harper & Row, 1987).

page 60   "The language of worldview has become widespread": a development traced thoroughly in David K. Naugle, *Worldview: The History of a Concept* (Grand Rapids: Eerdmans, 2002). Another recent helpful book is J. Mark Bertrand, *Rethinking Worldview: Learning to Think, Live, and Speak in This World* (Wheaton, Ill.: Crossway, 2007).

page 61   "World views are perceptual frameworks": Brian J. Walsh and J. Richard Middleton, *The Transforming Vision: Shaping a Christian World View* (Downers Grove, Ill.: InterVarsity Press, 1984), pp. 17, 32. All italics in original. The four questions are first stated on page 35. Wolterstorff's summary is found on page 10. Both Walsh and Middleton later moved decisively toward considerations of embodiment and living out a cultural vision shaped by the gospel, but their later works are unfortunately not as frequently cited by those who continue to promote the language of worldview, perhaps because of their increasingly radical critique of modern Western culture. See J. Richard Middleton and Brian J. Walsh, *Truth Is Stranger Than It Used to Be: Biblical Faith in a Postmodern Age* (Downers Grove, Ill.: InterVarsity Press, 1995); and Brian J. Walsh and Sylvia C. Keesmaat, *Colossians Remixed: Subverting the Empire* (Downers Grove, Ill.: InterVarsity Press, 2004).

page 62   "One of the leading proponents of worldview, Nancy Pearcey": Nancy Pearcey, *Total Truth: Liberating Christianity from Its Cultural Captivity* (Wheaton, Ill: Crossway, 2005).

CHAPTER 4: CULTIVATION AND CREATION

page 67   "human cultures have the strange yet fortunate property of always being full": Albert Borgmann, *Technology and the Character of Contemporary Life* (Chicago: University of Chicago Press, 1984), p. 116.

pages 70-71 "Barbara Nicolosi, a screenwriter and Christian leader in Hollywood": Barbara Nicolosi, "Let's Othercott Da Vinci," Christianity Today Movies, May 3, 2006 <www.christianitytoday.com/movies/commentaries/other cott.html>. Nicolosi is the director of Act One, an exemplary training program for young screenwriters, and first published this article on her blog at <churchofthemasses.blogspot.com>.

page 72   "gross receipts": all figures here and in chapter twelve are from <www .boxofficemojo.com>.

page 74   "John Cage and Pierre Boulez": Jeremy S. Begbie, *Theology, Music, and Time* (Cambridge: Cambridge University Press, 2000), pp. 179ff. Also of note is Jeremy Begbie, *Resounding Truth: Christian Wisdom in the World of Music* (Grand Rapids: Baker Academic, 2007).

page 74   "as abstract expressionist Makoto Fujimura writes of Pollock": Makoto Fujimura, "An Exception to Gravity," *re:generation quarterly* 7, no. 3 (2001).

page 76   "most demanding forms of cultivation are *disciplines*": among the many excellent resources on spiritual disciplines, perhaps the most enlightening is Dallas Willard, *The Spirit of the Disciplines: Understanding How God Changes Lives* (San Francisco: Harper & Row, 1988).

CHAPTER 5: GESTURES AND POSTURES

page 78   "How have Christians related to the vast and complex enterprise of culture?": on this topic, in particular, of the making of many books there is no end. In addition to H. Richard Niebuhr's classic *Christ and Culture* (see chap. 11), two recent books have approached this subject in helpful ways, closely related to my own sixfold typology of condemning, critiquing, copying, consuming, cultivating and creating. (For the perfect alliteration, by the way, I am indebted to my friend Jared Mackey, who alliterates as only a Baptist pastor's kid can.) Dick Staub, in *The Culturally Savvy Christian: A Manifesto for Deepening Faith and Enriching Popular Culture in an Age of Christianity-Lite* (San Francisco: Jossey-Bass, 2007), focuses on popular culture in particular and calls us to be "aliens, ambassadors, and artists" within it. T. M. Moore, in *Culture Matters: A Call for Consensus on Christian Cultural Engagement* (Grand Rapids: Brazos Press, 2007), takes a more historical approach highlighting the exemplary figures of Augustine, the early Celtic Christians, John Calvin, Abraham Kuyper and Czeslaw Milosz. Readers who compare these books to the present one will see that, as Moore suggests, there is indeed much common ground on which a Christian cultural consensus can be built in our generation.

page 82   "the project of accommodating Christian faith to new cultural developments": as Christian Smith and his colleagues have demonstrated in *Secular Revolution: Power, Interests, and Conflict in the Secularization of American Public Life* (Berkeley: University of California Press, 2003), these changes in once distinctively Christian institutions were accelerated by financial incentives, often provided, ironically enough, by Protestant laymen like John D. Rockefeller.

pages 87-89   The story of CCM is engagingly told in Mark Joseph, *The Rock & Roll Rebellion: Why People of Faith Abandoned Rock Music and Why They're Coming Back* (Nashville: Broadman & Holman, 1999), which was one of the first books to give voice to many artists' disillusionment with CCM's parallel artistic universe.

page 88   "I've got the blood of an innocent man all over me": Petra, "All Over Me," *More Power to Ya*, Rivendell Recorders, 1982.

pages 96-97   "my years serving with a campus ministry": Happily, other ministries on campus made up in part for my own blind spots. Other stories that unfolded during those same years are told in Kelly Monroe Kullberg, ed., *Finding God at Harvard: Spiritual Journeys of Thinking Christians* (Downers Grove, Ill.: InterVarsity Press, 2007 [1996]), and her subsequent book *Finding God Beyond Harvard: The Quest for Veritas* (Downers Grove, Ill.: InterVarsity Press, 2006).

CHAPTER 6: THE GARDEN AND THE CITY

The themes in this chapter (and in this book as a whole) are thoroughly and creatively explored in Albert M. Wolters, *Creation Regained: Biblical Basics for a Reformational Worldview* (Grand Rapids: Eerdmans, 2005 [1985]).

page 103   "Biblical scholar Richard Middleton": J. Richard Middleton, *The Liberating Image: The Imago Dei in Genesis 1* (Grand Rapids: Brazos, 2005), which is also a helpful current summary of scholarship on the topic.

page 104   "there is an *ex nihilo* . . . quality to human creativity as well": Robert C. Neville gives this idea a full philosophical explication in *God the Creator: On the Transcendence and Presence of God* (Chicago: University of Chicago Press, 1968).

page 108   "deposits of precious minerals": Thanks to Makoto Fujimura for pointing out the cultural significance of these minerals to me.

page 110   "between the wilderness and the theme park": Although I've taken the metaphor in a different direction, my thoughts on the wilderness, the theme park and the garden were spurred by Leonard Sweet's introductory essay in *The Church in Emerging Culture: Five Perspectives* (El Cajon, Calif.: Youth Specialties, 2003). Neal Stephenson's essay *In the Beginning . . . Was the Command Line* (New York: Avon, 1999) also offers provocative thoughts on theme parks. Albert Borgmann offers an important, more positive, alternative reading of the role of wilderness in human experience at several points in *Technology and the Character of Contemporary Life* (Chicago: University of Chicago Press, 1984).

INTERLUDE: THE PRIMORDIAL STORY

Readers interested in a succinct, accessible summary of the various ways of reading Genesis in light of contemporary cosmology and anthropology may want to consult Deborah B. Haarsma and Loren D. Haarsma, *Origins: A Reformed Look at Creation, Design, and Evolution* (Grand Rapids: Faith Alive Christian Resources, 2007).

CHAPTER 7: THE LEAST OF THE NATIONS

page 121   "Every good story has a twist": This quality of great storytelling is explored by Robert McKee in his book *Story: Substance, Structure, Style and the Principles of Screenwriting* (New York: Regan Books, 1997)—and of course was explained by Aristotle before him.

page 129   "the exile forced Israel to grapple with the implications of its faith": These themes are helpfully explored in Paul D. Hanson, *The People Called: The Growth of Community in the Bible* (San Francisco: Harper & Row, 1986).

CHAPTER 8: JESUS AS CULTURE MAKER

page 137   "contemporary New Testament scholar N. T. Wright": As of this writing Christian Origins and the Question of God comprises three volumes: *The New Testament and the People of God* (Minneapolis: Fortress, 1992), *Jesus and the Victory of God* (Minneapolis: Fortress, 1997), and *The Resurrection of the Son of God* (Minneapolis: Fortress, 2003). Those familiar with Bishop Wright's scholarship will recognize that part two of this book is unabashedly dependent on his work.

pages 143-44 "There is very early evidence of the Christians meeting on the first day of the week": Wright, *Resurrection*, pp. 579-80.

CHAPTER 9: FROM PENTECOST . . .

Craig S. Keener, *The IVP Bible Background Commentary: New Testament* (Downers Grove, Ill.: InterVarsity Press, 1994) has brief background material on Acts 2 and Acts 13, and in general is an exceptionally helpful reference on the cultural context of the New Testament.

page 156   "33 million Christians by 350": Rodney Stark, *The Rise of Christianity: How the Obscure, Marginal Jesus Movement Became the Dominant Religious Force in the Western World in a Few Centuries* (San Francisco: HarperSanFrancisco,

1997), p. 10.

page 157   "The best of our brothers lost their lives in this manner": quoted in ibid., p. 82.

page 157   "conscientious nursing *without any medications*": ibid., p. 89.

page 157   "many of these neighbors, seeking new friends and family": ibid., pp. 91ff.

page 159   "*Central doctrines of Christianity*": ibid., pp. 209-11.

CHAPTER 10: . . . TO REVELATION

page 167   "The contents of the City will be more akin to our present cultural patterns": Richard J. Mouw, *When the Kings Come Marching In: Isaiah and the New Jerusalem* (Grand Rapids: Eerdmans, 2002), pp. 20, 24.

page 168   "There is no need to read the negative passages as insisting": ibid., pp. 29-30.

page 168   "Spears will have to become pruning hooks": this insight is also Mouw's.

page 170   "Heaven is a place on earth": this is also the title of an excellent book on this subject, Michael Eugene Wittmer, *Heaven Is a Place on Earth: Why Everything You Do Matters to God* (Grand Rapids: Zondervan, 2004).

CHAPTER 11: THE GLORIOUS IMPOSSIBLE

pages 177-78 "My friend Gary Haugen was in Rwanda": a story he tells in Gary A. Haugen, *Good News About Injustice: A Witness of Courage in a Hurting World* (Downers Grove, Ill.: InterVarsity Press, 1999).

page 179   "Those who offer [the fifth type of answer]": H. Richard Niebuhr, *Christ and Culture* (1951; reprint, San Francisco: HarperSanFrancisco, 2001), p. 45.

page 182   "The conversionist": ibid., p. 195.

CHAPTER 12: WHY WE CAN'T CHANGE THE WORLD

page 188   "searching for phrases *with* and *without* quotes": After I drafted this chapter, the phenomenon of breathlessly inflated Google searches was given a proper takedown by David Pogue, "Disproving Search Results," *New York Times*, December 4, 2007 <pogue.blogs.nytimes.com/2007/12/04/disproving-search-results>.

page 189   "as outsiders like Alan Wolfe and insiders like Ron Sider have documented": Alan Wolfe, *The Transformation of American Religion: How We Actually Live Our Faith* (New York: Free Press, 2003); Ronald J Sider, *The Scandal of the Evangelical Conscience: Why Are Christians Living Just Like the Rest of the World?* (Grand Rapids: Baker, 2005). Note, however, that Sider has been critiqued for conflating nominal evangelicals with those who actually are deeply involved in their church communities. The latter group does seem to show real, substantial and durable differences with mainstream American culture, while the former, as Sider laments, does not. See John G. Stackhouse Jr., "What Scandal? Whose Conscience?" *Books & Culture* 13, no. 4 (2007), pp. 20ff.

page 191   "An extensive body of literature has shown that most actively managed mutual funds": well summarized in John C. Bogle, *Bogle on Mutual Funds: New Perspectives for the Intelligent Investor* (Burr Ridge, Ill.: Irwin, 1994). While this book is dated in certain respects, its fundamental conclusions have only been confirmed in recent years.

page 195   "Gladwell, in his fascinating book": Malcolm Gladwell, *The Tipping Point: How Little Things Can Make a Big Difference* (Boston: Little, Brown & Company, 2000).

page 199   "Lars Ulrich memorably testified before Congress": Kristina Stefanova, "Music Industry Gurus Testify on Capitol Hill Against Free Music Downloads," *Washington Times,* July 13, 2000, p. B7.

CHAPTER 13: THE TRACES OF GOD

pages 202-3 "Second Inaugural Address": the text is available at <www.bartleby .com/124/pres32.html>.

page 209   "God . . . makes known his redemptive purposes for us *through* both the powerless *and* the powerful": I first formulated this idea as I read Ronald A. Heifetz, *Leadership Without Easy Answers* (Cambridge, Mass.: Belknap, 1994), which also has deeply shaped my thinking on power reflected in chapter fourteen.

page 209   "two-thirds of American philanthropy actually goes to institutions . . . that primarily serve the rich": "Patterns of Household Charitable Giving by Income Group, 2005," The Center on Philanthropy at Indiana University, summer 2007, p. i <www.philanthropy.iupui.edu/Research/giving_ fundraising_research.aspx>.

page 213   "the letter to Philemon": Norman R. Petersen's fascinating book *Rediscovering Paul: Philemon and the Sociology of Paul's Narrative World* (Minneapolis: Fortress, 1985), although it wears a certain amount of postmodern skepticism on its sleeve, is an impressive and provocative exploration of the many ways that Paul intervenes to "change the world" that both master and slave, as well as the whole community, inhabit.

CHAPTER 14: POWER

page 223   "power is a fluid capacity that must be maintained": I thank an anonymous reviewer for the insight and the wording of this phrase.

page 224   No one has documented the rise of evangelicals to cultural power more thoroughly and insightfully than D. Michael Lindsay, *Faith in the Halls of Power* (New York: Oxford University Press, 2007).

page 225   "I'm counting on you to help me with some contacts": Susan Schmidt and James V. Grimaldi, "Panel Says Abramoff Laundered Tribal Funds," *Washington Post,* June 23, 2005, p. A1.

page 228   "Richard Foster chooses the word *service*": Richard J. Foster, *The Challenge of the Disciplined Life: Christian Reflections on Money, Sex and Power* (San

Francisco: HarperOne, 1989), pp. 175ff.

page 232 "Smokey Mountain": The story of Father Ben Beltran and Smokey Mountain is told in an article by Jane Sutton, "Telling It on the Mountain" <www.urbana.org/_articles.cfm?RecordId=343>.

page 234 "as Tina Brown's biography makes excruciatingly clear": Tina Brown, *The Diana Chronicles* (New York: Doubleday, 2007).

CHAPTER 15: COMMUNITY

page 239 The distinction between absolutely and relatively small creative groups and many of the underlying themes of this chapter were suggested by Randall Collins, *The Sociology of Philosophies: A Global Theory of Intellectual Change* (Cambridge, Mass.: Harvard University Press, 2000).

page 242 "the average number of 'friends' [on MySpace]": InterMix Media investor presentation, June 1, 2005, slide 15. A more recent informal study of first-year college students at the University of North Carolina, Chapel Hill, concluded that students had 111 Facebook "friends" at the end of their first semester: Fred Stutzman, "Unit Structures: Student Life on the Facebook" <chimprawk.blogspot.com/2006/01/student-life-on-facebook.html>.

CHAPTER 16: GRACE

page 261 "My dear children, without suffering": "The Light of Mother Teresa's Darkness—Part 2," ZENIT news service, September 7, 2007 <www.catholic.org/featured/headline.php?ID=4846>.

pages 261-62 "If we are to be kingdom-announcers": N. T. Wright, *The Challenge of Jesus* (Downers Grove, Ill.: InterVarsity Press, 1999), pp. 188-89.

FURTHER READING

Several magazines, weblogs and institutes consistently stretch my thinking and spur my imagination, and I recommend them for anyone who wants to continue the conversation about Christians and our creative calling.

Books & Culture: A Christian Review <www.booksandculture.com>
Brewing Culture <www.brewingculture.org>
The Center for Public Justice <www.cpjustice.org>
The Clapham Institute <www.claphaminstitute.org>
Culture Is Not Optional <www.cultureisnotoptional.com>
Diary of an Arts Pastor <artspastor.blogspot.com>
Fermi Project <www.fermiproject.com>
Hearts & Minds BookNotes <www.heartsandmindsbooks.com/booknotes>
Image: A Journal of the Arts and Religion <www.imagejournal.org>
International Arts Movement <www.iamny.org>
Mars Hill Audio <www.marshillaudio.org>
Serious Times <www.serioustimes.com>
The Work Research Foundation <www.wrf.ca/comment>
The Yale Center for Faith and Culture <www.yale.edu/faith>

Index

ABOUT ANDY CROUCH

Andy Crouch is executive editor of *Christianity Today*, where he is also executive producer of This Is Our City, a multi-year project featuring documentary video, reporting and essays about Christians seeking the flourishing of their cities. He is the author of *Playing God: Redeeming the Gift of Power* and *Culture Making: Recovering Our Creative Calling*, which won *Christianity Today*'s 2009 Book Award for Christianity and Culture and was named one of the best books of 2008 by *Publishers Weekly, Relevant, Outreach* and *Leadership*. His writing has appeared in *The Wall Street Journal* and in several editions of *The Best Christian Writing* and *The Best Spiritual Writing*.

Andy serves on the governing boards of Fuller Theological Seminary and Equitas Group, a philanthropic organization focused on ending child exploitation in Haiti and Southeast Asia. He is a senior fellow of the International Justice Mission's IJM Institute and a member of the Board of Advisors for the John Templeton Foundation. He lives with his family in Swarthmore, Pennsylvania.

From 1998 to 2003, Andy was the editor-in-chief of *re:generation quarterly*, a magazine for an emerging generation of culturally creative Christians. For ten years he was a campus minister with InterVarsity Christian Fellowship at Harvard University. He studied classics at Cornell University and received an M.Div. summa cum laude from Boston University School of Theology. A classically trained musician who draws on pop, folk, rock, jazz and gospel, he has led musical worship for congregations of five to twenty thousand.

Visit <http://culture-making.com> for more of Andy's writing, a study guide for group discussion of this book, and to learn more about cultural creativity.